Humanistic education
DEVELOPING THE TOTAL PERSON

Humanistic education

DEVELOPING THE TOTAL PERSON

ROBERT E. VALETT

California State University
Fresno, California

ILLUSTRATED

THE C. V. MOSBY COMPANY

Saint Louis   1977

Printed in the United States of America

Distributed in Great Britain by Henry Kimpton, London

The C. V. Mosby Company
11830 Westline Industrial Drive, St. Louis, Missouri 63141

Library of Congress Cataloging in Publication Data

Valett, Robert E
    Humanistic education.

    Bibliography: p.
    Includes index.
    1. Education, Humanistic. I. Title.
LC1011.V275   370.11'2   76-46354
ISBN 0-8016-5212-X

GW/VH/VH 9 8 7 6 5 4 3 2 1

To
Eric, who has helped me
recognize the need for
a more humanistic education

I hear—and I attend
I see—and I remember
I feel—and I wonder
I care—and I aspire
I speak—and I relate
I reflect—and I understand
I love—and I transcend
I experience—and I act
And so do I become.

Preface

The process of human evolution and development continues to be a struggle for survival. Persistent wars, famine, and a host of natural disasters impress us with the necessity to learn how to relate more adequately to others and our environment. But we are now becoming aware that our major problem is to understand ourselves and to be able to direct our behavior into more meaningful ways of living. As always, the evolutionary process is excruciatingly painful as we learn to live with ourselves and others.

Unfortunately, we have been slow in accepting the legitimacy of self-study and the way in which perception, feelings, and behavior are inextricably related in the full presentation of the self and its relationship to and transactions with others. It is amazing that, although we have obvious reflections of widespread personal and social disintegration in the statistics of suicide, crime, unemployment, governmental dishonesty, mental illness, family disorganization, drug addiction, venereal disease, and school and social dropouts, relatively little time and effort have been devoted to affective-humanistic education. It is my belief that this form of education should receive priority in the schools. The problem of human survival and continued development is now largely one of educating wholesome persons to use their skills and abilities fruitfully in living harmoniously within themselves and with others in a mutually supporting community. Schools can be much more effective in this regard than they have been in the past. With the rapidly growing understanding of the importance of the affective domain in education, we are faced with an exciting and challenging opportunity to design programs for total human development.

The purpose of this book is to help educators and others develop humanistic education programs. It assumes that affective education should be an intrinsic part of a child's education along with the more traditional cognitive and psychomotor education. I hope that this book will enable educators to design programs that are effective in helping children to understand themselves and others, to develop more positive self-concepts, to be able to express their feelings, hopes, and aspirations more adequately, to become more self-determining and actualized persons, and to achieve greater personal and social maturity. Although the book has been written primarily for teachers, it should also be helpful to other students of the helping professions, parents, and administrators who are interested in the implementation of humanistic education.

Acknowledgments are due the many people who have stimulated me to write this book. The suggestions and requests for help from numerous teachers of the educationally handicapped and behaviorally disturbed are most appreciated. Special acknowledgment must be accorded to Carl G. Jung, whose theories and teachings, as exemplified in his *Collected Works*, have been primarily instrumental in influencing my ideas on human potentialities and humanistic education. Appreciation is also extended to my wife, Shirley Bellman Valett, without whose help and constructive criticism this work would have been impossible.

Robert E. Valett

Contents

1   *What is humanistic education? 1*

2   *Human needs and educational goals, 9*

    The need for humanistic education, 11
    Human needs and education, 13
      Physical security, 13
      Love, 14
      Creative expression, 15
      Cognitive mastery, 16
      Social competency, 17
      Self-worth, 17
    Developmental stages and education, 20
      Psychomotor stage of growth, 20
      Cognitive stage of growth, 22
      Affective stage of growth, 23
    Summary, 24

3   *Developing the humane person, 27*

    The basic learning abilities, 28
    Educational process and human potentialities, 34
    Becoming a person, 37
    Premises for constructing a human development program, 40

4   *Affective-humanistic objectives, 43*

    Goals, 43
    Objectives, 47
      My self checklist, 49
    Programs, 50

Taxonomy of affective objectives, 52
   Level one: Understanding basic human needs, 53
   Level two: Expressing human feelings, 53
   Level three: Self-awareness and control, 53
   Level four: Becoming aware of human values, 53
   Level five: Developing social and personal maturity, 54
Summary, 54

5   *A humanistic rationale*, 57

Stage one: Understanding basic human needs, 59
Stage two: Expressing human feelings, 61
Stage three: Self-awareness and control, 63
Stage four: Becoming aware of human values, 65
Stage five: Developing social and personal maturity, 67
Summary, 70

6   *Curriculum guide for humanistic education*, 73

An affective education program, 76
   Stage one: Understanding basic human needs, 76
   Stage two: Expressing human feelings, 84
   Stage three: Self-awareness and control, 93
   Stage four: Becoming aware of human values, 100
   Stage five: Developing social and personal maturity, 107

7   *Pilot studies*, 115

Mental health projects, 115
Achievement motivation, 116
Reality therapy, 117
Self Enhancing Education (SEE), 117
Social Learning Curriculum, 119
Rational-emotive education, 119
Man: A Course of Study, 120
Confluent Education, 121
The Louisville experiment, 122
Behavioral science education projects, 122
Human Development Program, 123
Psychological education in secondary schools, 124
Philadelphia Affective Education Project, 125
Summary, 126

8   *Commercial models*, 129

Human Values Series, 129
Dimensions of Personality, 130
Focus on Self-Development, 131
Transactional Analysis, 132
Developing Understanding of Self and Others, 133
Inside/Out, 134
Self Incorporated, 135

Toward Affective Development, 135
Becoming, 136
Transcendental Meditation, 137
Values orientation programs, 138
   Meeting Yourself Halfway, 138
   Making Sense of Our Lives, 138
   Lifeline, 138

9 *Learning resource materials, 141*

Primary resource materials (kindergarten to grade 3), 142
Elementary resource materials (grades 4 to 6), 143
Secondary resource materials (grades 7 to 12), 145

10 *Experiential activities, 149*

Human involvement programs, 149
Expressive art, drama, and music, 152
Humor, 153
Inspirational literature, 155
Self-awareness and evaluation, 156
Educational games, 163
   Black Attaché Case game, 163
   Social-personal simulation games, 163
Interpersonal growth activities, 164

11 *Humanistic behavior modification, 171*

Basic principles, 172
Social reinforcement techniques, 174
Social identification and modeling techniques, 178
Self-regulation and control techniques, 179
Program evaluation techniques, 183
Teacher self-evaluation, 183
Humanistic implications, 186

12 *The humanistic community, 189*

The quest for values, 190
Encouraging human aspirations, 194
Some humanistic components, 195
Political concerns, 197
Implications for teaching, 199
Conclusion, 201

13 *Professional training, 205*

Personal qualities, 205
Training models, 206
   Freedom to Learn model, 207
   Teacher Effectiveness Training, 207

Schools Without Failure, 208
Affective curriculum models, 209
Formal training programs, 210
    University of California, Santa Barbara, 210
    Boston University, 210
    California State University, Fresno, 211
    Humanistic Psychology Institute, 212
    Other formal training programs, 212
    Continuing education, 213
    Designing local training programs, 216
Summary, 218

References, 220

Humanistic education

DEVELOPING THE TOTAL PERSON

Developing a sense of awe and wonder is part of humanistic education.

The first and overarching Big Problem is to make the Good Person.

A. H. MASLOW (1969)

CHAPTER 1

What is humanistic education?

"HUMANISTIC EDUCATION" is education that is concerned with the development of the total person. It is concerned with designing and providing learning experiences that will help people at all ages and stages of life continue to develop our uniquely human potentialities. It is concerned with facilitating our growth and changing our behavior so that we may become more wholesome, balanced, self-actualized, and responsible persons.

How does this differ from traditional education or from most contemporary education? It differs primarily in the human goals and models that we set for ourselves and our children. As civilization and its cultural technology continue to advance, education is forced to adapt and change as well. In most societies, traditional education has been concerned with providing the basic skills necessary to ensure cultural survival. These skills have usually consisted of such important things as reading, writing, figuring, solving common arithmetic problems, and even acquiring some work capability.

Over the centuries, most contemporary or modern educational systems have gradually expanded to include other goals as well. For instance, most schools now recognize the importance of enabling pupils to acquire some degree of physical exercise, strength, and health; to become more aware and appreciative of aesthetic values; and even to develop some civic awareness and responsibility. Accordingly, over the last 50 years or so, schools have significantly increased their offerings in physical education, art and music, and the social sciences. Contemporary education, then, changes to attempt to meet the minimal needs of people in a given society.

But modern education is limited and very shortsighted. Its emphasis has been on adjustment and adaptation to the prevailing culture and its technological needs. In contrast, humanistic education attempts to prepare persons to "go beyond" and transcend immediate personal and societal needs and goals. The emphasis in humanistic education is to teach persons how to cope more adequately with today

1

and prepare more effectively for tomorrow. Humanistic education attempts to integrate all learning in meaningful ways to enable the learner to adapt more effectively and also to plan, care, aspire, and create a more complete and wholesome way of life for everyone.

Let us look at two hypothetical examples of humanistic education programs in action. Both Jefferson Elementary School and Edison High School have incorporated the best of traditional education (acquisition of basic skills) and contemporary education (vocational adjustment) with some additional humanistic (future-oriented, transcendent) learning opportunities for their students.

Jefferson Elementary School

Children want to go to Jefferson Elementary School. The absentee and tardiness rate is the lowest in the city. Parent participation in all school affairs is unusually high. But most of all the children appear happy, and they are obviously learning as indicated by superior awards in the performing arts plus good achievement test scores in the basic skills. Other tests also show that Jefferson's pupils have good self-esteem and are highly creative, although their general learning ability is lower than that of children in many other schools in the district.

The most outstanding characteristic of Jefferson's program is that it is a uniquely nongraded school that actually allows children to make continuous progress toward individualized educational objectives. Each child proceeds at his own rate of learning and is rewarded for doing so. Pupils move from room to room and to various learning centers, laboratories, and instructional resource rooms with purpose and ease. Much of their time is spent in small basic skill study groups and supplemental individualized study projects.

Everyone is also involved in several humanities study groups, which include art, singing, drama, and instrumental music. Throughout the year, children engage in a broad social studies program of community field trips, social service projects, and cultural and historical studies with visiting speakers and discussion leaders (many of whom are parents). Every child also belongs to a friendship guidance group that meets frequently to discuss and solve the numerous interpersonal problems that occur in all schools, to improve children's social skills, and to plan special social events such as athletic, playday, and party activities.

In this school, all pupils help to set their own learning goals and objectives. Teachers write a personal letter to parents twice a year describing the progress the child has made during the preceding months. At the end of the year a conference is held between teacher, parent, and child to plan the most suitable educational program for the next year.

Edison High School

All students at Edison High must demonstrate minimal proficiency on a functional reading, mathematics, and social science examination before they are allowed to graduate. The following items from the examination illustrate a few of the skills required:

- Reading: Complete a three-page formal job application.
- Arithmetic: Compute deductions from a simulated paycheck (federal and state income tax, Social Security tax, union dues, medical insurance, and wages earned per hour).
- Social studies: Visit a city council or other governmental board meeting and write a report discussing in detail the pros and cons of a major issue being considered.

Among other things, all students at Edison must take and pass at least one course in each of the following areas:

Basic English and writing

Family life education (including child care training)

Drug education

Vocational career planning

Driver education

Personal psychology (self-actualization and control)

Music

Art, drama, or industrial arts

Future history and world affairs

Community work experience

Individualized sports or adaptive physical education

Ethnic, cultural, or comparative religion studies

Edison students spend considerably more time off campus in community learning activities (such as hospitals, child care centers, and local industries) than most other high school pupils. They are also significantly more motivated to learn than typical adolescents, and the incidence of behavior problems (and delinquency) is dramatically lower than that of comparable schools.

The preceding examples illustrate some of the attributes of humanistic education in practice. These are, of course, incomplete examples, since humanistic education also consists of many additional programs and learning experiences.

In recent years there have been reports of several new humanistic programs, some of which have proved to be quite successful. A number of documented programs have demonstrated the importance of certain fundamental goals and procedures. Although actual research findings will be discussed in some detail in Chapter 7, a few of them are relevant here. The following case vignettes will help to introduce the more important principles, which will concern us throughout this book. The source of each of these program illustrations is given; although the specific research results are real, the persons described are all fictitious characterizations.

Self-discipline: Betty is participating in the Affective Education Development Program at Olney High School in Philadelphia. She has been involved in a number of intensive learning activities to help her improve her self-concept, to develop meaningful and satisfying relationships with others, and to acquire increased self-control (Gollub, 1971).

Today, Betty is part of a senior classroom group that is simulating a failure situation in real life. Everyone is involved in the discussion and in modeling ways of dealing more effectively with the problem presented. As Betty acts out her personal solution to the problem, one of the students says, "Yeh! That's the way to do it!" Later, the group writes a brief evaluation of what they have been doing.

Since she joined this new program, Betty's attendance at school has risen dramatically, and it is much better than that of other students who are not in the affective education program. She has also made significant improvement in personal discipline and now is rarely referred to the administration for such problems.

Continuous progress: In the Canfield-Crescent Heights School in Los Angeles, the pupils seem to learn without being coerced. A group of second-grade boys is reading. Other groups are doing arithmetic, science, and social studies projects at their own individual paces. They all seem to talk, share their ideas, and move about freely. At a later time, they all move to discussion groups where they become personally involved in ethnic studies and express their basic feelings about their racial identity and aspirations.

At this school, parents have a major say in determining its unorthodox goals—a love of the learning process, healthy self-images, and the ability to make independent but wise decisions. Parents indicate that significant progress has been made toward these goals, and their children also score above the national average on standardized reading and arithmetic tests (McCurdy, 1975).

Self-expression: When the time came to watch *Inside/Out* on the classroom television set, Georgia could hardly wait to see what was to be presented. This was the seventh film to be shown in the weekly programs that Georgia looked forward to with enthusiasm.

The story on the television screen was about a blind girl named Donna who had to learn to be herself as well as she could. As Georgia watched the drama unfold, she began to see and understand how persons come to accept the things that make them different from others and how the process of becoming a person is in many ways the same for everyone (*Inside/Out,* 1972).

Following the television presentation, all of the children participated in a discussion of what they had seen and felt. Then they engaged in an activity of listing and sharing the various ways in which they were different but capable persons. When Georgia went out to recess she felt much better about her own person and her limitations, which so often frustrated her.

Self-understanding: Alan ran into his special resource classroom screaming, "Everyone in this school hates me—they all hate me—but I'm going to get them good!" Immediately, the teacher and other pupils gathered around him and sat down to talk. Then Tim said, "Man, that's your child talking and it's about to get you in real trouble!"

On the chalkboard, the teacher sketched several circles, labeled them "parent," "adult," and "child," and drew a lot of arrows going back and forth between them. Diane went to the board and drew some more arrows and showed Alan the kind of transaction that had occurred between him and another boy in the hallway. Then everyone discussed Alan's feelings and what might be done to help him cope with the situation.

This was the third week that Alan had gone without a fight. It seemed that he was getting better at talking things out instead of fighting, and everyone was wondering how long it would last. In one survey, 85% of parents polled thought that programs like this should be taught in the schools (Harris, 1969, p. 161).

Problem solving: Marie, Tom, Bob, Jamie, and Elaine are all working together as a group in their fifth-grade class in Niles, Michigan. They are busy making thumbprints on construction paper and writing short stories about human likenesses and differences. Shortly thereafter, they join the class for a lesson on problem solving during which they participate in defining the problem and in generating alternative cooperative solutions.

These children are part of 3,054 students in 118 classrooms, first through sixth grade, who are involved in the Project Alpha affective education program. Progress evaluations show that 72% of the children have grown in self-esteem and that strong community and professional support exists for continuing the program (Project Alpha, 1975).

Self-renewal: It was midmorning as Sam entered his high school classroom in Hartford, Connecticut. Quietly, he moved to join the group of teenagers who began to settle down in various parts of the room. Sam got into a comfortable sitting position on a soft rug near one side of the room. Then he closed his eyes.

As the teacher suggested that the group get comfortable and relax, everyone became still and began to breathe deeply. Within a few seconds, Sam appeared at ease and then became tranquil. He sat with his palms up on his lap and softly began to repeat a pleasant sound to himself. The other persons in the room were also meditating in similar ways. After about 15 minutes, the teacher rang a small bell and everyone opened his eyes and moved into a discussion group.

After one semester of meditation, Sam's grade point average increased significantly. His anxiety level also dropped considerably as judged by both parental and self-evaluations (Bloomfield et al., 1975, pp. 234-235).

Developing attention and concentration: Sitting down beside Mark, the teacher slowly drew the design as the boy watched. Then Mark drew the design, but with great difficulty and many errors. Mark started again, and this time his teacher instructed him aloud as he worked. In a few minutes, Mark began a new design while talking aloud to himself; softly he instructed himself: "Draw the line down, down, now more to the right—that's it; now up to the left. Boy, I'm doing good so far." On the next task, Mark did the drawing while whispering to himself. Finally, he drew a similar drawing while instructing himself covertly. When he had finished, he recorded his performance in his own record book and said, "Good, I did it!"

As one of several hyperactive-impulsive boys in a special education program, Mark had continued to improve his self-control and performance. Prior to receiving this form of special education, he had been repeatedly suspended from school for his poor attention and highly distractible behaviors. Now he was being taught to instruct himself and to control and monitor his own behavior (Meichenbaum and Cameron, 1974, pp. 265-269).

Self-determination and achievement: Harry had been in continual trouble with the law. After his most recent theft, he was suspended from school for a while and placed on probation. When he returned to school he was placed in a program for delinquent boys.

In this program, Harry was given the freedom to select his own learning activities. As soon as he realized that he had to keep busy doing something that would not annoy or disturb others, Harry selected a mechanics project to work on. His teacher told him his scores on an achievement test and then helped him get underway with his self-initiated mechanics project. From time to time, Harry would go to his teacher for special help and advice and to find special materials and sources of information.

Four months later, Harry was retested on the Stanford Achievement Tests; his score increased almost 15 months in reading and arithmetic. Since Harry was well below average in general intellectual ability, this gain was thought to be a highly significant one that resulted in part from his project (Williams, 1930).

Self-assertion and esteem: Eleven-year-old Peri was demonstrating her notebook on human emotions to her group. For some time now, she had been collecting pictures and stories of basic feelings such as happiness, sadness, worry, and many others. She had also added several stories of her own, including one of her feelings about learning to play kickball and another story about how she felt the first time she tutored a younger child in reading.

A few months ago, Peri had been an introverted, withdrawn, and unhappy child with few social skills and no friends. She had, however, always been a superior reader. Now Peri was more open and expressive, and she increasingly participated in social and physical activities. She was also actively involved in teaching several younger children to improve their reading.

One day, Peri told her special resource teacher, "This is the best school I have ever attended. The kids like me better and are more friendly—and I am getting less shy." Peri's mother says, "She has improved 95 percent," and her teachers also agree that she is becoming a much happier child (Valett, 1973, pp. 142-146).

These examples illustrate several common attributes of humanistic education. All of them are concerned with helping learners improve their thinking and problem-solving abilities. But they are also concerned with helping people deal more adequately with their feelings and emotions. The unique aspects of these programs is their emphasis on enabling pupils to re-create personal energies and to go beyond (or transcend) their immediate situation by aspiring to actualize some undeveloped human potentiality.

Humanistic education stresses the importance of developing the whole person. The balanced development and interaction of our unique potentialities for thinking,

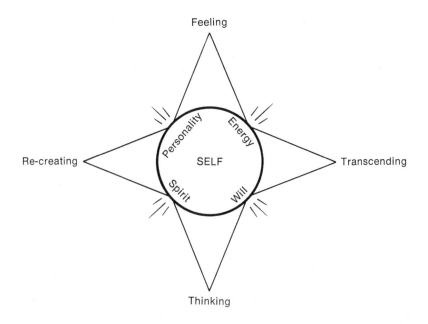

feeling, re-creating, and transcending are presented in the schematic diagram shown above.

When our education is a balanced and integrated one, we feel capable and full of energy. We then begin to experience a sense of personal wholeness and find ourselves in "good spirits" and full of life. A balanced personality is a zestful and willful one; our central self extends itself to encounter life in meaningful ways. These concepts will be expanded in more detail in other chapters of this book.

Education, then, is a process of developing human faculties and abilities. Humanistic education insists that this process be concerned with developing the whole person, which includes affective-emotional skills and abilities as well as cognitive and physical or psychomotor ones. And the final goal of humanistic education is to produce a good and relatively happy person who is capable of living a creative and meaningful life.

In summary, then, let us consider some of the major principles of humanistic education. Many of these principles have already been introduced in the examples presented. All of them will be elaborated on throughout the remainder of this book.

Considerable agreement exists that these principles need to be recognized as basic for planning and implementing humanistic education programs:

- Humanity is engaged in a continual process of "becoming and evolving" to higher levels of conscious awareness and being.

- Human abilities, skills, and potentialities can be actualized and developed through proper education.
- Humanity is capable of learning how to develop "good" human potentialities and more effective supporting social systems.
- People can learn how to become more balanced, complete, effective, and happy persons.
- *Self*-development and social responsibility are the final goals of education.
- The most important thing about a person is the human spirit to love, create, and transcend.
- Persons act and behave in accord with their values, dreams, and aspirations.
- People need to develop personal and social goals and values to live by.
- Cognitive learning is dependent on the effective-emotional state and the self-confidence and esteem of the person involved.
- Basic "self-knowledge" (self-awareness, understanding, acceptance, expression, assertion, control, and self-renewal) is the fundamental knowledge to be learned by all persons.
- A humanistic educational system furthers the continuous progress of persons at their own rates of learning through the provision of individualized objectives and programs.
- The humanistic educator is essentially a facilitator who guides and supports the learner in the process of becoming a unique person.

This chapter has introduced some of the fundamental concepts and principles of humanistic education. The remainder of this book will elaborate on these ideas and will also present numerous other models of humanistic education programs.

The emphasis throughout this book is on the practical educational applications of relevant humanistic theory and research. Teachers and other human facilitators will find most of this material of immediate value in designing their own programs. The reader should consider the summary discussion questions and activities at the end of each chapter as transitional to material yet to be presented. Humanistic education must be experienced in order to be understood—I hope that the reader's interest and experiential involvement will be furthered by this book.

DISCUSSION QUESTIONS AND ACTIVITIES

1. List and share several of your own unique abilities and human potentialities.
2. What do you feel are the most important things in life that people need to learn?
3. Discuss some things that you have aspired to. How have your aspirations affected your behavior?
4. To what extent do you think that elementary school pupils can help set their own learning objectives?
5. Assuming that you could help select the topics for an ethnic studies class or for a comparative religions class (at Edison High School), what specific ones would you include?
6. Describe something you have done to re-create and renew your own self-energy.
7. Give an example of how you have personally experienced one of the principles listed on pp. 6 and 7.
8. Should education help persons to meet human needs? Why or why not?

Children need to explore and discover their environment.

The goal of education is . . . to assist students to become individuals who are able to take self-initiated action and to be responsible for those actions; who are capable of intelligent choice and self-direction, . . . who work, not for the approval of others, but in terms of their own socialized purposes.

CARL R. ROGERS (1942, p. 384)

CHAPTER 2

Human needs and educational goals

EDUCATION IS A PROCESS of systematic experiences by which the individual learns how to live. The educational process itself is largely determined by the beliefs, aspirations, values, and affluence of the culture in which the individual finds himself. Historically, the structure of the educational process has been largely determined by those unique beliefs and values regarding human nature and the needs of the individual relative to those of society. Traditionally, social and cultural needs have received primary consideration, while individual needs and aspirations have been of secondary concern; this may have been a wise course of action in the early days of human history when the emphasis was on basic survival, but these priorities now need to be reversed.

No one questions the importance of survival itself; the critical issue is with the *quality* of survival and the direction of human evolution and social organization. When Cro-Magnon man struggled to raise his young, his efforts were geared to the constant realities of acquiring food, shelter, and protection from the ever-present dangers of a threatening physical environment. With the gradual acquisition of skills such as the control of fire and the development of simple tools, he quickly learned to modify and in some respects control the environment. The goal of adaptation and environmental control has continued to be, and will always be, the first concern in the mind of educators whether they be parents, teachers, or governors. But we no longer live in a primitive society. We have gradually progressed through such simple social and educational systems as those of the tribe and clan to the increasing de-

9

mands of the village and township and now to the complexities of the modern state and nation.

People quickly learned that through community of interests they increased their chances for survival. The problem of who was to decide what was best for the individual and the tribe was quickly settled by the obvious value of power. Authority over others was given to the most powerful leader, who made the final decisions as to what the society should do and in what direction it should go. This leader—chief, king, or dictator—then took appropriate steps to ensure that the people would learn how to contribute to and protect that society. A division of labor gradually developed, with a hierarchy of skills to be learned. At the apex, of course, were the warriors as the protectors of the society. Next came the priests, who were charged with the protection and enhancement of the emerging cultural values and who served as advisors to the leaders and as moral teachers and guides of the populace. At the bottom were the workers and the artisans, who were taught the tedious skills and assigned the mundane tasks necessary for perpetuation of the social organization. The primary skill to be learned by everyone was the use and refinement of weapons. With gradual technological advance, the need for improved systems of communication and the storage and transfer of knowledge became apparent. So societies created written language structures, built libraries, and established formal instructional systems— and schools came into being.

But schools were highly selective. Their purpose was to teach the selected few how to better understand the existing cultural values and symbols and how to contribute to their support through the development of required reading, writing, or technical motor skills. Such instruction was usually short term, mechanical, rote, and presented with forceful discipline that included the frequent administration of corporal punishment. Seldom, if ever, did the system recognize individual needs or inclinations or give any attention to the emotional and esthetic feelings or humanistic aspirations of the pupils. Although some exceptions exist, education of the masses has developed from this sterile background.

The traditional educational system did its job very well. It did train warriors and technicians who built and protected nations and empires, and it did acquaint the masses with its cultural values and the desire to nourish and defend them. It inspired a respect for power and for knowledge and an increasing desire for people to be able to communicate more readily regarding the ideas and values inherent within their culture. Gradually, there emerged a consciousness that knowledge itself was power and that the individual or society with such knowledge had a strength that could even supersede raw muscle power. With the emergence of such an insight and the belief that knowledge and power were interrelated, mass public education received an impetus that is still with us today.

With increasing literacy, self- and social awareness began to evolve and eventually reached the point of critical analysis—a dangerous point at which the people became ever more capable of analyzing their own cultural myths, values, and social-political systems and that inevitably resulted in personal and social strife, revolution, and continued social reorganization. Throughout the world, empires and social systems began to be challenged with new ideas and ways of living. The seed of democracy planted in ancient Greece continued to grow and spread in many forms—the impact of Christianity on Rome, the reformation in Europe, the American, French, Russian, Chinese, and "Third World" revolutions—that have culminated in the widespread surge for freedom and self-determination widely evident today.

Today the concerns of humanity are different. The demands on education have changed. The concern with the development of human faculties, abilities, and skills for elementary personal and social survival is no longer sufficient by itself. Although the traditionalists would attempt to confine education to the teaching of such basic skills as reading, writing, arithmetic, and perhaps some specific occupational training as well, most conservatives have recognized that this must be broadened to include general cognitive development. They argue that intellectual abilities must be fully developed and that it is essential that such things as the scientific method and the principles of acquiring, analyzing, evaluating, and using knowledge must also be taught. These are laudable goals that recognize that the mere acquisition of knowledge—information and facts—is insufficient if the individual is incapable of fully understanding, critically evaluating, and applying what he has learned.

But the acquisition of knowledge and continued cognitive development alone are insufficient goals for modern education; such an education is incomplete. People are more than computing machines that digest and process data to reach some objective conclusion. An education that produces intelligent computers capable of conquering the world, conducting suicidal religious children's crusades, organizing bloody inquisitions, developing super crematoriums as "final solutions to the Jewish problem," or justifying the indiscriminate annihilation of village populations in foreign wars is an inhumane and grossly inadequate education. Equally inadequate is the development of "Watergate" mentalities and distorted values that attempt to justify criminal political acts and Big Brother surveillance of the citizenry. There is no question but that people need to continue to develop rational powers of thinking and problem solving. To develop an "intelligent problem solver" is indeed a highly desirable goal of education. But it is only one goal and no longer the most important one, as it is now secondary to human survival.

THE NEED FOR HUMANISTIC EDUCATION

In the advanced countries it is now possible for a person to survive and live a relatively long life with only the most rudimentary skills in reading, writing, and computing. He can, in fact, be a rather poor problem solver with limited intellect and still continue to exist for years to come. Although the quality of this individual's life would undoubtedly leave something to be desired, he certainly lives much much longer than his caveman counterpart, for whom poor problem solving practically assured a very early demise. We have finally controlled our environment to the point that physical survival alone is not our compelling concern. Our technology has been developed to the extent that it can assure our survival, and we no longer need cringe in terror at the demands of the elements or the uncaged ferocity of the beasts of the forest. Our survival is no longer dependent on those external environmental forces historically perceived as beyond our control. What *is* crucial to our survival and continued evolution, however, is the degree to which we are now able to develop awareness of and control over our irrational propensities and inclinations. We are our own worst enemy, and somehow we must learn that it is the "beast within ourselves" that needs to be understood and changed through the process of meaningful education while concomitantly developing our uniquely human positive potentialities.

The development of emotive abilities, the shaping of affective desires, the fuller expression of aesthetic qualities, and the enhancement of powers of self-direction and control should receive instructional priority. It must be recognized that the primary purpose of education is to develop individuals who will be able to live joyous, humane, and meaningful lives. Education is perceived here as a lifelong process of developmental experiences. Effective education changes people in accord with the goals or objectives of the system. Educators are charged by society to bring about certain desirable behavioral changes in their pupils. Presumably, these changes are the result of clearly desirable goals and relevant experiences designed to accomplish these ends. Humanistic education recognizes the primary importance of the development of those social and personal skills essential to living in human society. Its intent is, as Sylvia Ashton Warner (1964) asserts, "to help children grow up in their own personal way into creative and interesting people."

This is not to disparage traditional cognitive development, excellence, and achievement. Humanistic education is concerned with the development of the whole person, including affective, motor, and cognitive abilities; but it stresses the primacy of affective and emotive development over the cognitive and motor aspects of behavior. The person who lives a joyous, humane, and meaningful life is a well-educated person. He has learned to deal with the harsh realities of existence and to experience the joy and exhilaration of living in a demanding and ever-changing world. He has learned to temper the harsh realities of existence with humane consideration and compassion for his fellow human being and to confront the brutal aspects in self and society. And he has learned to identify with something in his life worth working and striving for, which gives meaning to his existence. In so doing the educated person has learned how to use his physical, cognitive, and intellectual skills to more humane ends. He has, in the words of Alvin Toffler (1971), expanded his adaptive capacities, learned to relate to others, inculcated moral values, and developed the capacity needed to "control change and to guide his own evolution."

Humanistic education insists that the individual not be manipulated by some superimposed social ethic. He is not a toy to be computer programmed by those who "know best" what is good for him and the society in which he lives. Rather than be trained and programmed to fit the manpower needs of society and to pledge unquestionable allegiance to a king or dictator, each person must be educated to be able to understand, analyze, and meet his own personal needs as well as those of society.

humanistic education is one in which the individual is helped to become a self-directed, responsible, self-realized, and social human being. The effective educational program is one that recognizes and provides for individual needs through varied experiences that are personally and socially relevant. Effective humanistic education must begin with an assessment of human needs.

HUMAN NEEDS AND EDUCATION

There are many human needs and numerous ways of categorizing and describing them. If education is to prepare individuals to live joyous, humane, and meaningful lives, it must be concerned with helping to prepare them to more adequately cope with human needs. If a person proves incapable of meeting his needs together with those of others in his social system, it is improbable that he will be able to live a joyous, humane, or meaningful life. We might think that the schools have been teaching pupils how to meet human needs for years, but this has been proved to be a false assumption. As a result of an extensive survey of American schools by a team under the direction of John Goodlad (1969), Dean of the School of Education at UCLA, he reported that "we were unable to discern much attention to pupil needs, attainments, or problems as a basis for individual opportunities to learn." Humanistic education insists that meaningful learning can only result when pupil needs, problems, and attainments have been assessed and become the basis for the instructional programs. Children's basic needs may be categorized into six major areas as described here.

Physical security

Without basic physical security, learning becomes a difficult, if not impossible, task because the individual's energy is devoted to coping with his anxiety and fear of questionable survival. The functional needs to be met are for food and balanced diet, adequate housing, sufficient clothing, and good physical health and basic self-help skills.

Food and balanced diet

The hungry child is a poor learner. Many children arrive at school with empty stomachs that cause inattention and lack of energy during the day. We know that physical energy depends on adequate blood sugar levels. We also know that malnourishment such as protein insufficiency retards neurological development and produces intellectual defects. The implications are clear that parents and educators must cooperate in meeting this basic need much more adequately than they have in the past. In addition to family education regarding nutrition, school breakfast and lunch programs may have to be expanded and nutritional snacks such as orange juice provided at strategic learning periods throughout the day. Educators may also have to become more intimately involved in social welfare, community planning, and political movements to ensure that this need is met.

Adequate housing

The child who lives in grossly inadequate and crowded quarters is handicapped in learning. Lack of beds and sleeping space and poor or missing utilities negatively affect his health. Constant interruption and stimulation interfere with his ability to concentrate, read, or study. Meeting this need requires obvious social planning and intervention.

Sufficient clothing

Clothing is sufficient if it covers the child to the extent that it protects him adequately from the elements and does not evoke derision from his peer group or community. Children still remain out of school because parents have not been able to obtain shoes, coats, rain gear, and other essential items. Although many schools do have cooperative "clothes closets" that receive donated goods from the community, this is hardly the most desirable way of coping with what is essentially a broad socioeconomic problem involving employment and welfare policy. Schools should continue to assess the needs of pupils in this regard and to provide for them on an emergency basis but, again, broader involvement is required for this need to be met.

Good physical health and basic self-help skills

It should be obvious that the child with impaired vision, poor hearing, infected adenoids, and other apparent health defects will have difficulty in learning. Other children with dental anomalies, orthopedic problems, and similar disabilities not as readily apparent and those who have not acquired essential self-help skills such as toilet, washing, and eating habits usually experience educational difficulty. Until these individual needs are adequately diagnosed, understood, and met through correction or remediation, learning academic skills may be a waste of time if not an impossibility. Again, the school is limited in what it can do in this area. But many countries, for example, New Zealand, provide school health and dental services that have proved significantly effective in eradicating local and national health problems and in meeting individual needs. Such existing models can well serve as a basis for other governmental and educational systems to improve in this area.

Love

Everyone has a need for love, especially children in the process of growing and becoming. Education must recognize this elemental need and provide for it through such means as personal acknowledgment and attention, sensory-physical stimulation and interaction, and continued interpersonal involvement and warmth.

Personal acknowledgment and attention

The child needs to be acknowledged as an individual in his own right who is different from others in numerous respects but equal to them in needs and rights as a person. He needs to be attended to and praised for his unique strivings and accom plishments. Education must reorganize itself so that the individual is not lost or submerged in the faceless group. The school must be changed to systematically provide personal acknowledgment and attention to all pupils.

Sensory-physical stimulation and interaction

Love is experienced through acknowledgment and sensory-physical interaction with others. Children need to be touched, patted, hugged, tickled, squeezed, spanked, and kissed. Unfortunately, schools have been grossly lacking in positive physical interactions with pupils but seldom lax in negative stimulation such as spanking. Of course, the reverse should be true. Teachers and principals should become the source of positive interaction—a pat on the back here, a squeeze there, and an occasional kiss for younger children. Such positive associations with the learning process and his teachers by the child can drastically change his entire perception of self and the life he lives. Of course, educators need to exercise careful discretion in this area, but there is no question but that this human need can be met much more effectively within the educational process than it has been in the past.

Continued interpersonal involvement and warmth

Once the more essential love needs have been met, the need for continued interpersonal involvement and warmth is evident. The child needs to feel that the significant others in his life such as his teachers really care about what he does and how he feels. This is involvement on a higher level in which the teacher engages the student in a warm and supporting atmosphere to examine what he is doing and what he feels worthy of learning. The involvement of the pupil with others is a need fundamental to all further learning.

Creative expression

Once the needs for security and love have been satisfied, the individual becomes capable of coping with his distinctly human needs involving expressive, symbolic, and social skills. His need to express himself can be met through educational provisions that promote sensory exploration and development, expressive joy, and divergent and flexible production.

Sensory exploration and development

The opportunity to develop his sensory capacities must be provided through improved early childhood and elementary education programs. The child needs to learn to listen to the multitude of sounds in his environment, to become more visually astute to the colors and forms presented to him, and to experience the sensation of such varied textures as water, mud, paint, and sand. Both creative expression and later cognitive development are dependent on realization of the need for multisensory stimulation. Schools can easily extend their programs in this area by providing sand tables and auditory and visual stimulus materials and by increasing the number of excursions and opportunities for such exploration.

Expressive joy

If the need for creative expression is realized, the child will be able to express his feelings of joy. To develop, to produce, to create, to bring into existence something unique to the individual is a cause for celebration and joy. The child needs to learn that learning and creating are in themselves joyous experiences. The need to express such joy must be recognized and provided for as an integral part of the educational experience.

Divergent and flexible production

The goal of creative expression is not convergent or stereotyped production or achievement. It is instead the development of divergence, spontaneity, and flexibility—to create an openness and confidence in exploring new media and problems that the child will confront in life. Where education has traditionally emphasized convergence, more opportunities are now required for creative exploration and can be provided through a reemphasis of the arts and the expansion of innovative and experimental approaches to teaching the traditional subject matter disciplines.

Cognitive mastery

All persons need to acquire proficiency in thinking and problem solving. The continued development of intellectual capacity is dependent on the satisfaction of these needs: developmental-cultural experiences and opportunities to acquire and obtain general information; analyzing, evaluating, and judging problem situations, and achieving relative competency in basic learning skills.

Developmental-cultural experiences and opportunities to acquire and obtain general information

The traditional classroom is a rather sterile place for learning. It must be broadened to include the community and the culture—indeed, the entire world—in which the learner finds himself. The need to encounter varied life experiences and to become knowledgeable of the world demands alternative educational experiences to those presented in limited books within the four walls of the school classroom. Excursions and trips of all kinds, community work experiences, outdoor education, and individual community study projects are all means available to this end.

Analyzing, evaluating, and judging problem situations

General information and facts must be processed through the rigors of intelligent thinking. We now know that the rational critical and evaluative powers not only need to be developed, but *can* be developed through specific instruction. To survive, the individual needs to become more proficient in the selection, judgment, and application of the data he has accumulated.

Achieving relative competency in basic learning skills

No matter where he finds himself, each person will be called on to use certain basic skills in daily living. These will include large muscle, sensory, perceptual, and language skills. The child desperately needs to learn the rudiments of his primary language and its expression in oral and written form. He needs to compute, to purchase, and to measure. He must learn to listen, to discriminate, to follow directions, and to move appropriately to the many demands of his environment. These needs will continue to form the content of much of the educational program.

Social competency

Although some social needs have been provided for through schooling, most of this has been incidental. The educational system must now be deliberately constructed to meet the individual's needs for peer group acceptance and interaction, a moral and ethical sense of right and wrong with personal self-controls, and social responsibility and helping others.

Peer group acceptance and interaction

It is good and proper that many friendships are made in school. School is a socializing experience that begins with purposeful instruction and help in relating to others in the immediate environment. This is a critical need since, without such a relationship, no meaningful interaction with the environment can occur. There are numerous ways that teachers can structure their programs to make group interaction and coming to know and relate to others a possibility.

A moral and ethical sense of right and wrong with personal self-controls

In the final analysis of individual behavior, most learning has moral and ethical implications. Schools have always taught conventional morality through the actions of their teachers if through nothing else. Moral education and the inculcation of moral values are shared with the home, church, and community organizations, but there is no escape—nor should there be—for the school. Children today desperately need moral guidance, and a meaningful education must provide it more effectively than it has in the past. There is no question but that the child must learn to judge that helping someone in need is right and that inflicting pain or humiliation on a person is wrong. Morality is learned, and the virtues of life can be taught; the need is great, and education must help the child acquire these values.

Social responsibility and helping others

A person does not live by his individual efforts alone; the fullness of life depends on living successfully with others. The individual needs to develop an awareness of others, to care for and assist them, and to share in the responsibility of deciding and working for the betterment of all. The educational process should enable him to gradually understand and assume greater social responsibility. The need to care and be responsible is within us, and its fulfillment contributes to a more humane existence.

Self-worth

Many needs are summarized in the need for self-worth, which cannot be realized until the fundamental needs for physical security, love, creative expression, cognitive mastery, and social competency have been met, at least in part. The need for self-worth consists of the following components: personal worth and dignity, acceptance of personal strengths and weaknesses, and realistic self-confidence and independence.

Personal worth and dignity

All persons need to believe they are valuable and worthwhile in their own right. If their more basic needs have been met, they will develop a sense of uniqueness, personal identity, and dignity in their existence and accomplishments. The awareness of such a need and its importance can be fostered only by an education that treats the learner with respect.

Acceptance of personal strengths and weaknesses

Education is an ongoing experience by which the child becomes ever more conscious of himself. His developing consciousness needs to confront the reality of personal strengths and limitations. Most schooling has resulted in the awareness of distinct limitations, shortcomings, and failures on the part of the learner. What should be drastically improved in education are instructional systems such as continuous progress, ungraded, no-fail school organizations in which the child's strengths and assets are reinforced and developed to their fullest while weaknesses are minimized. The child needs to feel good about himself and what he can do.

Realistic self-confidence and independence

When his other needs have been met, a person still needs to feel self-confident and become reliant on his own judgment as a mature individual. Only in this way does he become independent of others to the extent that independence and freedom are possibilities. The goals of education demand that this need be met before education can be judged to be effective.

In the illustration on p. 19 the basic needs of children are presented in a psychoeducational hierarchy for teacher evaluation. It is not essential that each child be systematically evaluated in great detail to develop an effective educational program. What is necessary, however, is that the teacher be fully aware of the importance of these needs and use them as a frame of reference in selection of instructional objectives and teaching methodology. For children with pronounced learning problems it is always wise to evaluate these needs in some detail and to discuss them with a experienced colleague. It is also helpful to involve parents in the assessment of their child's needs, which can be done through the use of the chart during a house visitation or teacher conference.

Children should be involved in the evaluation of their own needs wherever possible. This is usually done in informal discussion with the teacher, with the child judging to what extent his needs have been met. With the help of the pupil, the parents, and an interested colleague or administrator, it is possible to determine to what extent the child's needs are being met, what other evaluation is necessary, and

CHILDREN'S BASIC NEEDS

A Psychoeducational Hierarchy for Teacher Evaluation

Student's Name _____ Age_____ Teacher _____

Children have essentially six basic areas of needs that must be met in part by appropriate education if learning is to contribute to continued growth and development. It is especially important to evaluate the student with a learning problem carefully in order to determine how the educational program can be arranged more effectively to meet the needs of the child.

On the following chart, mark the rating for each need that most accurately completes this sentence: *This student's need for _____ appears to have been realized:*

BASIC AREAS OF NEEDS	Very well	Well	Some-what	Very little	Not at all
6. **Self-worth** • realistic self-confidence and independence • acceptance of personal strengths and limitations • an awareness of personal worth and dignity					
5. **Social Competency** • social responsibility and helping others • a moral-ethical sense of "right" and "wrong" with personal self-controls • peer group acceptance and interaction					
4. **Cognitive Mastery** • achieving relative competency in basic learning skills • analyzing, evaluating, and judging problem situations • developmental-cultural experiences and opportunities to acquire and obtain general information					
3. **Creative Expression** • divergent and flexible production • expressive joy • sensory exploration and development					
2. **Love** • continued interpersonal involvement and warmth • sensory-physical stimulation and interaction • personal acknowledgement and attention					
1. **Physical Security** • good physical health and basic self-help skills • sufficient clothing • adequate housing • food and balanced diet					

Describe in your own words what you feel to be the priority needs of this child:

how a meaningful learning experience might be designed. As his needs are met and as he is received and nourished, so will he live. A proper education should enable him to live well.

DEVELOPMENTAL STAGES AND EDUCATION

Although human needs are always with us, there are stages of growth and development during which some needs are dominant over others. Education must carefully consider these developmental stages of growth to determine their implications for teaching. As a result of the work of Bloom (1956) and Krathwohl et al. (1964) a taxonomy of educational objectives has been developed; it has been organized into three major domains, or areas of concern. These areas have been termed the psychomotor, cognitive, and affective domains of education and can be traced back to the classical Grecian emphasis on the person as an integration of mental, physical, and spiritual abilities and potentialities. Such a view has been largely substantiated by the findings of developmental psychology, and the formulation of psychomotor, cognitive, and affective objectives of education has become widely accepted. Any consideration of educational goals and human needs is incomplete without proposing a structure in which they might be realized. If we view each domain as a stage of human growth with distinctive educational implications, we can specify a number of skills and abilities that evolve in part as the result of the learning process. Let us briefly examine each of these components in terms of their contribution to humanistic education.

Psychomotor stage of growth

The psychomotor stage is characterized by the struggle to develop body movement and control of one's body in a given environment. This concept is portrayed by the drawing of a child on all fours attempting to move through space (p. 21). The effort is complicated by the nature of the many muscles, bones, nerves, and sensory processes involved in body movement and control. The young child experiences his body as a puzzle box to probe, to extend, to fit together, and finally to integrate and coordinate for the spatial demands at hand. The skills and abilities to be developed are gross motor (those having to do with large-muscle activity such as throwing), sensory-motor (those having to do with the psychophysical integration of fine and gross motor activities such as are required in balance and rhythm tasks), and perceptual-motor (which have to do with the functional utilization of primary auditory, visual, and visual-motor skills such as those required in following directions, discriminating symbols, and drawing).

The learning process involved in the development of these psychomotor skills and abilities must be primarily concerned with motor and manipulative exercises. The first step in the process is to expose the learner to a rich environment that will stimulate his unconscious potentialities; fondling, deliberate talking to, and playing with infants are perhaps the most common examples of planned stimulation, but the

GROWTH STAGES	SKILLS AND ABILITIES	LEARNING PROCESSES
Affective	Social and personal	Emotive development • Personal transcendence • Self-identification and expression • Feeling and intuiting
Cognitive	Conceptual Language	Symbolic development • Thinking • Verbal expression • Conscious awareness
Psychomotor	Perceptual-motor Sensory-motor Gross motor	Motor development • Concrete relationships • Sensory exploration • Unconscious stimulation

Developmental stages and education.

same process is involved in teaching older children specific games and in the rehabilitation of brain-injured and other handicapped persons.

The next step involves opportunities for the learner to openly explore his environment under his own initiative and concomitantly to refine his varied sensory
modalities through touching, seeing, hearing, tasting, and sensing what surrounds
him; this varies significantly from the first step in that, initially, the child is deliberately manipulated by the forces in his environment, whereas at this step *he* initiates
the action and moves out to engage the world. As a result of movement in and
exploration of his world, the learner begins to manipulate objects and people and
eventually to form elementary concrete relationships. He comes to understand that
milk goes with bottles, shoes with feet, barking with dogs, leaves with trees, pictures and symbols with books, etc. The learning process here depends on the concrete material and equipment and extensive opportunities for direct physical contact
and manipulation of the environment. Although psychomotor development continues throughout life, the child gradually begins to comprehend his surroundings
and to rely on more cognitive abilities in coping with his problems.

Cognitive stage of growth

The cognitive stage of growth is characterized by the struggle of the individual to
use and manipulate symbols in the control of his environment. Instead of continually
dealing with concrete forms of reality, the learner begins to rely on representations of
that reality such as pictures, words, and numbers. He now begins to understand and
know his world through the manipulation of these representations and the growing
understanding of their relationships. This stage is portrayed on p. 21 by the individual contemplating his existence. The contemplated life is largely one of self-
examination of one's actions, thoughts, and feelings and is essential to the full development of the person. The kinds of skills and abilities to be developed during this
stage are largely language and conceptual in nature. Language skills have to do with
oral and written expression such as those skills commonly covered in speaking,
reading, and writing curriculums. The conceptual abilities are linguistic and symbolic
but have to do with the functional level of the kinds of critical concepts represented
in basic arithmetic and science programs dealing with sets, classification systems, and
logical thinking.

The learning process involved in the development of cognitive abilities is primarily concerned with the introduction and manipulation of cultural symbols. The initial
step is in developing a conscious awareness of oneself and one's environment that
evolves out of the concrete relationships experienced earlier. The awareness to be
developed is that experience and reality can be represented by symbols acquired
through systematic instruction. Thus the "tools" (words, numbers, etc.) for understanding and acquiring further knowledge are carefully presented in a sequential
curriculum. Once awareness and basic skill have been acquired, the learning process
is one of extended verbal expression. It is only through expression of cognitive skills
that the child becomes proficient in their use and application. The final step in the

process is the development of thinking to the point that the learner can not only express the essential language and conceptual skills he has learned but he can also deal with them abstractly, relate one concept to another, formulate new ideas, critically analyze his own thought processes, and move on to the creation of more profound symbols and systems.

As with psychomotor skills, cognitive development is a lifelong process. Much of it has occurred before formal education begins. But a great deal of it is shaped during the school years by the nature of the learning process in which the child finds himself. As important as cognitive development may be in education, it is but one domain in human life. The third and culminating stage is affective, which requires careful consideration.

Affective stage of growth

The affective stage of human growth is characterized by the awareness of feelings and emotions and their expression in continually refined interests, attitudes, beliefs, and value orientations. Affective development is intimately related to psychomotor and cognitive development and, like them, continues from birth to death. Most human behavior is finally determined by the person's affective-emotional state, which sifts the motor and cognitive inputs of experience.

The premise of this book is that the affective domain of human development has been seriously underrated in education as determined through curricular offerings and methods of school organization. The school can be much more influential than it has been in the past if it wishes to be so. It should be clearly recognized, however, that the educational system cannot in and of itself produce mature personalities and emotionally sound persons, since the quest for maturity is a lifelong developmental process with inherent maturational and experiential limitations in early and middle childhood and adolescence. But this does not mean that affective needs cannot be more fully attended to throughout the years of school or that improved programs to teach basic social and personal skills cannot be implemented.

The affective domain is pictorially represented on p. 21 by an upright person with outreaching arms and hands. All people reach out in personal hope and aspiration and in their feelings for continued development. The skills for such development are essentially social and personal ones required to effectively relate to oneself and to others. The abilities to accept oneself, to make friends, and to cope with social demands and responsibility are illustrative of those to be developed in part through the affective learning process.

The process itself must be designed around emotive concerns, problems, and subjective aspects of living. These are the human *qualities* of life that form the psychological glue or cement by which the individual holds himself together. The basic step in the learning process is one of dealing with feelings and subjective intuitions. The need is to explore the modes of emotion, feeling, and human concern and for the child to learn that these are legitimate areas of study and investigation without undue arousal of guilt or anxiety. From exploration, awareness, and understanding, the learning process must move to the intricacies of self-identification and expression, for it is here that the young learner must begin to face himself, to form his identity, and to moderate and control his expressive behavior. The learning process must also attempt to enhance those skills whereby the person's emotional development may result in personal transcendance. Acknowledgeably difficult as it may be, the educational system must be designed to culminate in rational, ethical, and altruistic behavior on the part of emotionally sound individuals.

SUMMARY

Educational goals have changed with the historical development and needs of humanity. Initially concerned with transmitting the rudimentary skills required for physical survival, humanity gradually shifted its focus to cognitive and academic development. Humanistic education proposes that the traditional emphases on physical and academic disciplines are grossly inadequate by themselves. If education is to be effective, the final result must be persons capable of living joyful, humane, and meaningful lives. To accomplish this purpose, affective and emotional objectives must be given more prominence within the curriculum.

The curriculum must become individualized and be based on the unique needs and accomplishments of each child. Educators must assess the learner's needs for physical security, love, creative expression, cognitive mastery, social competency, and self-worth. The school can adapt more readily to individual pupil needs if it recognizes developmental stages of growth and attempts to specify psychomotor, cognitive, and affective objectives for all children. An effective learning process is one that enables the pupil to acquire or develop the specific skills and abilities needed to solve his motor, cognitive, and affective problems. *Total* human development must become the aim of modern education.

DISCUSSION QUESTIONS AND ACTIVITIES

1. Discuss some of the historical beliefs about human nature and how they have influenced education.
2. How important is it today for everyone to become skilled in the use and refinement of weapons?
3. List several goals common to the American, French, Russian, and Chinese revolutions.
4. Do you think it is possible that our educational system could develop "1984-type" persons as described in George Orwell's famous novel? Explain your answer.
5. Write an example of how "man is his own worst enemy."
6. Think of yourself as you were in the sixth or seventh grade. Now complete the Children's Basic Needs form (p. 19) for yourself as you were at that time. What were your own priority learning needs at that time in your life?
7. List some psychomotor skills that you had trouble learning.
8. What do you consider to be the most important cognitive skill that a person must acquire? Why?
9. List several emotive concerns and problems of adolescents that might be included in an affective learning curriculum.

We learn to love and care for others.

*We seek for each individual the chance to be a whole person, free
of fragmentation that plagues modern life—fragmentation of intellect
and emotion, work and play, job and family, man and nature.*

JOHN W. GARDNER (1970)

CHAPTER 3

Developing the humane person

A BROAD CONSENSUS now exists that education must be concerned with the total person, with the development of all human potentialities to the fullest possible extent. This is, of course, a long-range ideal goal, but it can provide direction for the educational process. The trend toward designing education to meet human needs and concerns has even been formally recognized by governmental bodies, as exemplified by a report of the Joint Committee on Educational Goals and Evaluations of the California Legislature (1970, p. 4); this committee formally states that "the process of setting goals for education must include an assessment of the individual and collective needs for society." The report then considers how these varied needs can be determined and how educational systems might then be held accountable for them. With the growing awareness that traditional education has been constrictively narrow and inadequate in its provisions for human needs, there has been a clamoring for change that has been furthered by the popular media, and it has had a demonstrable effect in practically every community throughout the land. Writers such as John Holt (1970) have prompted a crusade on educational reform by pointing out that the answer to What makes a good education? is only found in the conceptualizations of what it is that makes a good life—and that the development of individuals to live a good life is the fundamental business of education. So it appears that the process of educational reform is well underway. The fundamental questions have been asked, the demand for relevance to individual and social needs has been accepted, and the quest for new models and accountability procedures has begun.

Humanistic education insists that the individual be provided with the chance to become a whole person. It agrees with Gardner that the fragmentation of intellect, emotion, and life functions must be countered through meaningful programs that integrate a person into a unique human being. But we must do more than merely

27

provide a chance that this will occur. What is required is cooperative effort between professional and lay groups to ensure that curricular offerings and school organization will be redesigned to accomplish the stated objectives. Whereas the traditional approach has usually offered a chance for the individual to become a whole person, the reorganization of education must be such that it assumes responsibility for the probable realization of this noble goal. As reported by the White House Conference on Children (1970, p. 123), "the curriculum, objectives, and structure of our present educational system are largely products of another age—responses to the needs of a society immersed in the rapid transition from rural/agricultural to urban/ industrial life styles." Curricular design and reorganization to meet current human needs is a major undertaking that must involve a continuously ongoing process of development and evaluation. Although many curricular models and designs are possible, those that seem most promising for total humanistic education appear to stem from developmental learning theory and research.

Developmental learning theory recognizes stages of human growth and their educational implications. It acknowledges that individual and social needs are reflected in motivational patterns for learning; concomitantly, it accepts the feasibility of viewing psychomotor, cognitive, and affective development as being realized in part through the specification of educational objectives and subsequent individualized programming. It also acknowledges that specific skills and abilities can be developed through instruction at opportune times in a well-designed environment for learning. Through the careful study of human growth and development, it has formulated sequential hierarchies of skills and abilities that can be considered as a frame of reference for curriculum development. These "basic learning abilities" should become the subject matter content of the modern school. Let us now consider them in some detail.

THE BASIC LEARNING ABILITIES

There are numerous ways of defining basic learning abilities. The one presented here is derived from a consideration of those critical behaviors or operational functions in which a person needs to become proficient to live the good life. It assumes that he must acquire these proficiencies through the developmental and learning process of education, and it assumes that all of these skills and abilities are important in their own right and as such constitute a proper subject matter for education.

The basic learning abilities are presented in six developmental levels that include skills from the psychomotor through the cognitive and affective domains of educational objectives. Each of these levels and the abilities included in it are as follows:

Level one: gross motor abilities (those required in the development and awareness of large muscle activity)

- *Rolling:* the ability to roll one's body in a controlled manner
- *Sitting:* the ability to sit erect in a normal position without support or constant reminding

- *Crawling:* the ability to crawl on hands and knees in a smooth and coordinated way
- *Walking:* the ability to walk erect in a coordinated fashion without support
- *Running:* the ability to run a track or obstacle course without a change of pace
- *Throwing:* the ability to throw a ball with a reasonable degree of accuracy
- *Jumping:* the ability to jump simple obstacles without falling
- *Skipping:* the ability to skip in normal play
- *Dancing:* the ability to move one's body in coordinated response to music
- *Self-identification:* the ability to identify oneself
- *Body localization:* the ability to locate parts of one's body
- *Body abstraction:* the ability to transfer and generalize self-concepts and body localizations
- *Muscular strength:* the ability to use one's muscles to perform physical tasks
- *General physical health:* the ability to understand and apply principles of health and hygiene while demonstrating good general health

Level two: sensory-motor abilities (those required in the psychophysical integration of fine and gross motor activity)

- *Balance and rhythm:* the ability to maintain gross and fine motor balance and to move rhythmically
- *Body-spatial organization:* the ability to move one's body in an integrated way around and through objects in the spatial environment
- *Tactile discrimination:* the ability to identify and match objects by touching and feeling
- *Directionality:* the ability to know right from left, up from down, forward from backward, and directional orientation
- *Laterality:* the ability to integrate one's sensory-motor contact with the environment through establishment of homolateral hand, eye, and foot dominance
- *Time orientation:* the ability to judge lapses in time and to be aware of time concepts

Level three: perceptual-motor abilities (those required in primary auditory, visual, and visual-motor functioning)

- *Auditory acuity:* the ability to receive and differentiate auditory stimuli
- *Auditory decoding:* the ability to understand sounds or spoken words
- *Auditory-vocal association:* the ability to respond verbally in a meaningful way to auditory stimuli
- *Auditory memory:* the ability to retain and recall general auditory information
- *Auditory sequencing:* the ability to recall prior auditory information in correct sequence and detail
- *Visual acuity:* the ability to see objects in one's visual field and to differentiate them meaningfully and accurately
- *Visual coordination and pursuit:* the ability to follow and track objects and symbols with coordinated eye movements
- *Visual form discrimination:* the ability to differentiate visually the forms and symbols in one's environment
- *Visual figure-ground differentiation:* the ability to perceive objects in foreground and background and to separate them meaningfully
- *Visual memory:* the ability to recall prior visual experiences accurately

- *Visual-motor memory:* the ability to reproduce prior visual experiences by motor activitiy
- *Visual-motor fine muscle coordination:* the ability to coordinate fine muscles, such as those required in eye-hand tasks
- *Visual-motor spatial-form manipulation:* the ability to move in space and to manipulate three-dimensional materials
- *Visual-motor speed of learning:* the ability to learn visual-motor skills from repetitive experiences
- *Visual-motor integration:* the ability to integrate total visual-motor skills in complex problem solving

Level four: language abilities (those required in total psycholinguistic functioning)

- *Vocabulary:* the ability to understand words
- *Fluency and encoding:* the ability to express oneself verbally
- *Articulation:* the ability to articulate words clearly without notable pronunciation or articulation problems
- *Word-attack skills:* the ability to analyze words phonetically
- *Reading comprehension:* the ability to understand what one has read
- *Writing:* the ability to express oneself through written language
- *Spelling:* the ability to spell in both oral and written form

Level five: conceptual abilities (those required in concept attainment and general reasoning)

- *Number concepts:* the ability to count and use simple numbers to represent quantity
- *Arithmetic processes:* the ability to add, subtract, multiply, and divide
- *Arithmetic reasoning:* the ability to apply basic arithmetic processes in personal and social problem solving
- *General information:* the ability to acquire and utilize general information from education and experience
- *Classification:* the ability to recognize class identities and to use them in establishing logical relationships
- *Comprehension:* the ability to use judgment and reasoning in common sense situations

Level six: social abilities (those required in social problem solving)

- *Social acceptance:* the ability to get along with one's peers
- *Anticipatory response:* the ability to anticipate the probable outcome of a social situation by logical inference
- *Value judgments:* the ability to recognize and respond to moral and ethical issues
- *Social maturity:* the ability to assume personal and social responsibility

The developmental levels of basic learning abilities are presented in the figure on p. 31. Gross motor skills form the basic level of the hierarchy, and an illustrative ability is crawling—portrayed by the baby crawling. Crawling is a developmental skill, beginning with creeping and extending to complex target-oriented programs furthering neurophysiological integration. Children should be provided with ample opportunity to crawl and should be taught specific body coordination skills through varied crawling activities. There are fourteen basic gross motor abilities, each with distinctive educational implications. It is assumed that these abilities are as inher

EDUCA-TIONAL OBJECTIVES	SKILLS	EXAMPLE
Affective domain	Social skills (value judgments)	
Cognitive domain	Conceptual skills (comprehension)	
	Language skills (fluency and encoding)	
Psycho-motor domain	Perceptual-motor skills (visual-motor integration)	
	Sensory-motor skills (body spatial organization)	
	Gross motor skills (crawling)	

Developmental levels and basic learning abilities.

ently important as the "higher abilities" on more advanced developmental levels. A developmental learning program must begin with the assessment of individual needs, skills, and abilities to provide the essential data for the prescriptive instruction to follow.

The second level consists of sensory-motor skills such as the body-spatial organization abilities demanded in such games as table tennis. The educational rationale is that body awareness and control of movement in space should be taught through imitative and exploratory exercises with provisions for special playground activities and programs designed for use within the regular classroom. There are seven sensory-motor abilities on this level, all of which are concerned with the integration of both fine and gross motor skills.

Level three consists of fifteen perceptual-motor abilities. Five of these have to do with auditory perception: acuity, decoding, auditory-vocal association, memory, and sequencing. There are also five that cover visual perception: acuity, coordination and pursuit, form discrimination, figure-ground discrimination, and visual memory. The last five are concerned with visual-motor perception and include visual-motor memory, fine muscle coordination, spatial-form manipulation, speed of learning, and visual-motor integration. The picture of the child holding a modern art painting represents the use of visual-motor integration skills, reflected in artistic production, demanding that eye and hand work smoothly together; many educational experiences can be planned to provide opportunities for such integration to develop.

Language skills are found on the fourth developmental level. Seven basic learning abilities, including reading and writing, are found here. Another language skill on this level is fluency and encoding—the ability to express oneself verbally, as is found in occasional encounters between baseball players and umpires. There is no doubt that fluent verbal expression and communication develop gradually as a result of experience and verbal stimulation and that education must recognize that, when the child has the need to express himself and feels free to do so, he should be rewarded and encouraged to engage in extended forms of verbal communication. All of the language abilities are built on more fundamental sensory and perceptual modalities such as auditory memory and visual discrimination. Careful attention must be given to the developmental sequence and interrelatedness of all language and perceptual abilities.

On the fifth level are grouped the six key conceptual abilities of number concepts, arithmetic processes, arithmetic reasoning, general information, classification, and comprehension. The ability to comprehend one's actions is represented by the figure working on the automobile motor. Comprehension develops through experience resulting in increasing attention and in the understanding of varied situations and their implications for problem solving: general exploration, directive instruction, and practice in making inferences and behavioral responses are essential in any relevant educational program. The ability to comprehend requires the use of judgment and reasoning in commonsense situations and involves proficiency in most of the lower level skills listed in the hierarchy.

The culminating level of development concerns social skills. There are four major developmental abilities: social acceptance, anticipatory response, value judgments, and social maturity. Each of these is a critical skill that is built on the other developmental abilities, since social competency demands considerable motor, sensory, perceptual, language, and conceptual integration. One of the most critical social skills is the ability to make value judgments, illustrated by those students who have learned an effective sense of right and wrong and who are able to control their actions and demonstrate proper behavior. It is apparent that children need to be taught consistent standards of right and wrong in keeping with their culture so that they may develop respect for the common humanity and dignity of all people. Pupils should also be instructed in the respect for individuality and the values of democracy and, to this end, education should enable the child to develop from egocentric to rational altruistic behavior. The ultimate development of social skills and abilities is a final criterion for determining the success of all prior education.

Contemporary education will become humanistic when it provides for the fullest possible development of *all* of these abilities. Most of the gross motor, sensory-motor, and perceptual-motor skills fall into the psychomotor domain of educational objectives. Conceptual skills, language skills, and some perceptual skills are found in the cognitive domain. The affective domain of educational objectives covers emotional and subjective behaviors, largely involving social and personal skills on the final developmental level, although, as indicated before, there is dependence on many other lower level skills and abilities in the cognitive and psychomotor domains. Traditional education has stressed the development and remediation of language and conceptual skills, and these all-important abilities must continue to be given considerable weight in any meaningful program. The developmental approach stresses the evaluation and systematic programming of *all* human skills and abilities. One organizational model for practical use is presented in *Programming Learning Disabilities* (Valett, 1969); developmental and remedial lessons and programs for all of these basic learning abilities will be found in *The Remediation of Learning Disabilities* (Valett, 1974). Those interested in diagnosis and evaluation approaches to the basic learning abilities should refer to *The Psychoeducational Inventory of Basic Learning Abilities* (Valett, 1968) for concrete behavioral tasks on beginning, middle, and advanced developmental levels that can become the basis for appraisal by the classroom teacher or educator concerned.

Although all developmental levels and abilities are important and need to be provided for more adequately in modern education, the emphasis in this book is on means whereby social and personal skills can be more fully developed. I strongly concur with the recommendation of the White House Conference on Children (1970, p. 78) that all schools should place special emphasis on the process of ethical reasoning and value formation, and that stress should be on "practice in discussing and arriving at individual ethical choices, with emphasis on both individual and social responsibility." Such an emphasis demands that formal education be more aware of the process involved in developing humane individuals who are capable of living meaningful lives. The process involves much more than providing systematic individualized instruction, as we will see when we now consider the other elements involved in becoming a humane person.

EDUCATIONAL PROCESS AND HUMAN POTENTIALITIES

The educational process must be systematically and deliberately designed for the eventual realization of human potentialities. This process is schematically represented by the figure on p. 35, which stresses the developmental stages involved. The fundamental building blocks in the process are the basic learning abilities that form the content of the curriculum. Once the individual has developed the essential gross motor, sensory-motor, perceptual-motor, language, cognitive, and social skills, he has the personal material and abilities with which to construct his life. But the mere acquisition and development of these separate skills by themselves is insufficient. What is finally demanded of the person is that he integrate his skills and abilities in a unique way so that his potentiality as a distinctive person may be realized in action and total behavior. For such an integration to take place, the educational process must itself possess an *élan vital* or spirit whose very essence is continually involved with and committed to the self-evolvement and integration of each person within the system.

This is a never-ending process, since education continues throughout the life span of the individual, wherever he may find himself. But the school can and must be organized to introduce the basic learning abilities in a systematic way with continual reinforcement and integration throughout the period of formal education. The complexity of this operation is represented in the figure on p. 35 by the many varied patterns and designs of the stepping stones for each developmental stage. In application of these skills and abilities to life situations, the learner must attain some balance between personal and social demands. It is as though the individual is continuously struggling on a balance board to maintain himself as he becomes aware that his personal needs and demands do not always coincide with those of society. A compromise of contrasting needs and demands inevitably must occur. And the dynamics of the compromising process require an awareness of the self and its human potentialities.

The self is best construed as the unique seed or makeup of the human individual with its germ of potentialities, unrealized abilities, predispositions, and inclinations. The self is within the person in the form of genetic qualities, including those distinctive propensities inherited through the evolution of the human species. These include collective tendencies from racial and cultural inheritance, which appear as strivings for symbolic expression that gradually emerge from the unconscious of the individual. The educational systems of the society, whether they be family structure, cultural ceremony, or formal curriculum, all combine to form and shape the way in which the self gradually emerges from its unconscious state. As the dreams, tendencies, images, archetypal strivings, and abilities begin to unfold and be integrated into conscious awareness and behavior, the person is moved to action. The self, then, is

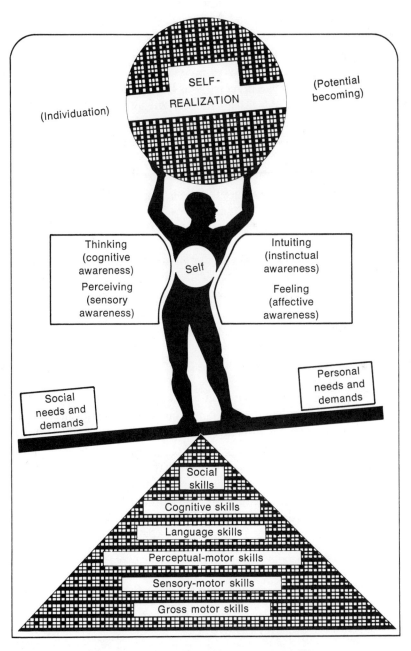

Educational process and human potentialities.

the source of psychic energy that is finally realized in individual patterns of behavior and life-styles.

Human behavior, however, is the result of many tendencies interacting with the environment. And many of these tendencies we share in common with other members of the animal kingdom. We are, after all, primate animals with many raw and primitive urges that, unless refined by humanistic education, can result in truly savage and animalistic expression. Several modes of functioning are open to us. We move and behave largely in accord with our feelings and emotions, or what we have called our affective awareness: every response to our environment has an affective component in terms of how we perceive it as being congruent with our needs, our beliefs, and our aspirations. We also function as perceptual organisms, bombarded by the distinctive stimulus qualities of sound, color, texture, etc., and we eventually become aware of their impact in our lives; artists of all types tend to rely on increased sensory and perceptual awareness as their primary mode of functioning. There are also intuitive propensities within us that may hold great potentiality of the individual: human instinctual awareness is something that is only now beginning to be understood, but the possibilities of knowing, understanding, and behaving accordingly as a result of developing such untapped qualities as extrasensory perception, "creative inclinations," and symbolic imagery require our attention. Of course, we are also thinking animals who function through judgment, reasoning, and being able to manipulate cultural symbols in the course of problem solving; the continued development of cognitive awareness will always be a form of human expression and educational concern.

But other animals also feel, sense, intuit, and think, even though their inherent limitations are greater than ours. What makes the human animal a humane person is the way that he struggles to achieve an integrated balance between the many modes of functioning and the extent to which he is able to realize his unique self-potentiality. This process of ever striving for increased consciousness, for potential becoming, for balance and individuation in one's life-style ideally culminates in self-realization. Few people ever achieve complete wholeness or self-realization in life. But the desirability and awareness of such a possible state of being is itself a reflection of distinctly human behavior that is worthy of development. And the educational process can reflect this concern by deliberately incorporating it in curricular design and organizational structure. This intent has already been proposed by the White House Conference on Children (1970, p. 78) through its description of what a twenty-first century person should be:

> We ask first then, not what kind of education we want to provide, but what kind of human being we want to emerge. What would we have twenty-first century man be?
> We would have him be a man with a strong sense of himself and his own humanness, with awareness of his thoughts and feelings, with the capacity to feel and express love and joy and to recognize tragedy and feel grief. We would have him be a man who, with a strong and realistic sense of his own worth, is able to relate openly with others, to cooperate effectively with them toward

common ends, and to view mankind as one while respecting diversity and difference. We would want him to be a being who, even while very young, somehow senses that he has it within himself to become more than he now is, that he has the capacity for lifelong spiritual and intellectual growth. We would want him to cherish that vision of the man he is capable of becoming and to cherish the development of the same potentiality in others.

This view of humanity demands a change in our cultural emphasis and the means for its implementation. The formal education system is but one social institution, and, although it may be instrumental in producing such a humane person, it cannot accomplish this task without concomitant redesign of other aspects of our culture. As we have seen previously, it is essential that the educator recognize that he must become involved in this redesigning of the social organization through exercising the rights and responsibilities of citizenship. For the child to become a humane person, the social and educational system must be structured in a way that not only allows or permits the child to do so but actually encourages and rewards him for achieving this kind of human development.

BECOMING A PERSON

The process of becoming a person involves interaction of the self with the total environment. Although we are shaped by our environment, we also have the power to determine the forms and structure of that environment through careful plan and design and by the resulting control or manipulation of those environmental factors deemed essential in producing humane individuals. It is not true that each person is an island unto himself, for that island of the self is shaped and formed by the huge environmental sea that surrounds it. The varied processes involved in becoming a humane person are portrayed in the figure on p. 38.

In the figure, we find a man standing on an island of struggle for personal integration. His life problem is to pull himself together—to integrate and balance his feelings, thoughts, sensory data, and intuitive inclinations with the demands of his own self-needs and those of his society as they are experienced through environmental demands and pressures. To accomplish this feat, he must develop a motivation and will to move or behave in ways that are meaningful to him. As Colin Wilson (1956) has expressed it, the human problem then becomes one of finding "an *act*, a definite act that will give him power over his doubts and self-questionings." In the final analysis, the action is evident in the distinctive movement and labor that give his existence some meaning. This is what commonly occurs through work and effort expended in some vocation or avocation, which is valued by the individual to the extent that he commits himself to the task.

Personal happiness can be seen in this scheme as something for which the individual reaches, strives, and hopes. It requires that he extend himself, that he struggle and exert energy and effort towards its realization. To move in such a purposeful way, the person is stimulated by his physical, social, and psychological needs and his struggle to maintain personal balance as he strives for realization of his values. It

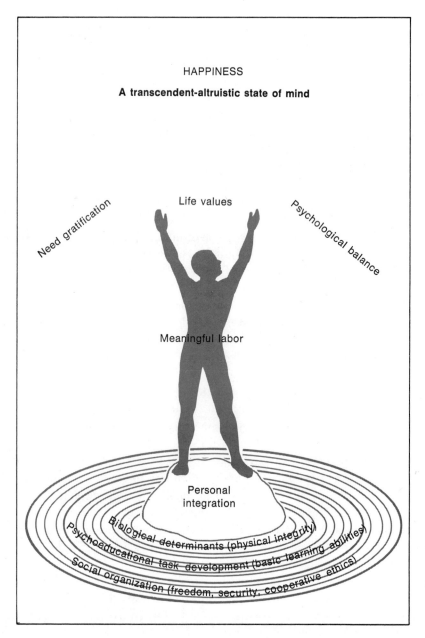

HAPPINESS

A transcendent-altruistic state of mind

Need gratification

Life values

Psychological balance

Meaningful labor

Personal integration

Biological determinants (physical integrity)

Psychoeducational task development (basic learning abilities)

Social organization (freedom, security, cooperative ethics)

Becoming a humane person.

should be noted that, as presented here, happiness consists of a transcendent altruistic state of mind in which the individual has partially realized his life values and in which his concern and commitment to the common good must also be reflected; this is the distinctive quality of a humane person, which differs critically from other possible forms of human development.

As we continue our struggle for personal integration and eventual becoming, our success is largely determined by our motivation, will, and personal values. The biological determinant includes genetically inherited structures, abilities, and propensities. It also includes our general physical integrity for coping with the environment. We are now engaged in a campaign of genetic intervention and control whereby defects may be altered or at least controlled (as phenylketonuria [PKU] has been by diet). Similar medical intervention may correct or modify physical anomaly or deformity through early operative procedures or prosthetic provisions. But such interventions require a planned design and a social will to such action that supersede individual whim and interest or mere educational awareness of the problem.

A second major determinant of personal integration is the extent to which the individual has acquired or developed proficiency in basic psychoeducational tasks. We have already referred to these tasks as the basic learning abilities and skills that are the tools for problem solving. These are the specific behavioral tasks or expectations that are presented to the child in a given learning or educational environment. We have seen that they are developmental in nature and range from gross motor, sensory-motor, perceptual-motor, language, and cognitive skills to social skills and abilities. The opportunity for exposure to and systematic sequential learning of critical psychoeducational tasks must be provided by the educational system. Certainly the structure and organization of this system is a major determinant of whether becoming a person is a possibility; this, too, is something that we can plan and design, and the plan and design must contain essential spirit and warmth to nurture the becoming *humane* person. It is as Carl Jung (1954, p. 144) has emphasized—the curriculum itself is only so much necessary raw material, " . . . but warmth is the vital element for the growing plant and for the soul of the child." What the educational system must provide is not just brilliant teachers, but teachers who can touch our human feelings and on whom we can look back with appreciation *and* gratitude.

Becoming a humane person, then, is a function of the biological individual interacting with the forces of society and its educational system. It is essential, of course, that the broader society itself subscribe to the goal of producing humane individuals and that such values be reflected in the way that the society structures itself and rewards humane behavior. It is here that much needs to be done in reordering our national priorities. If we are to truly provide opportunities for every child to learn, grow, and live creatively, we must shift societal priorities from those of military foreign aid, space exploration, military defense, and highway construction to those concerned with reducing pollution, increasing job training and employment, eliminating organized crime, and improving the schools. Support for such a drastic redirection of social efforts has already been indicated by the youth of the country as reported in a special study by *Newsweek* (1972, p. 44) magazine. Prominent citizens such as John Gardner (1970, p. 129), head of Common Cause, have also reported that the people now want a society that "puts human values above materialism, commercialism, technology, and the success ethic." When these priorities are considered in relation to other human demands, it is apparent that major social reorganization must accompany educational reform. The astute observer is aware that such a social reorganization has already begun and that we are, in fact, in the midst of a major social revolution that will affect all aspects of our culture. If a new cultural design results from a radical reorganization of national priorities, it may significantly promote the possibility of our becoming more humane persons.

PREMISES FOR CONSTRUCTING A HUMAN DEVELOPMENT PROGRAM

How, then, might we summarize the essential components of any program designed to further human development? Such a question must be concerned with the premises underlying an educational approach committed to the development of uniquely humane persons. The premises that have been presented and that form the basis for the educational program outlined in the balance of this book are as follows:

- Education is a process of developmental experiences by which the individual learns how to live.
- The primary purpose of education is to develop persons who will be able to live joyous, humane, and meaningful lives.
- Systematic, sequential educational experiences must be designed to enable people to cope with their needs for physical security, love, creative expression, cognitive mastery, social competency, and self-worth.
- Human development consists of psychomotor, cognitive, and affective stages of growth. Educational objectives and tasks can be specified for each growth stage.
- Education must begin with the assessment of individual growth patterns and needs relative to the collective needs of society.
- Developmental learning involves progressive acquisition of gross motor, sensory-motor, perceptual-motor, language, conceptual, and social skills and abilities. These skills should comprise the content of the school curriculum.
- Humanistic education emphasizes the importance of the developmental approach in the evaluation and subsequent programming of all human skills and abilities. It insists that all components of the educational system stress the development of human potential and the realization of ethical altruistic behavior.
- The development of self-awareness, self-expression, self-control, and value orientation should be given priority in the school curriculum.
- The realization of human potential or self-actualization involves biological, social, and educational determinants. We must learn to design and structure these determinants much more effectively than we have in the past.
- The entire learning environment must be designed to reinforce humanistic development. It must provide for continuous progress and movement toward individualized objectives and must reward rather than punish learners as they progress at their own rate. And it must provide preventive and remedial experiences as well as developmental ones. Learning must occur in an atmosphere of warmth and support that culminates in a psychologically integrated, self-confident humane person.

DISCUSSION QUESTIONS AND ACTIVITIES

1. What are some of the collective needs of our society that education must attempt to meet?
2. Carefully consider each of the basic learning abilities presented in the first part of this chapter. For each of the six levels described, indicate your strongest and weakest ability.
3. How might the schools provide more "practice in discussing and arriving at individual ethical choices, with emphasis on both individual and social responsibility"?
4. Describe a time and situation in which you felt yourself caught between personal and social needs and demands.
5. Define "self."
6. List several "raw and primitive urges" that must be refined by humanistic education.
7. Suggest a lesson plan (or program) that might help persons acquire some of the personal qualities desired in twenty-first century humans as described by the White House Conference on Children.
8. What are the distinctive qualities of a humane person?
9. Describe a teacher who contributed significantly to your development as a person. What were the unique qualities of this teacher?
10. List *your* top three national priorities.
11. Which one of the premises for constructing a human development program do you think is most questionable? Why?

Personal goals and objectives provide us with direction.

*Our most pressing educational problem, in short, is not how
to increase the efficiency of the schools; it is how to create and
maintain a humane society. A society whose schools are inhumane
is not likely to be humane itself.*

CHARLES E. SILBERMAN (1970, p. 203)

CHAPTER 4

Affective-humanistic objectives

THE PROBLEM IN CREATING a humane school system is that educational goals and curriculum and organizational procedures must be modified drastically. It is possible to place significantly more emphasis on the development of affective skills and abilities within the system, but this will require a greater awareness of the importance of humanistic education. This in turn requires educational leadership willing and able to reconsider educational priorities and to clearly specify long-range goals and instructional objectives in the affective domain.

Teachers must then be encouraged to give time and attention to affective education as an integral part of the total school program. Such encouragement must also include opportunities for teachers and administrators to experiment with new affective instructional programs and to work cooperatively for their continual improvement.

In-service training sessions and orientation meetings in affective education should begin with a consideration of possible goals, illustrative objectives, and available instructional programs. This chapter will present a number of such goals and objectives that may stimulate reactions from teachers and administrators concerned.

GOALS

Education has always been concerned with affective goals and objectives. Goals have usually been derived from societal and individual needs, as discussed in Chapter 1. With the gradual development of civilization, humanistic goals have been increasingly defined and clarified. The ancient Greeks were among the first to stress the importance of developing the total person, including physical, mental, and spiritual potentialities. But it was not until the eighteenth century, when Jean Jac-

Contrasting value orientations

Values	Traditional educational orientation	Humanistic orientation
Human beginnings and becoming	**Chance/evolutionary:** Human life and culture evolve in accord with evolutionary processes.	**Purposeful/evolutionary:** Human life and culture evolve in accord with individual aspirations and universal laws of nature.
Human potential	**Set:** Humanity is restricted by genetic endowment.	**Unlimited:** Humanity is only restricted by current environmental limitations, knowledge, and education.
Motivation	**Profit:** Human behavior is motivated by personal materialistic gain and profit.	**Satisfaction:** Human behavior is primarily motivated by intrinsic personal and social satisfaction.
"Progress"	**Material growth:** Human progress is determined by the rate of economic and technological development.	**Quality:** Human progress is the degree of conscious awareness and improved quality of life.
Ecology	**Exploitation:** Humans must control and exploit the natural environment for growth and profit.	**Harmony:** Humans must conserve and work in harmony with nature to further positive human evolution.
Morality	**Cultural/traditional:** The prevailing cultural mores (power, wealth, competition, "Puritan-Victorianism") must be taught.	**Transcendent:** Transcultural mores (love, cooperation, justice consciousness, etc.) must be emphasized.
Religion	**Secularism:** Religious education has no place in the public schools.	**Comparative:** Comparative religious concepts should be objectively taught in all schools.
Health	**Privileged treatment:** Poor physical or mental health is caused by the person and is his responsibility—"good health is a privilege."	**Rightful prevention:** Poor health is the result of personal-environment interaction requiring social education and prevention—"good health is a human right."

ques Rousseau (1762/1956) described the ideal education in *Emile*, that affective goals were specified in some detail; in that famous book, Rousseau outlined a curriculum for educating the "natural man" who would be capable of living and *feeling* life to its fullest possible extent.

Since then, modern philosophers have furthered the trend to clarify educational goals and their societal implications. A prominent example is Bertrand Russell' (1970, p. 47) insistence that "we must have some conception of the kind of person w wish to produce before we can have any definite opinion as to the education which w consider best"; this statement undoubtedly had much to do with the formulation c more specific goals such as those presented by the 1970 White House Conference o Children described in Chapter 3. Russell pointed out that educators may indeed b foolish if they produce results other than those for which they are aiming. He the aptly summarized the philosophical consensus that the educator must first have

Contrasting value orientations—cont'd

Values	Traditional educational orientation	Humanistic orientation
Work	**Capitalistic gain:** Full employment is not desirable or possible in a capitalistic society.	**Personal usefulness:** Full gainful employment is essential in a democratic and humanistic society.
General social goal	**Productive efficiency:** A futuristic scientific-industrial state of technologically efficient citizens.	**Self/social realization:** A futuristic community of self-actualizing persons.
Educational priorities	**"Basic skills":** Cognitive development and technical skills.	**"Affective abilities":** Total human development and personal and social effectiveness.
Educational "curriculum"	**Factual subject matter:** Reading Writing Arithmetic Speech History Geography Natural science Music Art Competitive physical education	**Principles of knowledge and living:** Language acquisition and development Applied mathematics Critical thinking and comprehension Functional mechanics Scientific methodology Comparative values and religion Psychology of self-actualization Consumer economics Community and world affairs Developmental health and biology Family planning Personal and cultural aesthetics Physical fitness and stress reduction Evolutionary government and civics

ght conception of human excellence and the good life; educators must be concerned with the development of the ideal character, which would consist of the constructive qualities of vitality, courage, intelligence, and sensitivity and which would produce a harmonious and affectionate human being.

More recently, professional educators have attempted to synthesize these concepts. The Educational Policies Commission of the National Education Association, for instance, proposed "cooperative self-realization" as the end goal of education and as specified subsidiary aims of civic responsibility, good human relationships, and economic efficiency. Similar educational goals have also been stated in numerous other ways—from such broad social aims as the abolition of war, want, and discrimination to highly precise statements of behavioral goals and objectives for the individual learner.

John Dewey (1950, p. 75) was among the first to propose that "the ideal aim of education is creation of power of self-control," which is to be developed by involving the pupil in experiences that are meaningful and purposeful to him. Today, there is widespread agreement that the essence of any self-actualization curriculum must be such that it makes persons aware that they can indeed help mold their basic selves and learn how to exercise a greater degree of control over their own lives (Gevarler, 1975; Mahoney and Thoresen, 1974; Maslow, 1970; Valett, 1974).

Educational goals and their corollary objectives, then, are finally derived from the value orientation of the society, its leaders, and educational philosophers. We have already seen how social evolution and the rise of civilization have resulted in the formulation of more humanistic aspirations. But we are still in the process of transition from the traditional to the more humanistic value orientations. It is helpful to contrast some of these specific value orientations, since they have obvious curricular implications that are emphasized throughout this book. Although the table on pp. 44 and 45 is oversimplified, it does pinpoint the major contrasting values of concern to educators. Such a consideration may enable us to clarify our own goals as persons and as educators and also help us design curriculums whereby such values may be more fully realized.

An educational goal should be thought of as a general statement of direction, aspiration, or intent over a long period of time. Goals are selected by society and its school system leaders and by teachers and pupils themselves. Goals provide broad directions and possibilities for program development and the selection of more specific teaching or learning objectives. Here are some examples of affective goals:

School system goals

- For pupils to arrive at individual ethical choices with emphasis on both individual and social responsibility.
- For pupils to develop interest in and appreciation of the fine arts.
- For pupils to develop their capacity to feel and express love and joy and to recognize tragedy and feel grief.
- For pupils to become more flexible and learn to meet rapidly changing demands on them without incurring excessive stress.
- For pupils to become more innovative and independently creative.

Teacher goals for pupils

- For Joan to be able to accept self-criticism.
- For my class to understand the importance of dignity and self-respect.
- For Tim and George to be able to show kindness and responsibility in caring for the hamsters.
- For Mike to become more self-sufficient rather than depending on peer approval for fulfillment.
- For Marie to be a more harmoniously integrated and happy person.

Pupil goals for self

- I want to control my temper and make more friends.
- Someday I hope to be a secretary and a happy wife.
- My goal is to become strong and powerful.
- I would like to be able to relax and not get so uptight.
- I hope to be able to use my abilities to help other people.

These goal statements are fairly representative of those found in humanistic education programs. In addition, psychologists (for example, Carl Jung, Abraham Maslow, and Sidney Jouard) have emphasized the importance of developing transcendent problem-solving goals: to go beyond the typical, to commit oneself to something aspired to, and to act divergently to realize such goals. Stated another way, we are not truly educated until we have formulated goals of self-communion and transcendence and until we have learned "to reach and touch and channel and witness our inner voices" (Heath, 1972), which are the deepest source of our creative-aesthetic-humanistic impulse.

All of these goals provide general direction but lack the specificity required for instructional purposes. It can be seen that, although they are affective goals because they deal with human feelings and emotions, they need to be described in more personally relevant terms if they are to become educationally meaningful. But, however they are operationally restated in more behavioral terms, their positive and purposeful essence remains the same. The purposeful essence of humanistic goals is briefly summarized in the following transitional terms:

to become aware	to dance	to play
to achieve	to dream	to renew
to assert	to feel	to risk
to aspire	to give	to sense
to build	to imagine	to serve
to care	to integrate	to sing
to change	to invent	to touch
to commit oneself	to laugh	to value
to create	to love	to wish

OBJECTIVES

It is essential that goals and objectives be clearly specified in all educational programs. Most teachers and therapists find it more difficult to formulate precise affective objectives than cognitive or psychomotor ones. However, it is possible to select highly specific affective learning objectives in the same way that most other teaching and learning objectives are established.

As a result of careful observation of pupil behavior the teacher can begin to refine general behavioral goals into more precise objectives that are directly relevant to pupil needs and developmental stages. What is required is a study of the educational history and concerns of the individual pupil. An individual educational objective states an attainable behavior that is compatible with general goals but that can be achieved in a given situation and time period. A good objective also outlines some actual performance expectations for the learner so that progress can be determined over instructional time periods involving appropriate lessons and programs.

For pupils with significant affective-emotional behavior problems the rationale for selection of appropriate objectives should be based on pupil needs and the diagnostic evaluation of the problem. The first step usually involves some form of direct systematic observation of the behavior over a period of time during which some notes and tabulations are made, as in the following example:

Daisy: Daisy, a 14-year-old maladjusted girl, was carefully observed in a class over 4 days for 30 minutes each day; during this time, she averaged nine major disruptions (such as coughing, walking around, speaking out, or annoying others with minor physical contacts) per class with no evidence of cooperation. Accordingly, one objective for Daisy was that she would cease being disruptive and manipulative of the class to the extent that she would cooperate on an assigned group project and would actually assist others in doing their work.

Here are some other similar examples:

Otto: Otto is an 8-year-old, behaviorally disturbed boy who repeatedly takes any article not belonging to him. He is constantly searching and looking for something to take at the most opportune moment. He wants attention, even if it is unpleasant and he has to steal to get it.

My objective is for Otto to learn to give some examples of someone taking something of his and how he would feel about it and to make suggestions to the discussion group as to how stealing might be stopped.

James: James is a 17-year-old boy with many emotional problems. He was carefully observed at the work center with various projects and work contracts. During initial vocational training he proved to be very rigid and narrow in his approach to different tasks. If he begins work in a given way, he tends to continue that approach, even though more feasible ways are rather obvious to everyone else.

My objective is that, on completion of this program, James will be able to give and explain at least two different possible ways to complete seven different work contracts. He will also be able to judge the alternatives and suggest the most feasible approach.

Shawn: Shawn is a 12-year-old educationally handicapped boy. At the present, Shawn seems to be unable to relate to male peers, and he relates in a silly manner to girls. He doesn't seem to care about himself or his appearance and is unaware of the effect that he has on others. Shawn presently comes to school with his hands, face, neck, and ears dirty. Most days his clothes are also dirty and he has a strong body smell. His general appearance is very unkempt.

The long-range goal is for Shawn to be able to relate to and be accepted by his peers; the immediate priority is for him to arrive in the class relatively clean and presentable.

The illustrations of Daisy, Otto, and James present rather specific learning objectives and conditions around which meaningful educational programs can be developed. The case of Shawn illustrates a long-range goal based on a specific rationale and suggests a possible behavioral priority that might be formulated into an instructional objective.

The following are examples of affective objectives developed by teachers after similar consideration of individual pupil needs and abilities.

Bobby: Bobby is 10 years old and socially maladaptive. He is socially immature and does not realize the effects of his own behavior. On completion of this lesson, Bobby will be able to give at least three logical alternative solutions to three social problem situations presented in photographs.

Al: Al is 14 years old and socially maladjusted. He will accept a term as president of the class self-government council. As president he will aid the council in developing the new behavior code and in leading all council meetings. He will also show some evidence of assisting other council members in carrying out their assigned duties.

Herb: Herb, 18 years old, is educable mentally retarded. On completion of these le sons, Herb will be able to maintain his own job rating card, demonstrating that he has successfully accomplished the following responsibilities:

- Arrived at work on time for 2 weeks straight
- Brought the necessary tools with him every day (gloves, wristwatch, apron, hat)
- Stayed on the job for 3 hours straight every day for 2 weeks
- Received no penalty marks from his work supervisor for the 2-week period

Martha: Martha is 12 years old and educationally handicapped. She will be able to participate in the class social discussion period by challenging at least two statements made by others. She will be able to support her challenge by presenting at least one other possible answer or solution for consideration by the class.

Jerry: Jerry, 16 years old, is emotionally disturbed and has a history of drug addiction. When Jerry has completed this learning program he will be able to express orally and in writing his personal feelings about "shooting up" (injection of hard drugs into the veins) and a concise statement that indicates an awareness of the possibility of overdose and death.

Alice: Alice is 17 years old and educable mentally retarded. On completion of the social training lessons, Alice will be able to act properly to successfully complete an employment interview arranged at C. K. Jones Company. Specifically, Alice will be able to dress appropriately, demonstrate poise, and verbally respond to interview questions regarding her experience, interests, and training work-experience programs.

In affective education it is extremely important to help the individual pupil formulate his own learning objectives and plan for accomplishing them. This is usually done through counseling and talking with him, during which time he comes to understand his current behavior better and develops a desire to learn new or more appropriate ways of behaving. Many guidance techniques and procedures are helpful in the process of enabling the pupil to obtain better self-understanding. Self-concept tests, inventories, and checklists are frequently used for this purpose.

My Self Checklist

One example of such an instrument is *My Self Checklist* (published by Fearon Publishers, 1973), which has been designed for use as an aid in determining pupil self-concepts. The main purpose of the checklist is to enable the pupil to express his feelings about how he currently perceives himself. His responses may then be considered along with those from other sources such as teachers and parents to help in formulating objectives for affective learning. *My Self Checklist* provides opportunities for the pupil to accept or reject such self-concepts as the following:

- I have many friends.
- I am a very shy person.
- I would like to be someone else.
- I am afraid of many things.

The list also has sections that permit the pupil to express his wishes, interests, requests for help, and strengths and weaknesses. As a result of considering his self-concepts and discussing them with the teacher or counselor, the pupil is often able to formulate broad goals and specific behavioral objectives for himself such as the following:

- I hope that next year I am happier than I am now.
- By Christmas I want to weigh 10 pounds less than I do now.
- I love poetry so much I hope to be able to write a long romantic poem by the end of summer school.
- I would like to be selected as captain of the soccer team this year.
- I want to be able to sit down and talk with my dad without getting upset and walking away.
- I want to make at least two new friends before the night of the Valentine Day dance.
- As a member of the Ecology Club I hope I do well enough to be elected an officer this school term.
- My objective is to quit biting my nails as soon as possible.
- Our class voted unanimously to request instruction on the use of marijuana and LSD.
- We want to spend more time learning about sexual feelings and ethics.
- The group would like to study about pollution and what the factory is doing to stop it.

PROGRAMS

Clear statements of general educational goals and specific objectives, however well formulated they may be, are inadequate by themselves. Objectives can only be realized if appropriate programs and resources are made available so the learner can begin to acquire or develop the desired behavior. Educational programs consist of a number of highly specific learning tasks and exercises that are commonly grouped together to form a lesson or series of lessons. Like educational programs in the cognitive and psychomotor domains, effective education programs can be designed either for groups of pupils or for individual students.

If the program is designed for an individual pupil and based on a diagnostic evaluation of needs, it is referred to as a prescriptive learning program. Most affective education programs for children with learning or behavior disorders should be prescriptive if they are to be effective. Effectiveness is usually determined by some form of pre- and posttest or evaluation procedure to see to what extent the pupil has learned the specified tasks or acquired the skills prescribed for him. An illustration of a summary prescriptive learning program for Martha, the 12-year-old educationally handicapped girl, follows:

Objective: For Martha to be able to participate in the class social discussion period by challenging at least two statements made by others. She will be able to support her challenge by presenting at least one other possible answer or solution for consideration by the class.

Pretest: Martha was carefully observed as a member of the class social discussion period for 16 days. During that time her participation was limited to barely audible yes or no answers to questions from group members. She was so hesitant and unsure of herself that she seldom looked at other members of the group.

Educational program: Martha was first paired off with Jane, who agreed to be her discussion helper. Both girls then listened to a tape recording of Indians discussing the topic "Why Indians Should be Allowed to Run Their Own Reservations." Discussion questions were presented in writing for the girls to think about. Jane responded first to the tape, and

Martha was asked to model and repeat Jane's argument in her own words. When Martha responded she was immediately praised by the teacher and Jane and rewarded by Jane with tokens. The same procedure was used for other questions until the fourth question, when Martha spoke first and was rewarded. The girls then took turns, and Martha was asked to challenge Jane on something she said. When Martha responded shyly she was encouraged by both Jane and the teacher and given tokens. On a subsequent tape, Martha was taught to reward herself with tokens when she challenged Jane. Four modeling sessions were held prior to reintroducing her to the discussion group.

Posttest: During her first reintroduction to the discussion group, Martha participated by making three statements and mildly challenging Tim on one of his remarks. Improvement continued during subsequent group discussions to the point that, after 5 weeks, Martha's special modeling program and reinforcement system were no longer necessary.

Space prohibits lengthy descriptions of other prescriptive affective education objectives and programs. However, the following list may serve to further illustrate the relationship of appropriate program design and posttest evaluation to goals and objectives.

Goals and objectives	Program design	Posttest evaluation
Willingness to take part in musical activities.	From nine records, selects and listens to three choral recordings.	Volunteers to sing in school chorus.
To be of service to a group of which he is a member.	Selected as a committee member for planning a class party.	Organizes social affair for group members.
To present an opinion on current issues he feels strongly about.	Is presented with information on varied topics and letters to the editor.	Writes a letter to the editor stating personal opinion.
To form judgments as to major directions in which American society should move.	Listens to the president's State of the Union speech and makes critical notes.	Joins a local student political organization.
To develop respect for the worth and dignity of human beings.	Serves on a study committee for the UNESCO project.	Volunteers service to UNESCO in the community.
To be able to leave home and mix socially with other children during a field trip.	Is rewarded for self-control during selected group activities at home and in school.	Relates socially to classmates during trip to the zoo.

It is not necessary, however, for all affective education programs to be prescriptive in the sense that all learning tasks and activities are individually designed according to the needs of each student. Prescriptive objectives and programs *are* essential for children with significant emotional, social, or personal problems. But most children do not have significant behavioral maladjustments that warrant individual therapy or prescriptive interventions.

What all children do have in common are certain affective and emotional needs that require understanding, expression, and development. These needs can and should be recognized and provided for in affective education programs for *all* children in our schools. Such a broad program is not prescriptive but "developmental" in the sense that it recognizes and provides for positive affective growth and development for all children.

Developmental affective education programs are designed for many purposes. These programs usually consist of a number of lesson and learning activities for use with certain developmental age groups with specified concerns or problems. All of these programs can be used with entire classes or small groups of pupils. They can also be used as resource material that can be modified or adapted for use in individual prescriptive programs. Chapter 9 presents a number of commercial affective education programs with stated purposes; they are widely used and serve as sources of varied tools and materials for accomplishing affective-humanistic objectives.

TAXONOMY OF AFFECTIVE OBJECTIVES

A taxonomy is a system for the classification of related concepts and ideas. In education there are several major taxonomies for the classification of goals and objectives. The three most widely accepted taxonomies for classifying psychomotor, cognitive, and affective objectives are those of Harrow (1972), Bloom (1956), and Krathwohl et al. (1964), respectively. These three classification systems are all arranged in developmental hierarchies that make it possible to consider appropriate objectives and their curricular implications.

Krathwohl et al.'s taxonomy of affective objectives has received increasing attention from the developers of humanistic education programs and materials. Their taxonomy consists of the following five stages:

- Receiving (attention, awareness, concentration)
- Responding (willingness, compliance, acting)
- Valuing (acceptance, preference, commitment)
- Organization (conceptualization, formulation)
- Value characterization (resolution, set)

This is indeed a helpful way of systematizing the many affective goals, objectives, and concerns that we have reviewed in this chapter. However, for purposes of practical educational planning and implementation this taxonomy is too abstract and lacks behavioral specificity.

Accordingly, a more functional five-level taxonomy has been developed for use throughout this book. All of the traditional objectives and levels of concern have been incorporated in the humanistic taxonomy of affective objectives that is presented here. Each level begins with specification of the major affective classification of behaviors, the general educational goal and objectives, and a rationale for its selection. An affective-humanistic education program designed for use by regular pupils should be organized developmentally around these goals and stated objectives for all lessons or learning activities. The purpose of all program materials and tasks should be to enable the pupil to accomplish the learning objectives and to approximate the long-term affective program goal. This taxonomy and the model program guide presented in Chapter 6 are organized on five developmental levels, or stages, and accomplishment of the goals and objectives at each stage is deemed prerequisite to full comprehension and accomplishment of program goals or objectives at the higher stages.

Level one: understanding basic human needs
General educational goal

For pupils to demonstrate their understanding and appreciation of how people attempt to meet their basic human needs of physical security, love, creative expression, knowledge, social competency, and self-worth.

Rationale

The history of humanity is a record of attempts to meet physical and psychological needs; continued human development is a process of increasing self-awareness and competency in understanding the self and how to meet its needs.

Level two: expressing human feelings
General educational goal

For pupils to be able to understand and express their feelings about major life concerns.

Rationale

Children need to learn to understand and express both positive and negative feelings. Human feelings should be studied as normal and desirable behavior that is important in human development. Ways of coping with human feelings at different stages of growth and development should be learned as part of general education.

Level three: self-awareness and control
General educational goal

For pupils to become more aware of their selves and their relationships with other people and to develop self-control.

Rationale

To effectively cope with personal and social demands and relationships it is necessary for the individual to become increasingly self-aware of his actions and their consequences. Children can learn to develop self-awareness, sensitivity to others, and appropriate self-control through systematic instruction, experience, and practice.

Level four: becoming aware of human values
General educational goal

For pupils to become aware of the major personal attitudes, social skills, and diverse values that influence human behavior.

Rationale

Successful living demands that the individual be able to relate to people in many stressful situations. Children must learn that people are motivated by many different personal and cultural values. Pupils must acquire those social skills that enable them to function in the community.

Level five: developing social and personal maturity
General educational goal

For pupils to improve their proficiency in predicting the personal consequences of their behavior, in gradually assuming social responsibility, in adapting to changing events, and in becoming increasingly able to transcend egocentric concerns, and in renewing their selves.

Rationale

Social and personal maturity is an important end goal in education. Children need to be taught what desirable behaviors comprise "maturity" and how and when these might be learned. Schools should provide varied opportunities and experiences for the continued development and acquisition of these essential behaviors.

SUMMARY

As we have learned, broad educational goals must be reduced to behaviorally stated objectives and teaching strategies. Developmental program goals such as those presented here should be translated into definitive objectives and purposeful learning tasks and activities. In the next chapter we will review selected research findings that support this developmental approach to humanistic education.

DISCUSSION QUESTIONS AND ACTIVITIES

1. Describe your own conception of the ideal man or woman.
2. How would we know if a person had finally learned or developed "cooperative self-realization"?
3. Do you agree or disagree with Dewey's ideal aim of education? Explain your answer.
4. Select two contrasting value orientations presented in the table on pp. 44 and 45 and give an illustration of each.
5. List one or two personal goals or objectives that you feel very strongly about.
6. Propose an alternative affective learning objective for one of the children described in this chapter.
7. Critique Martha's affective education program. Did it really accomplish the stated objective? What other educational strategies might also have been used?
8. What is the common attribute among all posttest evaluation examples presented on p. 51?
9. Give an example of an affective objective that would be classified on the top level of the taxonomy of Krathwohl et al.
10. Why is it important to have a rationale for educational objectives?
11. How could the humanistic taxonomy of affective objectives be used to clarify objectives for a high school "sex education" program?

We need to carefully consider why and what we are about to do.

The great teachers whom I have known are forever alert
to the fact that the individual, whether two or twenty years old,
can tell us more about his unrealized potentials than can
any norm prepared in any office.

GARDNER MURPHY (1958, p. 316)

CHAPTER 5

A humanistic rationale

TEACHERS CONCERNED with affective education create instructional programs for the development of individual potentialities. They do not emphasize normative performance or insist that their pupils learn or grow at the same rate or in the so-called normal way. Instead, much individual freedom is given to pupils to study themselves, to express their feelings in their own way, to develop values, and to search for meaningful personal goals and aspirations.

The affective education program goals and guide presented here are designed to involve students in the consideration of self and their relationship to others and their formulation of personal and social values. The program is built on Glasser's (1966) premise that "behavior changes when a person gets involved in something worthwhile" and that the primary role of the teacher is to work with the child to help him make a value judgment about something worthwhile. Accordingly, this program guide has been deliberately structured to involve repeated inquiries into self and social behavior that result in some form of value judgment and insight on the part of the learner.

The general program goal for affective education is symbolized in the design on p. 58, which represents a person in the process of developing social and personal maturity, or self-actualization. The figure presents a human form with arms and hands reaching up on a many-faceted, dynamic background. The figure represents the person in the process of human development through five levels of affective education: understanding basic human needs, expressing human feelings, self-awareness and control, becoming aware of human values, and developing social and personal maturity.

The rationale for these five levels, or stages, of humanistic education is based on

57

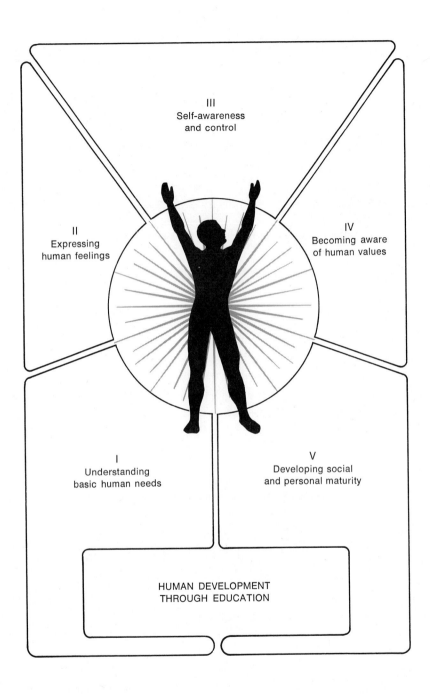

III
Self-awareness
and control

II
Expressing
human feelings

IV
Becoming aware
of human values

I
Understanding
basic human needs

V
Developing social
and personal maturity

HUMAN DEVELOPMENT
THROUGH EDUCATION

philosophical and empirical research. We have already surveyed the major philosophical contributions supporting affective-humanistic education. Most of the basic
theoretical concepts of humanistic psychology and education have been summarized
by Buhler (1971) in her statement that education must help the individual become a
person with a life goal of accomplishing something he believes in and is capable of
fulfilling through self-determination. The major question, then, is not What should
be learned or taught? but *Can* these humanistic goals and their constituent skills and
abilities be taught? If so, how? and To what extent is this possible in the schools?

Since research in humanistic education and psychology is relatively new and
limited, it will be years before these questions can be fully answered. But, however
limited our current findings may be, we do have substantial results available that
support a developmental approach to humanistic education. In this chapter some of
the more important and representative research findings that underlie these five
stages of humanistic development will be presented.

Each stage is presented with a statement of purpose and goals. These goals are
then proposed in the form of study units or lesson topics, which are illustrated in
detail in Chapter 6. Research results are then summarized in terms of their educational implications.

STAGE ONE: UNDERSTANDING BASIC HUMAN NEEDS

The purpose of affective education at stage one is to enable the child to become
aware of basic human needs and people's attempts to satisfy them in life. As Toffler
(1971) has stated, "Education should help create the consciousness needed for man to
undertake the control of change, the guidance of his evolution." The development of
such a consciousness should begin with a study of what humans actually need out of
life. The six proposed study units and possible lesson topics are as follows:

- *Physical security:* food, shelter, clothing, health
- *Love:* attention, friendship, caring, empathy, family togetherness
- *Creative expression:* exploration, painting, dance, song
- *Knowledge:* thinking, learning, discovering, explaining
- *Social competency:* helping others, playing together, living together in peace, working together
- *Self-worth:* confidence, personal strengths and limitations, freedom and indepen-
  dence, dignity and respect, self-esteem

There have been many notable studies on the importance of recognizing and
understanding basic human needs. Their essential place in human growth and mat-
uration has been recently summarized by Poland (1974), who categorized food, shelter seeking, elimination, and responsiveness as physiological needs, whereas sex,
care, language expression, and exploration are all seen as primary psychological
needs. Eysenck (1975, p. 270) has also summarized research on human biology and
genetics with the conclusion that, educationally, we must recognize and provide for
differences in human instincts, energy levels, personality, and intelligence. The

detailed studies of Gesell and Ilg (1946) were the first to spell out educational implications of childhood needs and maturational stages. But Maslow (1962, p. 379) was
the first to argue that human needs for love, curiosity, knowledge, and self-
actualization were basic and instinctoid and that, without their gratification, health
was impossible and "a loss of humanness would result."

We have known for some time that basic human needs are primarily met and
satisfied within the home and family. For example, Bloom's (1965) classic study
disclosed that 50 percent of a child's intelligence is developed between birth and age
4 years and that another 30 percent develops between the critical ages of 4 and 8
years; he also found that good parental models who "pressed" for such things as
language development, achievement motivation, and school attainment while
providing basic physical security and the opportunity to learn were the critical factors
in human development. However, the "educational program," within both the family
and the school, does make a significant difference. Perhaps the earliest attempt to
specify these differences for each developmental stage was that of Havighurst (1948)
who formulated behavioral definitions of the biological, psychological, and cultural
needs and their unique implications for education. Continued research has produced
more data substantiating the importance of understanding and meeting the basic
human needs.

We now know, for instance, that the basic element in human security is what
Harlow has named contact comfort. From his numerous laboratory experiments
Harlow (1971) has concluded that the roots of love are to be found in tactile-
kinesthetic contact, stimulation, and response. As a result of later research (1974) he
concluded that, if animals and persons are deprived of physical contact-solace-
security in early childhood, they develop maladaptive behavior patterns in adulthood. More recently, Rice's (1975) experimental study of premature infants treated
with systematic stroking, massaging, and rocking showed that significant psy-
choneurological gains and improved mental development occurred—with the most
immature infants making the greatest gains! Physical security, love, and stimulation
are indeed of basic importance and can be furthered through proper educational
experiences.

Creative expression and knowledge are also inherent human needs as disclosed
by research. Among others, the studies of Getzels and Jackson (1962) on creativity
are of particular importance to education. Their findings disclosed that creativity and
intelligence were two different things that were not very highly correlated and that
education for creativity is dependent on the development of preconscious, intuitive
processes and abilities that should emphasize playful, divergent discovery methods of
learning. The extensive research of Guilford (1967, p. 476) has similarly shown that
such precise cognitive skills and knowledge as divergent production, evaluative
thinking, and social abilities can be developed through appropriate educational practice and exercise. In his most recent work, Eysenck (1975, pp. 203 to 211) has called
for a recognition that good education leads to further inequality among persons as a
result of development of real differences in talent rooted in biological and genetic

predisposition; he also pleads for the further development in all persons of the affective personality traits of nurturance, cooperation, and sensitivity.

The integrative needs are those of social competency and self-worth. Substantial research has accumulated on the importance of the pupil's social, physical, and psychological self-concepts and how they affect learning and total behavior. In an early study, Brookover (1965) showed that a child's behavior is a function of how his parents perceive him and what they expect of him. Then Rosenthal and Jacobson (1968) established that positive or negative teacher expectation has a significant influence on student performance. The work of Black (1974) and others has also confirmed that the self-concepts and confidence of poor readers and other low achievers are detrimentally low. The extensive studies of Coopersmith (1967) on the implications of self-esteem for educational research and practice are well known and have shown that good self-esteem is associated with analytical thinking, persistence, creative ability, social independence, stability, and high self-expectations.

Historical and clinical data also support the importance of understanding and providing for basic human needs. For example, the lives of such persons as Buddha and Jesus give testimony to the necessity to love and create more fully. It is good to remember that our own Declaration of Independence also recognizes the needs and inalienable rights of persons, including life, liberty, and the *pursuit* of happiness. Government and its educational institutions are instituted to aid in this endeavor, and the evidence is that we have been making steady progress toward these common ends. Some current indications of our continued pursuit of happiness through legislation include a number of laws providing programs and funds for the handicapped, compensatory education for the deprived, equal rights for women and minority groups, and proposed national health insurance laws and laws to provide for full employment.

STAGE TWO: EXPRESSING HUMAN FEELINGS

The purpose of instruction at level two should be to help the child develop and express his feelings. As Jones (1969, p. 198) has written, "The matter of orchestrating appropriate degrees and forms of emotional and imaginal expression in support of cognitive skills is the teacher's to improve upon." But, for such orchestration to occur, children must be presented with curricular opportunities to study and to express their own feelings. The three proposed units and possible lesson topics are as follows:

- *Primary feelings:* love, anger, fear, faith, despair, pain, hope
- *Critical emotional concerns:* birth, loneliness, sadness, war, marriage, unemployment, peace, accidents, death, hurting others
- *Instincts and intuitions:* predispositions, fantasy, dreams, unconscious functions, will, peak experiences

Everyone has the right to feel. But somehow this right has not yet been widely accepted or legitimized; in many places, children's feelings continue to be denied, suppressed, and squelched. The importance of children being able to express their feelings as part of a constructive educational experience has been discussed by Fraiberg (1974) and others.

It was, however, the clinical research of the early psychoanalysts, Sigmund Freud and Carl Jung, that first demonstrated the importance of emotional expression. Freud's (1959, Chap. 5) work on repression showed that many psychological and psychosomatic problems may result from unduly restrictive conditions. Then Jung (1960) documented the positive transcendent functions of psychic energy as it appears in feelings and fantasy as attempts to integrate unconscious drives and instincts into conscious behavior. The constructive results of such positive emotional and instinctual expression are seen in the inspiration and productivity of uniquely artistic personalities (Michaelangelo, Picasso, Calder), musicians (Beethoven, Casals, Copeland), writers and poets (Dostoevsky, Whitman, Agatha Christie—who did not have a formal education), and even scientists, for example, Edison, Einstein, and Szent Gyoergyi.

Research shows that we must all learn to constructively express our primary feelings (love, hate, etc.), to cope with the critical emotional problems in life, and to acknowledge and develop our deepest intuitive and instinctual potentialities. If we fail to do so, we risk developing what Maddi (1971) has termed existential sickness which is marked "by the belief that one's life is meaningless, by the affective tone of apathy and boredom, and by the absence of selectivity in actions."

Numerous studies and experimental programs have been designed to determine the effect of emotional education. One of the earliest successful attempts to further emotional expression and development was that of Bullis and O'Malley's (1947) human relations program for classroom use. Since then, research in this area has expanded rapidly. Typical findings have been that feeling- and behavior-oriented discussion groups do help children learn about themselves and others (Myrick and Kelly, 1971). We also know from such studies as that of Cole et al. (1969) that self-concepts can be modified through role-playing and modeling of emotional feelings and problems. Most of these findings were incorporated into the first intensive applied research study of a carefully designed affective education program in the Philadelphia public schools, which successfully tried to "legitimize feelings, clarify them for the student, and suggest a variety of behaviors which he can use to express them" (Borton, 1974).

In recent years, research with many educational implications has been done in the area of intuitive functions and potentialities. Stanley Krippner (1970) has reported on a number of studies in which hypnosis was successfully used in various special education programs to decrease emotional tension, increase motivation, and improve academic achievement. Parapsychological research has also produced interesting findings such as the discovery through the use of Kirlian photography that persons emit light energy fields ("coronas") in different emotional states that can be controlled by training and personal will ("Parapsychology," 1974). Similarly, the psychokinetic effects of emotional states and willful functions have been demonstrated in work at the Stanford Research Institute using psychics such as Uri Geller

("Uri Geller," 1974). Much of the research on paranormal functions has been summarized by LeShan (1974), who concludes that many of our intuitive powers and abilities can be enhanced through proper education. For example, LeShan has demonstrated that psychic healing is a reality and that, to some extent at least, it is a learned ability that can be acquired or enhanced through specific education and practice.

A humanistic and affective education must provide the proper learning experiences for the development of the emotive powers and potentialities of humanity. Nobel prize–winning molecular biologist Szent-Gyoergyi (1974) has concluded from his extensive research that there is an innate drive in living matter to perfect itself through the flow and transfer of vital energies and that this energy "builds its own evolving structure and mechanisms of expression." We must learn to feel these vital energies more fully and to further their positive expression in our life. In the words of astronaut-scientist Mitchell (1974), we need to "recognize the validity of the nonrational cognitive processes" and learn to cultivate peak emotional experiences in our lives.

STAGE THREE: SELF-AWARENESS AND CONTROL

The purpose of units and lessons of level three should be to help the child think about and develop self-awareness and control. It should build on the child's previously acquired understandings of human needs and forms of emotional expression and should move on to a direct study of self-consciousness, awareness of others, and selected problems of self-control. The instructional program should attempt to get at the ways in which people handle the "titanic emotions" so well described by Eldridge Cleaver (1968, p. 148):

> I seek a lasting relationship, something permanent in a world of change, in which all is transitory, ephemeral, and full of pain. We humans! We are too fragile creatures to handle such titanic emotions and deep magnetic yearnings, strivings, and impulses.

Children must learn not only how to express feelings but also how to become more aware of these feelings in themselves and others; they must deal with the question of why humans have trouble in controlling themselves and in what way they may begin to learn to control their titanic emotions, yearnings, and impulses. The following three units and possible lesson topics are proposed for this level:

- *Self-consciousness:* "Who am I?" life functions, sensory awareness, cognitive awareness and problem solving, personal needs
- *Awareness of others:* sensitivity to others, attention, faith, helping, cooperating
- *Problems of self-discipline:* yelling, tattling, fighting, lying, grouchiness, rudeness, jealousy, selfishness, stealing, destructiveness, accepting criticism, self-control and regulation

Benjamin Franklin was the first American to stress the importance of self-awareness and control and to devise and record a successful program for their accomplishment. In his *Autobiography*, Franklin (p. 124) reports experiments on himself in which he systematically developed a number of personal virtues (such as temperance, order, moderation, tranquility, and resolution) through the use of a rather exact behavior modification tabulation system. Abraham Lincoln also emphasized the importance of personal resolution in one's life, and his advice to others was to "always bear in mind that your own resolution to succeed is more important than any other one thing."* It seems that, as a people, Americans have always valued self-awareness and control, but it is only recently that we have acquired a scientific and educational technology for its actual realization. The research in this area is now so voluminous that only representative samples can be cited here.

Much of the research on the development of human consciousness has been summarized by Ornstein (1972) and shows that the left brain hemisphere specializes in analytical, rational thinking such as verbal language and mathematical and linear functions; the right hemisphere is predominately concerned with synthetic and intuitive patterns of thought, including such things as artistic endeavors, facial recognition, and spatial relationships. Orstein suggests that we are being dominated by the left hemisphere and that what is needed is a more *complete* education to balance and integrate the abilities and functions of both sides of the brain. Ornstein's work has been taken very seriously. On February 28 and 29, 1976, the first conference entitled "Education of Both Halves of the Brain" was held at the University of California, Berkeley, and featured research findings from both education and neuropsychiatry. Some of these findings have already been incorporated into experimental programs for the development of the metaphoric and intuitive processes of the human brain (Samples, 1974).

The possibility of self-control through biofeedback has also received much recent attention. Jacobson's (1948) early experiments with progressive relaxation procedures demonstrated that a person could learn to control tension and anxiety. With a monitoring apparatus that "feeds back" data on his psychophysiological status of being, the person can be signaled that he is thinking, feeling, or doing specific things that are either helpful or detrimental to physical or emotional health. By such means the person can "learn new ways of coping behaviorally with his environment, or he may be able to alter his life style in such a way as to keep his physiological processes within safer limits" (Schwartz, 1973).

Most of these self-control methodologies have already been used in education. The successful use of electromyographic biofeedback with hyperactive children has been reported by Braud et al. (1975). The combined use of relaxation, attention training, and biofeedback apparatus with school children has been researched and reported by Simpson and Nelson (1974). Another noted researcher, Brown (1970) has shown that theta brain rhythms of 4 to 7 cycles per second have been associated with serenity and creativity and that conscious awareness and control of these rhythms can be developed through proper training and education.

Many of these findings have been incorporated in a variety of new curriculum offerings. One of the most controversial of these has been the Silva Mind Control

---

*Attributed to Lincoln by Carl Sandburg in his poem "The People Yes."

rogram, which has attempted to integrate numerous self-awareness, regulatory, iofeedback, and intuitive development techniques (McKnight, 1973). A professor of nathematics, Taylor (1974), has also reported on attempts to develop "superminds"; mong other things, these attempts disclosed highly unusual psychokinetic powers in everely retarded children. An ESP curriculum guide for use with secondary students has even been developed by McConnell (1971), a research professor of iophysics at the University of Pittsburgh, with the stated purpose of furthering a deepened understanding of scientific method and a renewed sense of wonder to-ard man and his potentialities."

But even more research and attention is being given to the possibilities of expand-ag human consciousness and control through natural means. The cybernetic en-ineer Gevarter (1975) has concluded that the cerebral cortex evolves its ideas and umanistic value system from the use of consciousness and its uniquely intuitive ognitive processes; he has proposed that education should be concerned with in-reasing one's personal awareness through increased problem-solving approaches cusing on self-esteem. One of the earliest experiments along these lines was con-ucted years ago by Williams (1930) with slow-learning delinquent boys who were astructed through self-selected and self-initiated learning projects, which resulted in chievement test gains of four times the normal expectancy. Other experiments on elf-initiated learning, self-awareness training, and self-regulation and control have roved promising with both normal and exceptional pupils (Ross, 1969).

Consequently, we can expect to see an increasing number of self-actualization rograms and curriculums such as those by Valett (1974), Samples and Wohiford 974), and many others presented later in this book. It is now clear that, as Toffler 971, p. 484) has written, we are "faced with the power to create a new ecies . . . to assume conscious control of evolution itself," and we must rise to this aallenge and learn to anticipate, design, and control our own future.

TAGE FOUR: BECOMING AWARE OF HUMAN VALUES

The primary purpose of activities at level four is to help the child think about and ecome more aware of the major human values. It should be developed on the remise proposed by Maslow (1962, p. 198) that "the human being needs a amework of values, a philosophy of life, a religion or religion-surrogate to live by ad understand by, in about the same sense that he needs sunlight, calcium, or ve." The three proposed study units and the lesson topics deal with the many aings that people find of value in their lives:

- *Skills for social living (manners):* courtesy, kindness, friendliness, honesty, cheer-fulness, cooperativeness, respect, tolerance, personal conscience
- *Personal and social commitment:* love, wealth, power, knowledge, religion, ser-vice, aesthetics
- *Cultural values:* liberty, independence, work, justice, democracy, thanksgiving, freedom

Educational research on value formulation, character education, and the devel-ment of moral behavior began in earnest with the Hartshorne and May (1928-1930) studies during the 1920's. Among other things, these studies showed that positive character traits could be developed through educational programs conducted in public schools and that the results of such programs could be determined by tests, checklists, and other kinds of evaluation instruments developed for that purpose. For the next 40 years or so, relatively little interest was displayed in this area. During the turbulent 1960's it became apparent that our prevailing cultural values were being openly challenged, and school districts again became interested in the establishmen of character education programs. Typical of these was the Valley Vista Elementary School character education program, which was started in 1971 and which resulted in such positive behavior changes that vandalism bills for the district dropped significantly ("Character Education," 1971). With the advent of the "Watergate affair," the resulting indictments of Nixon administration officials, and subsequent congressional investigations of illegal CIA and FBI activities, demands for reform were made and interest increased in providing more effective moral education and value orientation programs in the schools.

Kohlberg (1964) has conducted considerable research on moral and ethical development and has shown that children proceed from a premoral egocentric stage to conventional role conformity and, finally, with proper education, to a stage of self developed moral principles. For example, during the middle childhood elementary school years, most children are on the "conventional level" of moral development and interpersonal agreement, social acceptance and peer conformity to prevailing group mores take precedence in determining their actual behavior. The final stage of development is marked by the presence of a personal conscience and value orientation; Kohlberg states that education should stimulate the development of the individual child's own moral judgment and character.

In his work on developmental tasks and education, Havighurst (1948) emphasized the importance of value development. He specified that the tasks of middle childhood included developing conscience, morality, and a scale of values; these are accomplished in part within the schools through teaching about morality, punishments and rewards, models and examples, and peer group learning experience Later, Coopersmith's (1967) work on the antecedents of self-esteem emphasized the importance of parental models and firm guidance of their children in the total process of becoming a responsible person.

Considerable data are now available on the process of character education and the development of moral and ethical values. The studies of Bronfenbrenner (1962) in both the United States and the Soviet Union have shown how the peer group can be used to develop desirable character traits. A technology for reinforcing cooperation between children has been formulated in detail through the research of Azrin and Lindsley (1956). Their experimental work with disturbed children consisted of providing two youngsters with parts of puzzles that could only be completed together and with games demanding cooperative efforts for solution; when "cooperative behavior" was immediately reinforced with candy and tokens, significant improvement was made. Similarly, the Suomi and Harlow (1972) studies on the social rehabilitation of monkeys reared in isolation have been generalized to human populations and show that selected younger children can serve as healthy nonthreatening models of proper behavior for older disturbed individuals. The inappropriate behaviors of delinquent girls have also been modified through the use of educational therapy procedures that emphasize daily goal setting and evaluation and peer group reinforcement as outlined by Rice (1970). Keasey (1971) also found that higher stages of moral development were positively associated with and related to the extent of social participation in various clubs, groups, and social organizations for fifth- and sixth-grade children. Apparently, varied social contacts and active participation enable the learner to be introduced to numerous value systems and finally contribute to the formulation of a personal value orientation.

We also know that teacher values and expectations have a direct influence on pupil behavior. Rosenthal and Jacobsen's (1968) controversial study showed that poorly functioning primary pupils did better if the teacher expected them to improve. The qualities of good teacher models were then found to include the ability to be positive, accepting, perceptive, friendly, supportive, and "able to create a warmer social-emotional mood around their students" (Rosenthal, 1973). Aspy and Hadlock's (1967) studies also showed that effective teachers are empathic, congruent, and valuing of the student. Similar results have been obtained from White's (1974) study of "humanistic mathematics" and Swenson's (1974) study of the humanistic facilitation of achievement in first-year French.

Most of this research has been summarized by J. Raths (1974) in his article on strategies for developing values. Raths (who with L. Raths was an early pioneer in value-development education) concludes that the five major instructional procedures for teaching value clarification are as follows:

- A nonjudgmental attitude on the part of the teacher
- Teacher interest in and concern about students
- Peer group sharing of ideas about differing value orientations
- The ability to ask appropriate questions at the right time
- Teacher feedback during student-centered teaching

Research, then, has established that human values are both "caught *and* taught." While the importance of the teacher model cannot be overlooked, it is also apparent that the nature of the instructional program itself, with its carefully designed opportunities for learning about values, clarifying values, and formulating personal value orientations, is equally important. Humanistic education must provide more ample opportunity for students on all levels to develop moral and ethical value orientations if we are to continue to improve our lives and the society in which we live.

STAGE FIVE: DEVELOPING SOCIAL AND PERSONAL MATURITY

Stage five is the final instructional level in affective education. The purpose of these units and lessons should be to help the pupil think about and understand what social and personal maturity consists of and to help him develop some of the skills and behavior involved. Learning activities at this level should be built on John Dewey's (1931) proposal that "education must cultivate the social spirit and the power to act socially, even more assiduously than it cultivated individual ambition for material success in the past." The major question to be considered on this level is, What is the mature person? Four study units with possible lesson topics are proposed:

- *Predicting personal consequences:* foresight and self-restraint, anticipating others, accepting authority, expecting social judgment
- *Adapting to change:* self-development during family change, environmental change, technological change, governmental change, and personal misfortune
- *Assuming social responsibility:* family responsibility, social awareness and involvement, social commitment, assuming leadership, transition in the future
- *Transcending self:* pursuit of happiness, cultural transcendence, personal meditation and renewal, reverence for life, universal identification

In his final book, *The Farther Reaches of Human Nature*, Maslow (1971) summarized his research on the critical aspects of social and personal maturity; he concluded that education could help create the good and mature person by facilitating the development of a positive consciousness through focusing on the enhancement of intrinsic values, excellence, joy, and peak experiences. Coopersmith's (1968) studies also disclosed that the person with good self-esteem is most likely to be an active, creative, socially aware, capable, and balanced person. Recent studies contracted by the National Institute of Education showed that the overwhelming majority of high school graduates wished that they had been provided with a more individualized education with emphasis on developing goals and plans and more relevant preparation for real life (Petit, 1976).

The mature person must be educated to deal with the realities of life in a capable, creative, and transcendent way. He must also acquire the vitality, courage, and wisdom to make the most of his life and to foster within himself the motivational qualities of concern, will, and fortitude. Getzels and Jackson (1962, p. 135) have also characterized the mature and moral person as perceiving and admitting to personal shortcomings, holding to personal ideals, transcending such qualities as appearance and social acceptability, and "identifying with humanity beyond the immediate confines of his own group." Research also shows that these abilities to predict social and personal consequences, to adapt to change, to become responsible and altruistic, and to learn to transcend self can all be taught and developed through proper education.

Several of the studies already referred to indicate how social and personal maturity is acquired through education. The use of differential social reinforcement with modeling, role-playing, and directive verbalization of appropriate social behavior have all been shown to be effective instructional procedures by Bandura and Walters (1963) and others. Proper teaching strategies for the development of specific altruistic and sharing behaviors in normal children have been researched by Bryan and Walbeck (1970), Rogers and Vasta (1970), and Staub (1971). Similar procedures have been found effective by O'Connor (1971) in developing socially responsible behavior in withdrawn children. For example, all of these studies indicate that, through the use of positive peer tutors and such means as videotapes or films showing peers acting in desirable ways, maladaptive children can be taught to carefully observe, understand, and copy the desirable behavior and thereby practice the proper way of acting in a given situation. There is little doubt that adaptive and altruistic behavior can be directed and shaped through appropriate educational experiences.

But what about "self-transcendent" behaviors? Can these, too, be learned and influenced by education and, if so, *should* the schools be expected to provide such atypical learning experiences? Schools of all kinds have long recognized the importance of art, music, and drama as transcendent learning experiences, and many of the research findings in those fields have been incorporated in new or innovative educational programs. Until recently, however, very little evidence was available as to the importance of such transcendent behaviors as meditation and other self-renewal techniques.

In a recent publication, Bloomfield et al. (1975) discuss the dynamics of creative energy and intelligence and how they are enhanced through meditation. The most common meditative technique consists of learning how to relax and repeat a personal sound, or mantra (om, one, God, love, or one's own first name), and then to respond to its vibratory effect, which has the tendency to reduce mental activity and balance the nervous system; the extensive research results are quite impressive and have numerous educational implications. In a study with disadvantaged third-grade children, Linden (1973) found that meditation enabled them to become more field independent and increased their concentration and motivation. Other special meditation techniques have been used with 4- to 10-year-old children to help them to develop and integrate their sensory, emotional, and cognitive abilities. Studies with high school students have shown that meditation develops their capacity to learn and interrelate knowledge and "enables them to see coherence in, and give direction to modern life" (Bloomfield et al., 1975, pp. 225 to 226). Other studies have shown significant increases in grade point averages of meditating high school students (Bloomfield et al., 1975, p. 87). There is no doubt that, when schools provide quiet periods for meditation and supplement it with mild relaxation and yogalike exercises, pupils are able to concentrate better, to lower their personal anxiety levels to increase frustration tolerance, and thereby to improve academic performance.

Seeman et al. (1972) also found that college students who meditated over a 2-month period became more inner directed, self-accepting, spontaneous, and self-regarding. Highly significant increases in grade point averages were found among meditating college students by Heaton and Orme-Johnson (1974). Gowan and Ferguson have also reported significant decreases in anxiety, and increases in psychological health and self-actualization in meditating students (cited by Bloomfield et al., 1975). Equally impressive results have been found in nonschool populations such as prisons; for example, the Federal Correctional Institution in Seagoville, Texas, has reported that meditating inmates seem to develop inner peace and a sense of personal ethics and "inmates *not* practicing meditation were eight times more likely to be punished for antisocial behavior" ("Meditation High," 1976).

Training in social skills, adaptivity, responsibility, altruism, meditation, and other transcendent behaviors should all be a vital part of humanistic education. Some time ago, Havighurst and Taba (1949) called for an education program that would emphasize extending emotional experiences and experiential value building. More recently, Orstein (1972, Chap. 7) has outlined the "education of the intuitive mode," which is a new value synthesis of experiential practices involving physiological self-mastery, body energies, nonattachment, death, dreams, myth, and human intuition. In another integration of interesting research, Harman (1974, p. 667) of the Stanford Research Institute has concluded that schools in the future will emphasize the development of an evolutionary and future-oriented attitude that will foster the development of a "higher awareness and cosmic consciousness in man."

SUMMARY

In this chapter we have established an empirical rationale for a developmental taxonomy of affective-humanistic education. Five sequential stages (developmental levels) have been presented and substantiated. Each of these has been presented with illustrative goals and learning objectives. Many variations and modifications of these goals, units, and suggested lessons are possible.

The essential factor of professional concern should not be the amount of information presented or the methods used; the thing of vital importance is that the humanistic teacher must provide a warm and supporting learning environment in which the learner may desire to study affective skills and develop greater self-consciousness. For, as Jung (1954, p. 57) has stated, the child must above all learn to become properly conscious of himself through schooling. Without this consciousness the child "will never know what he really wants, but will always remain dependent and imitative, with the feeling of being misunderstood and suppressed." Therefore the teacher's conscious interest in the affective domain and the spirit by which he conveys this interest to the pupils remain the essential elements of any instructional program. Where such a spirit exists, the affective-humanistic education program guide presented in the next chapter can serve as a useful frame of reference for the professional concerned with the development of the total person.

DISCUSSION QUESTIONS AND ACTIVITIES

1. What is an instinctoid need?
2. List several problems that may prevent parents from providing basic physical security for their children.
3. How could creative and exploratory needs be more adequately provided for in the schools?
4. How might parents help improve their children's self-esteem?
5. Discuss how your own feelings may have resulted in some form of creative expression.
6. Should "bad" feelings be legitimized?
7. How might fantasy be used to further positive emotional development in education?
8. Read Benjamin Franklin's *Autobiography* and critique his behavior modification record keeping system.
9. Which side of your brain do you feel dominates your behavior? Why?
10. List as many different kinds of biofeedback as you can think of.
11. Discuss the values and problems in a self-selected or self-initiated learning project you have experienced.
12. Discuss some aspects of the "conventional morality" as it exists in your community.
13. Select a news article and picture that might be used in teaching about morality.
14. How long do peer group value orientations shape personal behavior?
15. Give an example of a mature person.
16. What place does work experience have in developing social and personal responsibility? How can this be furthered through the schools?
17. Discuss how school schedules might be modified to provide 15 minutes a day for meditation.

A humanistic curriculum is a multifaceted and balanced one.

*The evidence suggests that affective behaviors develop when
appropriate learning experiences are provided for students much
the same as cognitive behaviors develop from appropriate
learning experience.*

DAVID R. KRATHWOHL et al. (1964, p. 20)

CHAPTER 6

Curriculum guide for humanistic education

AN INTEGRATED developmental curriculum guide for affective-humanistic education is presented in this chapter. The guide is based on the taxonomy and research presented in previous chapters and is pragmatically illustrated by lessons and learning activities. It assumes, as Krathwohl suggests, that affective behavior can be developed through such purposeful and systematic instruction.

Although no attempt is made here to present specifics from other theoretical rationales, their contributions to this synthesis must be recognized. The work of Piaget (1932) in developmental psychology and on the moral judgment of children has contributed much to current educational thought and practice. Havighurst (1948) must be credited with spelling out teaching possibilities and educational implications of developmental tasks. Rousseau's (1762/1969) lessons for the social and emotional development of Emile have also been widely emulated. Kohlberg's (1968) model has renewed interest in the development of moral and ethical learning activities. Bronfenbrenner's (1970) work has contributed much to the creation of programs for developing the character traits of honesty, friendliness, self-reliance, and cooperation. Carkhuff (1972) has originated systematic resource models that show how children can learn from action programs integrating human experiences and value exploration. Practical program models have even been devised in the transcendent aspects of affective education, such as meditation in the schools, by Driscoll (1972) and others.

An attempt has been made here to integrate and synthesize these various contributions into a functional outline of a developmental affective education curriculum

73

Developmental affective education curriculum guide

Life stage	Personal orientation	Primary influence	Affective curriculum content	Educational process
Maturity	**Altruistic idealism:** "other" orientation, rational-expressive behavior	Ideal self	Developing social and personal maturity (self-actualization)	Questing goals and aspirations
		Significant others		Reality, work experiences
Adolescence	**Adjustment:** social awareness, social motivation	Society	Becoming aware of human values	Selective programming
		Friends (peers)	Self-awareness and control	Social experimentation, information processing
Childhood	**Assimilation:** identification, introjection	Parents	Expressing human feelings	Modeling and imitation
Infancy	**Egocentrism:** self-gratification, impulsive-feeling domination	Self (physical identify)	Understanding basic human needs	Need satisfaction

guide (above). In his famous work on human growth and identity, Erikson listed eight stages of development from infancy to old age; however, he failed to specify curriculum content or to provide illustrative learning experiences for use by educators. This guide acknowledges that the educational process itself continues throughout life but varies with different life stages and growth periods, but it then presents an outline that can also be used in instructional planning.

In this guide to affective education, four stages—infancy, childhood, adolescence, and maturity (adulthood)—and their educational implications are presented. Persons at each stage of human development have a unique personal orientation that varies from egocentrism to altruistic idealism. Correlatively, each person is primarily influenced, changed, and educated by himself, parents, friends, society, significant others, and his own ideal self-concepts.

Each life stage also seems to emphasize certain educational processes by which the person learns most effectively. For instance, the child first imitates and models his parents' behavior in his attempts at problem solving. Later he shifts his attention to processing information from friends and others and by experimenting with and selecting new modes of behavior. In late adolescence and "adulthood," actual work experiences and involvement in the real world and the search for meaningful goals and aspirations determine the individual's behavior.

The content of the affective-humanistic curriculum should provide numerous learning activities, exercises, and lessons that enable the pupil to understand and achieve the goals and objectives at each stage of development. Accordingly, curriculum lessons and experiences begin with stage one, understanding basic human needs, and progress upward through stage five, developing social and personal maturity.

As an instructional guide this outline presents a sound structure on which the teacher who has a conscious interest in the affective domain of education can build practical lessons for students. Although this guide has been designed to promote humanistic learning in the affective domain, it also involves cognitive and psychomotor skills and activities.

The remainder of this chapter consists of illustrative goals, objectives, and learning programs presented by developmental stages. Each stage is introduced by title, broad educational goal, and its rationale. Illustrative educational units, objectives, and performance criteria follow. Several educational programs with suggested learning activities for each unit complete each stage.

I hope that the interested teacher will find the sample affective education objectives, programs, and learning activities sufficient for experimental use with his own class. It must be remembered, however, that these are merely *sample* programs and lessons that must be adapted, modified, and supplemented for actual use with any particular class or individual pupil. The major purpose, then, of the sample objectives and programs presented here is to serve as a structural stimulus to those teachers who wish to develop their own meaningful affective-humanistic education programs.

DISCUSSION QUESTIONS AND ACTIVITIES

1. To what extent do you agree or disagree with the introductory quotation from Krathwohl et al.?
2. Critique the developmental affective education curriculum guide presented on p. 74.
3. Which of the educational processes presented on p. 74 is most well developed and used in the schools? Which do you feel is least used?
4. Review the stage-one sample learning program Living Together In Peace. Design another lesson on peace using the United Nations as basic subject matter.
5. Outline a stage-two (expressing human feelings) lesson having to do with pain and suffering.
6. Reconsider the goals and the rationale presented for stage three (self-awareness and control). Write a comprehensive autobiography in which you discuss your personal characteristics as listed under self-consciousness.
7. List some of your own self-control problems
8. To what extent do you feel the stage-four social skills and values could be taught as part of a regular social studies class?
9. Actually teach one of the six lessons listed under stage five (developing social and personal maturity). Then critique the lesson and suggest how it might be supplemented and improved.

AN AFFECTIVE EDUCATION PROGRAM

Stage one
UNDERSTANDING BASIC HUMAN NEEDS

General educational goal

For pupils to demonstrate their understanding and appreciation of how people attempt to meet their basic human needs of physical security, love, creative expression, knowledge, social competency, and self-worth

Rationale

The history of humanity is a record of attempts to meet physical and psychological needs; continued human development is a process of increasing self-awareness and competency in understanding ourselves and how to meet our needs.

Illustrative educational units, objectives, and performance criteria

1. Physical security: To be able to understand and appreciate that the need for physical security includes attempts to obtain adequate food, shelter, clothing, and health

Each member of the class will cut out and describe in writing four newspaper or magazine pictures depicting how people have attempted to meet their needs for food, shelter, clothing, and health.

2. Love: To be able to understand and appreciate that giving attention to others, friendship, caring and empathy, and family togetherness are all different aspects of the need to give and receive love

Each pupil will select, read, and discuss four different poems that express these aspects of human love.

3. Creative expression: To be able to understand and appreciate that dance, song, exploration, and painting are all major forms of the need for creative expression

Each student will do the following:

- Orally describe two folk dances from different countries.
- Play a recording of a favorite song.
- Write a brief description of a time he explored new surroundings.
- Bring in a picture of a painting he enjoys and explain why he enjoys it.

4. Knowledge: To be able to understand and appreciate that the need for knowledge involves the continual improvement of the skills of thinking, learning, discovering, and explaining

Each pupil will do the following:

- Write a formula that expresses specific thoughts or ideas.
- Demonstrate how learning to ride a bicycle occurs through responding to cues and continued practice.

- Select and perform a simple scientific experiment that demonstrates how people may discover new knowledge.
- Use a tape recorder to describe and explain the results of the scientific experiment; the class will judge the taped explanation for clarity and conciseness.

5. Social competency: To be able to understand and appreciate that people strive to become socially competent in the society in which they live by helping others, playing together, living together in peace, and working together

From the books listed on the provided reading list, each student will select, read, and describe in writing two stories that illustrate some of the above-specified ways that people satisfy their need for social competency.

6. Self-worth: To be able to understand and appreciate the human need to develop a sense of self-worth as reflected in personal confidence, acceptance of personal strengths and limitations, a striving for independence, and self-respect and dignity

The student will present an oral report, based on independent research, on how a person—Abraham Lincoln, Babe Ruth, Martin Luther King, Jr., Roberto Clemente, or some other person he knows—developed these qualities of self-worth.

Lesson topic
PHYSICAL SECURITY: FOOD

Lesson objective: To understand that the need for food is basic to our physical security and continued growth and development

Sample learning program (primary grades): Purpose: The purpose of this specific lesson is to understand why children like Nana may be hungry and how this might affect their behavior. Directions: Read the story about Nana and complete the questions and activities that follow.

Nana

Nana is 8 years old and she is always hungry. Last year her village did not have much rain, and most of the food plants did not grow very well. The people have been hungry ever since, as they only eat once a day. Nana feels tired most of the time.

---

1. Use crayons to draw and color a picture of this story.
2. How old is Nana?
3. Why did the plants in her village not grow very well? How does this affect how often the people eat?
4. How does Nana feel most of the time?
5. Define the word "famine" (you may use the dictionary).
6. What might other people do to help Nana and the villagers overcome their hunger?
7. Look through magazines or newspapers and find a picture of a hungry person. Cut it out and paste it on a sheet of paper. Then write a sentence describing the person you have selected.

Related activities
- List favorite foods for holiday meals.
- Collect pictures of special foods from other countries.
- Develop a desirable menu for breakfast, lunch, and dinner.

Lesson topic
LOVE: ATTENTION

Lesson objective: To understand that love is a very important basic human need that is expressed through the way we give and receive care and attention

Sample learning program (middle elementary grades): Purpose: The purpose of this specific lesson is to understand several different ways that love may be expressed. Directions: Use your notebook to write your answers to the following items.

1. In his play *Twelfth Night,* Shakespeare wrote, "Love sought is good, but giv'n unsought is better." What do you think this means about the need to love and be loved? What does it tell us about what happens to us when we love other people?
2. Dogs like to be petted and stroked and to be played with. Name some other animals that also like to be loved in a similar way.
3. How can you show another person that you care what happens to him?
4. Try to describe how it feels to be loved by other people.
5. We love and attend to different people in different ways. List several different kinds of love.
6. Read this proverb and then check what you think it means: "He may say that he loves you. Wait and see what he does for you!"
   _____ a. Love is telling someone you love him.
   _____ b. Love is doing something for others.
   _____ c. Love is telling someone you love him and then doing something for him.

Related activity
- Collect and discuss five different Valentine's Day cards that express different kinds of love.

Lesson topic
CREATIVE EXPRESSION: PAINTING

Lesson objective: To understand that painting is one form of the human need for creative expression

Sample learning program (middle elementary): Purpose: The purpose of this specific lesson is to enable you to understand how people might express their feelings through painting. Directions: Obtain some large newsprint, assorted colors of tempera paints, and a place to spread out on the floor and work.

1. Think of a time when you were very happy. Try to remember how you felt at that time. Paint a picture that attempts to express these happy feelings.
2. What other kind of picture might you have painted that would have expressed your feelings?
3. What are your favorite colors? Why?
4. The Indians used to paint pictures to express their feelings about their lives. Paint a picture about something that happened to you that was very important; try to express your feelings in the painting.
5. Bring in pictures of three paintings by different artists that express different feelings. Explain to the class what you think each artist was trying to express.
6. Why does painting help a person express his feelings?

Related activities

- Work cooperatively with two other pupils to prepare a joint painting depicting an unhappy feeling.
- Invite a local artist to talk to your class about how he attempts to express himself through painting.

Lesson topic
KNOWLEDGE: DISCOVERY

Lesson objective: To understand that the continuous search for the discovery of new knowledge is a basic human need

Sample learning program (upper elementary): Purpose: The purpose of this specific lesson is to understand some of the different ways in which people attempt to discover new knowledge. Directions: Arrange to visit a scientific laboratory in a local industry. If this is not possible, view a film on an industrial research laboratory. Answer the following questions.

1. Describe what you observed during your visit or film observation.
2. What are some of the things the laboratory was established to do?
3. List at least one new bit of knowledge that the laboratory has discovered.
4. Carefully observe a preschool child in his home. Describe his behavior.
5. What are some of the things that the child may have discovered while you were watching him?
6. Most people discover things through their new experiences of trial and error. Describe something that you discovered in this way and what you were doing.
7. List several instruments that help people to discover new knowledge.

Related activity

• Select an experiment from an elementary science book that you would like to do. Perform the experiment for the class and explain in detail what you are trying to do and what you discover.

Lesson topic
SOCIAL COMPETENCY: LIVING TOGETHER IN PEACE

> **Lesson objective:** To understand that people need to learn how to live together in peace
>
> **Sample learning program (middle elementary):** Purpose: The purpose of this specific lesson is to become aware that social cooperation, law, and justice are necessary for peace to exist. Directions: Read the story below. Use your notebook to complete the learning activities.

Tommy's decision

After school, Tommy went to Mr. Lucano's candy store. It was always fun to run and pick out candy. Tommy was in such a hurry that he knocked over the bread rack while going into the store. Mr. Lucano made him pick it all up, and by that time his favorite candy had been sold out. Tommy felt upset and angry as he left the store.

Later, after his baseball game, Tommy was riding his bicycle past Mr. Lucano's store. He saw two men get out of a car with what seemed to be guns. Then he heard shouting from inside the store.

---

1. Why was Tommy angry as he left the store?
2. What should Tommy do?
3. Use the dictionary to define law, justice, and peace.
4. To live together in peace, people must work together in making and following the rules under which they will live. Suggest a new rule that might help improve the social behavior in your class.
5. List three ways that you can work with friends to have a more peaceful school and neighborhood.
6. What do you feel are some of the problems you have in getting along with other people?
7. How do police officers help us to live together peacefully?

Related activity

- Collect several different posters of peace signs. Explain to the class what the symbols on the posters mean.

Lesson topic
SELF-WORTH: CONFIDENCE

> **Lesson objective:** To understand that all people need to develop a sense of self-confidence
>
> **Sample learning program (upper elementary):** Purpose: The purpose of this specific lesson is to help you decide what you might do to become more self-confident. Directions: Close your eyes and think of someone you know whom you feel to be a self-confident person. Complete the following activities.
>
> 1. Write a description of how this person acts that makes you feel he is self-confident.
> 2. Self-confident persons usually feel quite certain and secure about what they are doing; they feel that what they are doing is OK and they think, "I *can* do it." List some things about yourself that you feel confident that you can do well.
> 3. How confident do you think you would feel if you were a member of the UCLA basketball team that had the most straight wins in basketball history? Why might you feel that way?
> 4. Most people can learn to become somewhat more confident in their abilities if they have some help. What kind of help might make you feel more confident?
> 5. Complete this sentence: I do *not* feel very confident in _____.
> 6. Get together with a group of four other class members. Discuss several things that you all decide might be done to help someone overcome a lack of self-confidence.
> 7. In what way might a person become overconfident about his skills and abilities?
>
> **Related activities**
> - An old proverb says, "To thine own self be true." Explain to the class what this means to you.
> - Draw a picture of something you feel very confident in doing.

Stage two
EXPRESSING HUMAN FEELINGS

General educational goal

For pupils to be able to understand and express their feelings about major life concerns

Rationale

Children need to learn to understand and express both positive and negative feelings. Human feelings should be studied as normal and desirable behaviors that are important for our development. Ways of coping with human feelings at different stages of growth and development should be learned as part of general education.

Illustrative educational units, objectives, and performance criteria

1. Basic feelings: To be able to understand and express such basic human feelings as love, anger, fear, faith, despair, pain, and hope

On completion of these lessons, all students in this discussion group will be able to openly express four of the seven basic feelings listed above.

2. Critical emotional concerns: To become aware of the following critical emotional concerns common to most people and to be able to express one's feelings about these concerns:

Birth	Arguments	Peace
Loneliness	Success	Dreams and aspirations
Making friends	Getting married	Cooperation
Sadness	Personal misfortune	Human death
Failures	Accidents	Hurting others
War	Going away	

Each student will develop a notebook on five or more critical emotional concerns on the list consisting of newspaper stories and written notes expressing his personal feelings about these stories.

3. Instincts and intuitions: To become aware that human emotions and feelings are also expressed in such ways as dreams, predispositions, fantasy, myth, unconscious functions, will, and peak experiences

Each pupil will describe to the class a dream he has had and get members of the class to act it out with him.

Lesson topic
BASIC FEELINGS: ANGER

Lesson objective: To be able to understand that anger is a normal human feeling that can be expressed in socially acceptable ways

Sample learning program (middle elementary): Purpose: The purpose of this specific lesson is to help you consider several ways of expressing anger. Directions: Read the following story and complete the activities.

The dirty jerk

Sometimes Pete got so angry he would throw and kick things around. Once he threw a rock at a boy who called him names. His father said, "Pete, it's natural to get upset and feel angry at times, but you have to learn to express your anger in a better way." This was hard for Pete to do because he got so upset at times that he could not even think of other ways to express himself.

The next day, Pete was walking home from school and Joe began to tease him. Then Joe called Pete a dirty jerk. All of a sudden, Pete got mad! He reached for a rock on the ground—but then he thought of what his father had said.

---

1. What do you think Pete will do?
2. What are two other ways that Pete could use to express his anger?
3. Make some puppets from paper bags and put on a puppet show about the story "The Dirty Jerk." Take turns showing other ways for Pete to express his anger.
4. "Righteous indignation" is the expression of anger in socially desirable ways when you have a good reason for being angry (such as being called bad names). List several good reasons why people might get angry.
5. Think of a time when you got angry and lost your self-control. How did you act? How else *might* you have acted?

Related activity

- How many answers can you give for this riddle: Why is an angry man where he never is and never could be?

Answer: Because he is beside himself

Lesson topic
BASIC FEELINGS: HOPE

Lesson objective: To be able to express one's hopes for the future

Sample learning program (upper elementary): Purpose: The purpose of this specific lesson is to become aware of and to express several different hopes that people have. Directions: Bring to class some pictures that represent things that people have hoped for. Then do the following activities.

1. Present your pictures to the class and explain how they represent people's hopes.
2. Which one of the pictures that you brought to class might also express one of your own hopes?
3. What do you hope for in the future?
4. Below are some things that people have hoped for:

Fishing trip	New job
Picnic	Invitation to a party
New shoes	Visit from father

   Write several other things that you know people have hoped for.
5. If you were the following persons, what might you hope for?

   A prisoner of war
   A boy in an orphanage
   An old woman in a hospital bed

6. When people hope for things, they usually work and behave in such a way that their hopes might be realized. Describe something that you have hoped for that you finally realized.

Related activity

• List on the chalkboard the different kinds of things your classmates have hoped for. See if you can group or classify the different kinds of hopes according to the following:

Personal hopes
Hopes for other people
Other kinds of hopes

Lesson topic
CRITICAL EMOTIONAL CONCERNS: GETTING MARRIED

Lesson objectives: To be able to express one's feelings about marriage
Sample learning program (junior high): Purpose: The purpose of this specific lesson is to explore several feelings about marriage. Directions: Complete the following learning activities.

1. People get married when they find that they have common interests and that they love one another and wish to be together and care for each other. It usually takes months or years of going places and doing things together before people are sure they wish to spend their lives together. Some young men and women do not think carefully about marriage and what it requires of them. They may get married too quickly and be unhappy afterwards. Loving and caring for someone and raising a family is a big responsibility. Not everyone should get married. Explain in writing why someone you know got married.
2. What do going places and doing things together have to do with marriage?
3. When might a person get married too quickly?
4. Why shouldn't all people be married?
5. What do you feel are some of the desirable things about marriage?
6. What do you feel might be some of the undesirable things about marriage?
7. Why do many people go to a minister, priest, or rabbi to be married?

Related activity

• Bring to class a recent newspaper picture or article on marriage. Express your personal feelings about the picture or article and lead the class in a discussion of how they feel about it.

Lesson topic
CRITICAL EMOTIONAL CONCERNS: HUMAN DEATH

Lesson objective: To be able to express one's feelings about human death
Sample learning program (upper elementary): Purpose: The purpose of this specific lesson is to permit expression of feelings and attitudes about death. Directions: Read the following story and complete the learning activities.

The funeral

It did seem strange that she was only 16 years old. Tom felt that was pretty young to die and he had always thought of Beth as his older cousin who would live for many years. Now she was dead as a result of a terrible train wreck, and Tom found himself in a funeral home for the first time. He had never seen so many flowers before, and it made him feel strange to smell them as he passed the closed casket. The service was short, and then they drove behind the hearse to the cemetery where Beth was to be buried. It was then that Tom felt like crying.

---

1. How did Beth die?
2. What other ways do people die?
3. What is a hearse? Describe some different hearses.
4. Why do people have funerals?
5. What may have made Tom feel like crying?
6. Describe your personal feelings about death by writing them in some detail in your notebook.
7. Get together with a group of four other pupils. Together make a list of several "natural" and "unnatural" forms of death.

Related activities
- Write a description of a funeral or memorial service you have attended.
- With some friends, visit a cemetery and copy several epitaphs from head-stones. Discuss these with your class.

Lesson topic
CRITICAL EMOTIONAL CONCERNS: SCHOOL SUCCESS AND
FRUSTRATION

Lesson objective: To be able to express positive and negative feelings about school experiences

Sample learning program (upper elementary): Purpose: The purpose of this specific lesson is to express some of your feelings about school. Directions: Read the following story and complete the learning activities.

Old Bill

The other boys called him Old Bill. That was because he was 26 years old when he went back to school to learn to read, write, and count. Bill had worked in the fields since he was a boy, but now in the year 1884 he decided he wanted to go to school. At first it was very hard to sit with the children, but the teacher said he was welcome if he really wanted to learn. He already knew how to count some, and arithmetic was fun for him. Although he wanted to read most of all, he had to work hard at it. He really enjoyed it when he successfully read his first book.

---

1. Why do you feel that "Old Bill" wanted to go back to school?
2. How do you think he really felt about sitting with young children?
3. What did he seem to enjoy most in school?
4. What do you enjoy most in school?
5. What do you feel most upset about in school? What makes you "upset"?
6. Briefly describe in writing the most enjoyable year you spent in school.

Related activities
- Make a chart of all your school subjects and activities. After each subject or activity write whether you are "very successful," "somewhat successful," or "unsuccessful."
- How do you feel school could be made a more enjoyable place to be?

Lesson topic
CRITICAL EMOTIONAL CONCERNS: JOY

Lesson objective: To be able to express joy and celebration in life

Sample learning program (middle elementary): Purpose: The purpose of this specific lesson is to understand some ways that people express their feelings of joy and celebration. Directions: Have a class discussion about your favorite holidays; list them on the chalkboard and vote on their popularity. Complete the following activities.

1. Write in your notebook the holiday that you gave as your favorite. Explain why this is your favorite holiday.
2. Color a picture that shows how you last spent this holiday. Write a brief explanation of the picture.
3. Which holiday on the board was the least popular? Why do you feel it was the least popular?
4. Describe how you would feel if these things happened:

   Nobody celebrated your birthday.
   There was no Christmas vacation at school.
   The Fourth of July celebration was canceled in your town.

5. Why do people throughout the world have celebrations? List a celebration that is enjoyed in some other country than the United States and explain what is being celebrated.

Related activities

- With your class, select an occasion to celebrate and plan a party. Discuss why this event is being celebrated and the kind of party you will have.
- What do you plan to contribute to the celebration or party?

Lesson topic
INSTINCTS AND INTUITIONS: MYTH

> **Lesson objective:** To be able to feel and experience the importance of myth in our lives
>
> **Sample learning program (upper elementary):** Purpose: The purpose of this specific lesson is to feel and understand an American myth. Directions: Read the story below and complete the following activities.

Paul Bunyan

Paul was a great woodsman who lived and worked in northern Minnesota. It was said that he was so strong that he could blow a dozen trees down with one good sneeze. He would eat so much that it took four cooks several hours to make his breakfast of many giant flapjacks and 100 eggs. Paul had a pet ox that was so big that it took a day for blackbirds to fly between its horns.

---

1. Was Paul a real man?
2. Why do people like to hear stories about persons such as Paul Bunyan?
3. Would you like to have Paul for a friend? Why or why not?
4. Describe some other myths you have heard of and try to explain what they mean.
5. List some myths and fairy tales that people still believe in today.

Related activities

- Have a "tall story" contest in your class.
- Read a famous myth from another country (try to find a "classical" myth) and tell how it makes you feel.

Lesson topic
INSTINCTS AND INTUITIONS: DREAMS AND FANTASIES

Lesson objective: To be able to relate to and experience dreams and fantasies

Sample learning program (middle elementary): Purpose: The purpose of this lesson is to help you recall, feel, and understand the importance of a particular dream or fantasy. Directions: Place a pencil and sheet of paper by your bed before you fall asleep. The next time you dream, try to draw a picture of part of your dream as soon as you awake. Then complete the following activities.

1. Look at your picture and write down all the words or sentences that come to you about your dream.
2. Use a larger sheet of paper and color or paint a picture of the most vivid part of the dream you can remember.
3. Show your picture or painting to others and tell them about your dream.
4. Describe how the dream makes you feel.
5. Describe a dream that you had several times and that you remember quite well.
6. Why do people dream?
7. Share your favorite daydream or fantasy.

Related activities
- Make a class dream book of paintings and stories.
- Discuss how daydreams and fantasies might come true.
- Discuss the meaning of the word "symbols."

Stage three
SELF-AWARENESS AND CONTROL

General educational goals

For pupils to be able to become more aware of themselves and their relationships with other people and to develop self-control

Rationale

To effectively cope with personal and social demands and relationships, it is necessary for the individual to become increasingly self-aware of his actions and their consequences. Children can learn to develop self-awareness, sensitivity to others, and appropriate self-control through systematic instruction, experience, and practice.

Illustrative educational units, objectives, and performance criteria

1. Self-consciousness: To become aware of one's physical characteristics, sensory abilities, expressive language, talents, needs, sensitivity, and aspirations

On concluding these lessons, pupils will write a comprehensive autobiography in which they discuss their personal awareness of each of the characteristics listed above.

2. Awareness of others: To be able to become more aware of the physical and psychological needs and feelings of other people engaged in cooperative learning activities and games

Students will participate in three awareness games (such as Secret Message, Blindman's Faith, and Chin Ball Pass) and then orally describe their feelings about partners; the partner will respond to the expressed awareness of him.

3. Self-control: To be able to more adequately control and express undesirable behaviors such as the following: yelling, tattling, fighting, jealousy, rudeness, lying, destructiveness, and selfishness

For a selected behavior the pupil will demonstrate alternative ways of acting and will show a reduced frequency of the undesirable behavior as recorded on a self-tabulating chart.

Lesson topic
SELF-CONSCIOUSNESS: WHO AM I?

> **Lesson objective:** To become more aware of one's physical and psychological self
>
> **Sample learning program (upper elementary):** Purpose: The purpose of this specific lesson is to look at and describe yourself as well as you can. Directions: Select three different photographs of yourself taken at different ages. Paste them on separate pages in a notebook entitled "Who Am I?" Then complete the following activities.
>
> 1. Under each picture, write your name, age, the place where the picture was taken, and what you were doing at the time.
> 2. Describe your favorite hobby, activity, or interest (how did you really like to spend your time?) at the time each picture was taken.
> 3. Describe your health at the time each picture was taken. How healthy are you now?
> 4. How do you feel you look now? Describe your height, weight, eye color, hair color, and general physical appearance. If you wish that you might look somewhat different than you do, explain how you would want to look.
> 5. What are your present interests and hobbies? What do you now enjoy doing most of all?
> 6. Describe how you feel about yourself and the kind of person you feel yourself to be right now.
> 7. How do you think other people would describe the kind of person you are?
> 8. What kind of person do you feel you would like to become?
>
> **Related activities**
>
> • Roll out a large sheet of butcher paper. Lie down on the paper and have a friend trace your body outline. Then color in your clothes, your skin, and the rest of your body parts. Use your reflection in a hanging wall mirror as a model. Cut out your picture and hang it on the wall.
> • Write a brief paragraph describing how you feel about the picture of yourself you have just made.

Lesson topic
SELF-CONSCIOUSNESS: THE SOUNDS AROUND US

Lesson objective: To become more aware of the many sounds in and around us and how they affect our behavior

Sample learning program (upper elementary): Purpose: The purpose of this specific lesson is to explore the meaning of several sounds in our environment. Directions: Put your head down on the desk and be absolutely quiet for at least 3 minutes. Listen carefully to all of the sounds you can hear. Try to concentrate on what you hear and to remember it. Complete the following activities.

1. Use your notebook to list as many different sounds as you can remember.
2. Discuss your sounds with the class. List as many different sounds on the chalkboard as you can. Select one or two of the most unusual sounds that were listed and have everybody close their eyes and try to hear them. How many people were able to hear these unusual sounds?
3. Place your fingers in your ears with your arms and head on your desk. Close your eyes and listen quietly. Write down what you heard this time. Discuss what you heard.
4. List three very pleasant sounds that you enjoy. What makes them pleasant to you?
5. What are your favorite musical sounds or instruments? Why are these your favorite?
6. Some sounds such as police sirens are warning sounds. Describe several other kinds of warning sounds and what they mean to you.

Related activities
- Draw a picture of an animal that makes a warning sound.
- Bring to class a recording of a favorite sound and play it for your friends to hear. Explain to them how this sound makes you feel.

Lesson topic
AWARENESS OF OTHERS: ATTENDING TO OTHERS

Lesson objective: To be able to become more aware of the physical and psychological needs and feelings of other people who are engaged in co-operative activities

Sample learning program (upper elementary): Purpose: The purpose of this specific lesson is for you to become more attentive to what other people are saying and doing. Directions: Sit on the floor in a large circle of about 10 other boys and girls. Be sure to sit close enough so that you will be able to whisper to one another. Do the following activities.

1. Select a person to be the group leader, who is to think of a one-sentence "secret message." The leader then covers his mouth with his hands and whispers the secret message into the ear of the person on his right. That person then whispers the message to the next person on the right and so on until the message has been passed around the circle. When the message reaches the last person in the circle, everyone is to secretly write down in their own notebook what they thought they heard whispered to them.
2. Write down what you heard. Do not show the message to anyone else.
3. The last person to receive the secret message is to be first in reading what he heard to the group. Write down what the last person said he heard.
4. Is what you have written down the same as what the last person said he heard? If they differ, how do they differ? Do they mean the same thing?
5. Why do some people misunderstand what they hear from others?
6. Carefully attend to what another person is doing for 3 minutes. Try to write down everything he does or says during that time.
7. How well do you feel you were aware of what the person was doing that you were observing? Were you aware of everything he was doing? Why?

Related activity

• Some people never seem to listen to or care about others. Think of someone you have met who is like this and select a group of three or four classmates to role-play a scene. Ask the class to observe the role-playing and have them suggest ways to help such a person become more attentive to others.

Lesson topic
AWARENESS OF OTHERS: FAITH

Lesson objective: To be able to develop an intuitive awareness of and faith in other people

Sample learning program (junior high): Purpose: The purpose of this specific lesson is for you to become aware of your faith in others and in some things that you cannot see. Directions: Select a partner for Blindman's Faith. Have your partner blindfold you thoroughly so you cannot see. Your partner will then guide you around the room and out of doors for approximately 15 minutes, during which you will be given a number of things to touch and feel. Try to remember all that you do. After you remove the blindfold, complete the following activities.

1. Use your notebook to write how you felt and what you experienced while you were blindfolded.
2. Use the dictionary to define the word "apprehension."
3. Were you apprehensive at any time while you were being guided around blindfolded? Explain your answer.
4. What kind of faith did you have in the person who was guiding you around?
5. How do you think that persons who have lost their sight develop faith in themselves?
6. How do we develop faith in other people?
7. Now change roles and blindfold and guide your partner around. Write down where you took him and what you did.

Related activity
• People have learned to have faith in many things they cannot always see, such as faith in God, faith in democracy, and faith in science. What are some of the things that you are aware of that you have faith in?

Lesson topic
SELF-CONTROL: YELLING

> **Lesson objective:** To be able to more adequately control the tendency to yell at other people
>
> **Sample learning program (middle elementary):** Purpose: The purpose of this specific lesson is to consider alternative behaviors to yelling at other people. Directions: With a small group, go to a designated spot on the playground or to an empty room where you will not disturb others. Yell and scream for a minute as loud as you can. Now yell and scream at each other for a minute. Return to your class and complete these activities.
>
> 1. Quietly take turns describing to each other how it felt to yell and to be yelled at. Was it pleasant or unpleasant?
> 2. Sometimes screaming and yelling can be fun. For instance, screaming during a scary movie or during a game can be enjoyable. List two actual situations in which screaming and yelling are socially acceptable behaviors.
> 3. Most of the time it is unpleasant to be yelled at. Describe in writing a time when somebody yelled at you and it made you upset. How did you act?
> 4. Describe the last time you yelled at someone and upset them. What else might you have done?
> 5. Why do people yell and scream at one another?
> 6. Usually, it does not help to yell at another person. Why is this true?
> 7. If someone continually screamed at you, what might you do about it?
>
> **Related activity**
> • Beth was often upset because it seemed as though her family was constantly yelling and screaming at one another. She usually tried screaming back at them, but things only got worse. Beth wished that somehow they might stop all this and learn to get along without so much noise and disturbance. What could Beth do?

Lesson topic
SELF-DISCIPLINE: DESTRUCTIVENESS

Lesson objective: To be able to control one's destructive tendencies

Sample learning program (upper elementary): Purpose: The purpose of this specific lesson is to become more aware of constructive ways to express destructive feelings. Directions: Read the story below and do the following activities.

Smashing the train

For some time now, Bryan had felt cheated. His brother, Joe, was always being invited to parties and outings, but no one invited Bryan and he was 1 year older than Joe. Now Joe was invited to a special picnic at the park. When Bryan heard that, he went into his room, slammed the door, and started to play with his train. But the more he thought about the picnic and Joe, the madder he became. All of a sudden, he started jumping up and down and smashing the train. Then the door opened and his father came into the room.

---

1. What made Bryan upset?
2. How do you think he might have felt about destroying the train?
3. What else could Bryan have done about his feelings?
4. What do you think his father should do?
5. Everyone has destructive feelings at times. Describe a time when you felt like wrecking or destroying something. What did you do?
6. Many things are destroyed unnecessarily. Explain how the following things may be destroyed unnecessarily:

   Trees   Food
   Toys   Birds' eggs

7. What do you feel should be done about people who destroy things unnecessarily?

Related activity
- It is not always possible to repair or replace things that one has destroyed. For example, a good friendship can be destroyed through thoughtlessness. Write several things that a person might do that could destroy a good friendship.

Stage four
BECOMING AWARE OF HUMAN VALUES

General educational goals

For pupils to become aware of the major personal attitudes, social skills, and diverse values that influence human behavior

Rationale

Successful living demands that the individual be able to relate to people in many stressful situations. Children must learn that people are motivated by many different personal and cultural values. Pupils must acquire those social skills that enable them to function in the community.

Illustrative educational units, objectives, and performance criteria

1. Skills for social living: To be able to understand and demonstrate the value of courtesy, kindness, friendliness, honesty, cheerfulness, cooperativeness, respect, and tolerance in social living situations

The pupil will (a) define in writing each of the above skills, (b) role-play the definition with selected class members, and (c) orally evaluate the demonstration with other participants.

2. Personal and social commitment: To become aware of the values of love, wealth, power, knowledge, religion, service, and aesthetics and to understand why people have committed their lives to them

The pupil will demonstrate his awareness of these personal values by compiling a list of outstanding public figures who have been widely identified with each value; the pupil will also qualify in writing the extent to which he feels each person listed is committed to that value.

3. Cultural values: To become aware of our cultural values of liberty, independence, work, justice, democracy, and thanksgiving

On completion of these lessons the pupil will be able to discuss the theme and major characters in six different stories he has read that illustrate each of these cultural values.

Lesson topic
SKILLS FOR SOCIAL LIVING: KINDNESS

Lesson objective: To become more aware of the value of kindness

Sample learning program (middle elementary): Purpose: The purpose of this specific lesson is to consider several forms of human kindness and how they may be demonstrated in life. Directions: The following article was taken from a news report. Read it carefully and then complete the activities.

Thirty-one cats found in house

Following continual complaints of noise and disturbance from the neighbors, police obtained a search warrant to enter the residence of Mrs. Ola Parkins last week. What they found was 31 cats all over the five-room house and in a fenced yard. Mrs. Parkins told police that she had picked up sick and stray cats for years, as she could not bear to see them suffer without adequate care. Judge Haskins of the Municipal Court will decide the fate of the cats sometime next week.

---

1. Why were the neighbors complaining?
2. How was Mrs. Parkins being kind to the cats?
3. If you were Judge Haskins, what might you decide to do?
4. Cut out a picture of a cat from a magazine and paste it in your notebook. Try to find out the breed of cat and describe what kind of care it might require.
5. Why are some people more kind to animals than to humans?
6. In what way would you like people to be more kind and considerate of you?
7. In what way is it sometimes difficult to be kind to others?

Related activities

- Sometimes, people take advantage of the kindness of another person. Describe to your class how this might be done and discuss why people act this way.
- Write a brief paragraph describing how you might be more kind to other people.

Lesson topic
SKILLS FOR SOCIAL LIVING: TOLERANCE

Lesson objective: To become aware of the value of tolerance as an essential social and personal attitude

Sample learning program (upper elementary): Purpose: The purpose of this specific lesson is to be able to develop an understanding of and tolerance for different children. Directions: Read the following story and complete the activities.

Real differences

When Susan moved to her new town, she was placed in Mrs. Allen's seventh-grade history class. The first day of school was a real surprise to Susan, as she had never seen so many different people in one class before. Of the 29 children in her room, 10 were Chinese, including 3 who had just arrived from Hong Kong. 8 were white, 6 were black, 4 were Mexican-American, and 1 was a real American Indian. Everyone had different stories to tell and there were several new games to learn as well. It bothered her sometimes that everybody dressed so differently. She also wondered why they spent so much time studying modern Chinese and Mexican history.

---

1. What bothered Susan about her class?
2. Why do you think the class spent so much time studying modern Chinese and Mexican history?
3. What might Susan do to better tolerate the differences she found in her new school?
4. What are some of the different ways that people live that should be tolerated in others? Discuss this with your class.
5. Tolerance commonly means allowing another person to live his own style of life. List something that you feel should *not* be tolerated in others and discuss this with your class.
6. What are some of the things you have had difficulty in learning to tolerate in others?

Related activity

• Write several different experiences or things that people might do that would probably help them to become more tolerant persons.

Lesson topic
PERSONAL AND SOCIAL COMMITMENT: POWER

Lesson objective: To understand the value of power as an ability to act with strength to determine one's own life

Sample learning program (junior high): Purpose: The purpose of this specific lesson is to be able to contrast political, physical, spiritual, and military forms of power. Directions: Cut out a newspaper or magazine picture that illustrates some form of power. Place the picture in your notebook. Complete the following activities.

1. Write a brief description of the picture and try to explain what the people may be feeling and thinking.
2. People usually give power to their leaders to make the rules and regulations under which they live. Every person has some power in his vote as a citizen, and he must use it wisely to govern himself and others. List several different kinds of governmental representatives people can give power to.
3. Moses was a great leader of his people and had spiritual power that greatly influenced others. Write a paragraph about another spiritual leader and explain how he used his power.
4. An automobile represents a form of physical power that we can control to some extent. List two other forms of physical power we use in our daily lives and explain how they influence us.
5. More than 2000 years ago, Alexander the Great conquered the world of his time. As a young man he dreamed of power and believed that by ruling the world he would be able to bring peace and order to its people. What kind of power does a conqueror use?
6. Do you think that armies can bring peace and order to the world?

Related activity

- Discuss these questions with your class: Do you think it is undesirable to have power over others? How much power over yourself do you have? What kind of power do you feel is most valuable?

Lesson topic
PERSONAL AND SOCIAL COMMITMENT: SERVICE

Lesson objective: To become aware that being of service to other persons is highly valued in all societies

Sample learning program (upper elementary): Purpose: The purpose of this specific lesson is to be able to experience some of the satisfaction of being of service to other people. Directions: With your class, plan a visit to a home for senior citizens. Arrange your visit so you will have time to visit and talk with them. Do the following activities.

1. Outline several things that you might do during your visit that would be of service to senior citizens. Discuss these with your class and teacher.
2. Write a description of your visit, explaining what you actually saw and what you did that was of service.
3. There are many ways that people may be of service to others. For example, a scoutmaster is of service to the community as well as to the boys in his troop. List two other forms of community service.
4. How have people been of service to your school? How might you be of service to your school or community?
5. Who is most in need of service from others?
6. How might you someday need more help and service from other people than you do now?

Related activity

- Service to others has many rewards. Read the following story from Aesop's fables; then write what you feel the mouse might have thought when he saw the lion caught in the net.

The lion and the mouse

A mouse ran over the nose of a sleeping lion, who then woke up. The lion caught the mouse in his paw and was going to eat him, when the mouse said, "Forgive me, I did not mean to wake you up. I am sorry, please let me go." The lion smiled at the frightened little mouse and let him go.

Sometime later the lion fell into a rope net placed by some hunters, and he roared for help. The mouse heard him roar and ran to help him by nibbling the ropes. Soon the lion was free.

Lesson topic
CULTURAL VALUES: WORK

> **Lesson objectives:** To become aware of the value of work
>
> **Sample learning program (junior high):** Purpose: The purpose of this specific lesson is to understand that meaningful work helps both the individual and the society in which he lives. Directions: Cut out three newspaper pictures of persons involved in different forms of meaningful work. Paste the pictures in your notebook. Complete the following activities.
>
> 1. Under each picture, write a paragraph describing what kind of work the people in the pictures are doing.
> 2. Meaningful work provides us with self-expression and many rewards. List several different kinds of work and explain how self-expression may be obtained from these jobs.
> 3. It is often necessary to work at jobs that do not provide much self-expression. Describe such a job and explain how it may be rewarding in other ways.
> 4. List as many other rewards for working that you can think of.
> 5. Work is a way of doing something useful for yourself and others. Without cooperative work and labor, we would be unable to build a good society in which to live. Write a brief theme that describes some form of work you think you might be interested in doing someday. Get together with a group of four or five other classmates and discuss what you have written.
> 6. In many countries, children and students of all ages spend part of their school year doing some work that is useful to the society in which they live. Discuss with your class some of the jobs that you feel children could do to help contribute to a better society.
> 7. What could be done to provide work to every person who is capable of working?
>
> **Related activity**
> - Visit a place where one of your relatives is working and talk to him about his work. Write a paper describing what he does; if he would like to do some other kind of work, describe what that may be.

Lesson topic
CULTURAL VALUES: LIBERTY

Lesson objective: To become aware of the value of liberty

Sample learning program (upper elementary): Purpose: The purpose of this specific lesson is to be able to understand liberty as a state of freedom in which the individual can help to decide how he will live. Directions: Read the following story and complete the activities.

The wish of Claudius

Claudius was a 12-year-old boy in ancient Rome. He was born into slavery, as both of his parents were made slaves after being captured in a war. His parents had died when he was small, and Claudius continued to work in his master's kitchen. Claudius had often dreamed of what it would be like to be free and be his own master. He wished for his liberty more than anything else. One day, his master called him to his room with the other slaves and announced that he was making all of them free. Claudius was stunned and didn't know what to say or do!

---

1. Why was Claudius a slave?
2. Where else has slavery existed in the world?
3. Write down some of the feelings that Claudius might have had when he was made a free person.
4. Discuss with your class what a person has to do to be "his own master."
5. It is said that liberty must be earned by each generation of people. What could this mean?
6. Are you really free to decide how to live? Discuss with your class some of the limits to personal freedom.
7. Write a paragraph describing how your freedom to do whatever you wanted to do would affect other people and how it might interfere with their freedom.

Related activity

• Read the following proverb to your class and lead a discussion of what you think it means:

Nothing brings more pain
than too much pleasure;
nothing brings more bondage
than too much liberty.

Stage five
DEVELOPING SOCIAL AND PERSONAL MATURITY

General educational goal

For pupils to improve their proficiency in predicting the personal consequences of one's behavior, in gradually assuming social responsibility, in adapting to changing events, and in becoming increasingly able to transcend egocentric concerns

Rationale

Social and personal maturity is an important end goal in education. Children need to be taught what desirable behaviors comprise "maturity" and how and when these might be learned. Schools should provide varied opportunities and experiences for the continued development and acquisition of these essential behaviors.

Illustrative educational units, objectives, and performance criteria

1. Predicting personal consequences: To become more effective in self-restraint, in anticipating others, in understanding and accepting authority, and in expecting social judgment for inappropriate behavior

Given three pictures of different persons attempting to adapt to varied social demands, the pupil will list two alternative ways of responding to each picture.

2. Adapting to change: To become aware that people must continue to learn to quickly identify and adapt to technological changes, environmental crises, governmental changes, personal misfortunes, and fundamental changes within the family itself

The pupil will be able to identify in writing at least one major change in each of the above areas that has occurred in the last 5 years and to explain how this change has affected his own life.

3. Assuming social responsibility: To be able to demonstrate family responsibility, social awareness and involvement, social commitment, some contribution to personal and social progress, and the acceptance of peaceful means for effecting continued social change

The learner will demonstrate his assumption of social responsibility by maintaining a journal of his effort and contribution in two or more of the areas of concern listed.

4. Transcending self: To become aware that personal maturity requires the transcendence of immediate egocentric concerns and involves the continued pursuit of happiness, attempts to transcend one's own cultural limitations, personal meditation and aspiration, a reverence for life, and universal identification and altruism

The pupil will present to the class an oral biographical report on a person who has demonstrated some of these transcendent qualities of personal maturity.

Lesson topic
PREDICTING PERSONAL CONSEQUENCES: ANTICIPATING BEHAVIOR

Lesson objective: To become more effective in anticipating our own behavior and the actions of other people

Sample learning program (junior high): Purpose: The purpose of this specific lesson is to be able to predict what might happen in several different situations. Directions: Read the following story and complete the activities.

Some real action

It was a hot summer evening with nothing to do. As Al walked down the apartment steps and out the door, he wished something exciting would happen. Just then he saw his pal Paulo coming around the street corner with several guys. Al recognized three of them as boys who had been in continual trouble because of drugs and cutting school. Then Paulo came up and said, "Come on, Al, we're going to a place where there is some real action!"

---

1. Write what you think Al should do.
2. What do you think Al might be feeling?
3. Form a small group of four or five pupils and discuss why people need to be able to anticipate what their friends might do in certain situations.
4. With your group, discuss what this proverb means: "Look before you leap."
5. For each of the following behaviors, write what you would anticipate happening:

   Getting up late to catch the school bus
   Running across the street without looking
   Coming home late for dinner
   Not finishing a homework assignment
   Yelling and screaming at mother

Related activity
- Two personal needs that some people must anticipate are time required to walk to school and food required for a campout. List several things that *you* need to do that you must anticipate and plan for.

Lesson topic
ADAPTING TO CHANGE: TECHNOLOGICAL DEVELOPMENT

> **Lesson objective:** To become aware that people must continually learn to adapt to the many social and environmental changes in their lives
>
> **Sample learning program (upper elementary):** Purpose: The purpose of this specific lesson is to consider how several major technological changes have affected our lives. Directions: Read the following story and complete the activities.

Gasoline buggy

Jason was riding his horse along the old dirt road when he first heard the noise. It went "putt-putt-putt," a sound he had never heard before. When he turned his head, he saw it coming around the bend. He had heard them called horseless carriages, and they sure did look just like that. Jason's horse was nervous, but he held her reins close until the horseless carriage was right beside him. Then he hollered and let the horse go, and they quickly galloped away. Jason thought, "Who would be silly enough to buy one of those slow, noisy things anyhow?"

---

1. Draw or color a picture of the horseless carriage. Then write a paragraph describing how Jason felt about the new invention.
2. How do people feel about new inventions today?
3. With your class, discuss what makes a new technological development good or bad.
4. List some of the future technological changes you think you might see and have to adapt to.
5. Describe to your class the technological development you feel has made the greatest impact on your life. How has this affected you?
6. Discuss why it is difficult for many people to adjust to new technological developments.

Related activity

- There are many kinds of technological changes that have influenced how people live. We will continue to adapt to future changes. Indicate in writing how you think the following technological developments will change our life:

   Invention of the space rocket
   Invention of the computer
   Development of antibiotic drugs

Lesson topic
ASSUMING SOCIAL RESPONSIBILITY: SOCIAL COMMITMENT

Lesson objective: To be able to demonstrate the assumption of some form of social responsibility

Sample learning program (upper elementary): Purpose: The purpose of this specific lesson is to understand the importance of social involvement and commitment. Directions: Read the following story and complete the activities.

Picnic

When the alarm went off at 7:00 A.M., Denise remembered it was Saturday. It was a beautiful day and it felt great to just lie in bed. Then it hit her! This was the day she had signed up to help the Community Beautification Committee. A group of kids was going to clean up the junk on the corner lot on Main Street, cut the weeds, and plant flower boxes along the curb. Just then the telephone rang; it was Betty asking her to go on a picnic with her friends. Denise thought the picnic would be great on such a fine day.

---

1. Discuss with your class what Denise had committed herself to.
2. Discuss what you think she should do and why.
3. Social commitments are agreements to work with others for a common good. Discuss why a person might want to make commitments to other people.
4. What is a "social obligation"? List two or three examples.
5. Discuss what this proverb means: "Promises may get friends, but 'tis performance that keeps them."
6. Discuss why people often fail to keep their commitments.
7. Write a theme entitled "My Social Commitment." Describe some social concern that you feel strongly enough about and that you could commit yourself to do something about.

Related activity

- Form a class committee to list several community organizations that are committed to different causes. Visit one organization and obtain information for an oral report to your class.

Lesson topic
TRANSCENDING SELF: CULTURAL TRANSCENDENCE

Lesson objective: To become aware that personal maturity requires the transcendence of immediate egocentric concerns

Sample learning program (upper elementary): Purpose: The purpose of this specific lesson is to understand and appreciate some of the ways in which people attempt to transcend their own cultural limitations. Directions: Use the *National Geographic* magazine to find a story about how people live (or have lived) in another country and how they have contributed to the development of civilization. Complete the following activities.

1. Discuss the word "civilization" with your class. Consider several different definitions and how civilization continues to develop.
2. All cultures and societies are limited in many ways; for example, time and geography are two limiting factors. With your class discuss these limitations and add some other illustrations.
3. Write a brief paper describing what the country you have selected has contributed to the development of civilization.
4. We transcend our own society and culture by going beyond it to consider what other people in the world have contributed to our lives. For example, we have learned to appreciate German automobiles, Japanese electronic equipment, and French wines. List two other countries and some of their contributions to the world that have affected our lives.
5. Other cultures have also been the sources of varies ideas in science, literature, religion, government, art, and music. Consider Arabia, China, Egypt, and Italy; select one of these countries and, with several classmates, organize a group project to study the country and to report on some of the *ancient* values and contributions of this country.
6. If you could visit another country and live with the people awhile, where would you like to go and why?

Related activity

- All cultures and societies have a mythology. Write a definition of the word "mythology" and give an illustration of a myth and explain its source. Draw or color a picture of the myth and discuss with your class some of the reasons that cultures create myths.

Lesson topic
TRANSCENDING SELF: PERSONAL MEDITATION

Lesson objective: To understand and experience how personal meditation may help the individual to transcend his immediate problems and concerns
Sample learning program (junior high): Purpose: The purpose of this specific lesson is to experience and discuss a form of meditation. Directions: Read the following story and complete the exercises.

Magic rose

Since she was a little girl, Candy had loved roses. It may have been that way because her father grew them for a hobby and she learned to appreciate their beauty. Now she always kept a rose in her bedroom. Sometimes in the early morning she would wake to the smell of roses. As she lay in bed and looked carefully at the wonderful flower, she would feel good as she meditated about herself and the new day. She always treasured the silence of those moments with her rose.

---

1. Discuss with your class why Candy loved roses and how they helped her.
2. The silence and reflection of meditation usually relaxes people and renews their strength and energy. Bring a rose to class, place it on your desk, and make a colored picture of it. Now place the rose on your picture, fold your hands, and quietly look at it and think about its beauty. Be very quiet and meditate about the rose for 3 minutes.
3. Write a paragraph describing your thoughts and feelings during your meditation.
4. Join a small group of four or five pupils. Select one rose and place it in a water-filled vase on the floor. Sit in a circle around the rose, hold hands with people in the circle and look at the rose. With your eyes open, gaze at the rose for 2 minutes and meditate on its beauty. Now close your eyes and meditate on the rose for another 2 minutes or until your teacher requests your attention. Open your eyes and discuss your thoughts and feelings with your group.
5. Discuss why some people feel it is difficult to practice meditation and what is required to meditate successfully.

Related activities
- People meditate in many different ways and in many different places. List several different forms of meditation. With your class, write all the different forms on the chalkboard and discuss them.
- Write a brief paragraph explaining your feelings about why and when people should meditate.

Lesson topic
TRANSCENDING SELF: UNIVERSAL IDENTIFICATION

Lesson objective: To become aware of universal identification as a transcendent aspect of social and personal maturity

Sample learning program (upper elementary and junior high): Purpose: The purpose of this specific lesson is to consider how different people may become and act in the future. Directions: Read the following story and complete the activities.

Through the universe

They had been gone from Earth for exactly 5 months. Of course, they had spent 6 weeks on the moon station refueling for the long flight to Venus. Brad knew that there were many children already living in the space city on Venus. After all, this was the eighth expedition to make the trip. Nevertheless, he felt like a pioneer as he looked out of the windows at the bright stars surrounding him in the universe. Then he saw Osako coming through the door. She reminded him of Japan and the 10 other nations that also had volunteers on this flight. Brad felt close to his friends from throughout the world as he looked out on the beautiful universe. He wondered what his future life with his universal family would be like.

---

1. Draw or color a picture of what you think the spaceship may have looked like.
2. With your class, discuss what you think it might be like to live on a moon station for 6 weeks.
3. Try to put yourself in Brad's place and to feel what his present world on the spaceship might be like. Describe your feelings to your discussion group.
4. Write a paragraph describing what Brad's future life on Venus might be like.
5. All humanity is in the process of growing, changing, and becoming new and different. Discuss what you think Osako might hope to become in a new life on Venus.
6. Humanity is one large family living on the spaceship called earth. We are part of many forms of life throughout the universe. What other forms of life do you think may exist in the universe?

Related activity

- Write a theme describing what you aspire to become someday and what you hope the future of humanity will be. Discuss these ideas, aspirations, and hopes with your class.

Many humanistic education programs occur in natural settings.

We believe in the value of self-knowledge and of the examined life. We assume that this kind of knowledge is important for the individual, that it enables him more fully to realize his own potentiality and humanness, that it will affect how he behaves.

R. MOSHER and N. SPRINTHALL (1970)

CHAPTER 7

Pilot studies

MANY PILOT STUDIES and experimental affective-humanistic education programs have been conducted in the public and private schools. Most of the major studies with distinctive results and specific educational implications have been done since the end of the second world war. All of those reported here have introduced new curriculums for increasing the student's self-knowledge and the development of his human potentialities.

No single humanistic-affective learning program studied has been found to meet the needs of all pupils and teachers. It can also be said with assurance that no such program will be developed in the near future. However, the following programs can all be considered significant early pilot studies that will undoubtedly continue to contribute much to the improved design and implementation of future experimental curriculum projects in affective-humanistic education.

MENTAL HEALTH PROJECTS

Most of the early classroom experiments in affective education were designed on the mental health model. The attempt was to teach the principles of mental hygiene and to foster good mental health through instruction in human relations. Most of the early experiments were vague and unsuccessful because they dealt in broad generalities. A few exceptions were noted, however, and these contributed much to the development of more realistic approaches.

Bullis and O'Malley (1947) conducted a number of applied experiments in teaching human relations in the classroom. Their results were published in two books by the Delaware State Society for Mental Hygiene and became the basis for supplemental psychological consultation and developmental guidance programs in the public

115

schools. In the 1950's many of these findings were integrated into a unique instructional program by Ojemann (1959) of the University of Iowa, and they subsequently received widespread attention and use.

The American School Health Association finally surveyed the meager research available and in 1963 published a report on mental health in the classroom, which outlined in detail the essential topics and study units for use in public school programs from kindergarten through junior college. Four major units of study were suggested for each grade level:

- Unit I: Personality structure and development
- Unit II: Interaction of an individual with others, including influences of cultural patterns
- Unit III: Socioeconomic status and its influence on mental health
- Unit IV: Emotional climate in home and classroom

For each of these four areas of study the basic concepts to be taught at each grade level were specified together with appropriate learning experiences and materials that might be used. For example, one of the objectives for Unit III is "adjustment to loss or unfortunate circumstances," and some stories and discussion activities are suggested to help young children learn to adjust to disappointment in their lives. Even today this report remains an outstanding health education model for use on all grade levels.

ACHIEVEMENT MOTIVATION

Everyone has a need for achievement in all aspects of life. The drive or disposition to strive for accomplishment of psychomotor, cognitive, and affective goals and tasks is referred to as achievement motivation. More than 30 years ago, McClelland and his associates at Harvard University began studying achievement motivation. McClelland used a learning theory approach: all motives are learned; motives are affectively toned associative networks responding to meaningful stimulus situations.

Another researcher, Atkinson, theorized that any situation presenting a challenge to achievement by arousing an expectation of success will also present a threat of failure. Atkinson's approach to achievement motivation is focused on the resolution of conflict between the hope of success and the fear of failure. A number of Achievement Motivation Training courses were developed for use with schoolchildren. Much of the program is concerned with strategies to get pupils to take risks in playing games and in problem-solving situations and to increase their personal expectations. For example, participants would learn to play a game and then take risks to improve their performance on the next attempt. They were then taught to label and clarify their achievement thoughts and aspirations. Although not always successful, early studies did show some significant test gains in personality scores that measured "achievement needs"; significant gains in grade point averages for participants in some experimental classes also seemed to be promising. Many classes in achievement motivation strategies have been conducted with pupils from varied backgrounds and age levels, including Head Start preschoolers and regular and remedial elementary and secondary students.

As research into changing achievement motivation levels continued, the characteristics of high-achieving individuals were identified, and training programs to teach achievement motivation were developed (Alschuler et al., 1970). Teaching achievement motivation involves five steps or activities: games, self-awareness, positive thinking, realistic goal setting, and techniques or strategies for achieving selected goals. The training program is organized in weekly lesson cycles that involve systematic instruction by teachers and extensive self-evaluation by the students involved. Special games and instructional materials proved nonthreatening to low-achieving students. The program has had considerable success and has been used in industry, government, and private settings as well as in the public schools.

REALITY THERAPY

A number of new reality training and reeducation procedures have been proposed by Glasser (1965). Although his work was initially developed for use with maladaptive persons in therapy, it has since been expanded for use in schools as part of a preventive mental health program.

The stated purpose of reality therapy is to teach people to fulfill their own basic psychological needs: the need to love and be loved and the need to feel worthwhile to oneself and to others. These needs must be met in a way that maintains a socially acceptable standard of behavior and in a way that is not injurious to others. The earlier and more thoroughly we learn to fulfill our needs, the more satisfactory our lives will be, although constant relearning of solutions for meeting our needs is required as our lives and situations change.

The primary responsibility of a teacher is to discover the ways in which a child is not fulfilling his needs and then to work out a plan through which the child can be helped to meet those needs. Teachers must not remain objectively removed from their pupils but should become deeply involved with them, accept them as they are, and provide the proper education for them to move on. The program is a highly behavioristic one that stresses the importance of evaluation of the problem behavior, goal orientation, planning, commitment to stick with it, and suffering natural consequences.

This program emphasizes the morality of behavior and helps the student to face the issue of right and wrong. Through peer group discussions and activities it attempts to teach pupils to behave better and to fulfill their needs. It has received increasing acceptance as part of most good humanistic education programs.

SELF ENHANCING EDUCATION (SEE)

In 1957 the Cuperintino Union School District in California assigned special master teachers with guidance training to each school as an "agent of change" to identify the factors that seemed to limit learning. Self-esteem emerged as the most vital element in the learning situation, and an experimental program was started to improve self-concepts and pupil behavior.

From 25 students in an initial pilot class the program was expanded to cover more than 6000 students in 200 classes for elementary pupils. In 1966 a Title III grant permitted the program to include formal research in the San Jose and Menlo Park school district.

Research was based on the premise that the major underlying factor in underachievement is low self-esteem and that the most effective way to develop strong motivation, increase achievement, and develop socially productive behavior is by helping the child develop, increase, and expand his self-esteem.

Randolph and Howe (1966) then collaborated in developing an experimental program. Innovative lessons were developed around the following 12 objectives of pupil involvement:

- Student involvement in problem identification and solution
- Self-management
- Changing negative reflection to positive self-images
- Building trust in others
- Setting limits and expectations
- Freeing and channeling energy
- Overcoming unproductive repetitive behavior
- Changing tattling to reporting
- Developing physical competencies
- Making success inevitable
- Developing self-evaluation
- Breaking curriculum barriers through individualized instruction

The following lesson strategies in this program are specifically concerned with one objective, developing self-evaluation:

- Providing the pupil with test and performance information relative to his own expectations and actual achievement
- Providing the pupil with records, checklists, and other means to enable him to actually evaluate daily school performance
- Teaching pupils how to maintain their own records and rewarding them for doing so

Another general goal of this program is to help teachers become more effective models for their pupils and to enable them to provide more adequate opportunities in the classroom for children to grow and learn at their own rate. Much emphasis is placed on the development of teacher-pupil communication skills that are thought to result in increased pupil self-control, self-direction, and self-evaluation.

Most of the new lessons and approaches were found to be effective in accomplishing affective goals and objectives. It was concluded that trust in self and self-esteem can be increased through appropriate education. Since then the program has been adapted for use in many school districts concerned with improving elementary education.

SOCIAL LEARNING CURRICULUM

Goldstein (1974) and his staff at Yeshiva University created the Social Learning Curriculum program with its emphasis on social skills for exceptional children. The goal of the program is to develop more mature individuals who can think critically and act independently to such an extent that they are socially and occupationally competent. Social competence includes the ability to make relevant decisions and the ability to exhibit appropriate behaviors in such things as management of personal affairs so that the individual can establish and maintain independence.

The present format and content of the Social Learning Curriculum represent some 25 years of experience and research in classroom settings for special children. The current publication of the curriculum represents the culmination of initial development, field testing, teacher evaluation, and continual revision. Field testing with educable retarded children took place in 29 states and five foreign countries over a 6-year period.

The Social Learning Curriculum differs from earlier curriculums in that it introduces the self as a planned and central part of the total curricular sequence. The self is meant to be dealt with as an important object of study on all levels from the primary grades through high school. Furthermore, all other subjects are expected to be taught in terms of their relations to the self and what is learned about it. One of the aims of this kind of approach is to help each pupil develop an adequate self-identification, or positive self-concept. In its broadest meaning this implies that the student in the special class will be guided step by step toward a realistic picture of himself as an acting, reacting, and interacting being in a social setting.

This curriculum is well organized with detailed teacher manuals that present specific suggestions for teacher preparation, behavioral objectives, and reinforcement activities. For example, the stated objectives for the unit Recognizing and Reacting to Emotions are that the student should be able to identify specific emotions, causes of and changes in emotions, consequences of emotional reactions, degrees of emotions, and moods created by emotions.

The program itself consists of 10 phase books of 15 to 20 lessons each: *Perceiving Individuality, Recognizing the Environment, Interdependence, Body-Self Recognition, Recognizing and Reacting to Emotions, Sensory Interpretation, Communicating with Others, Getting Along With Others, Helping Others,* and *Self-Care.* Supplemental materials include stimulus pictures, workbooks, charts, transparencies, and related activities with a scope and sequence chart. It is perhaps the best researched and most well-developed affective education program for systematic use with young retarded children.

RATIONAL-EMOTIVE EDUCATION

In 1955 Albert Ellis developed what he termed a rational-emotive approach to therapy and education in which active experience, persuasion, directive learning activities, and affective homework assignments were all used. Since then this approach has been further adapted for use in the schools.

The Living School in New York City has pioneered in this approach, which provides regular cognitive education but divides the day into two main periods: one devoted to learning skills and the communication arts, the other devoted to personal expression and social interaction. Emotive expression, problem discussion, and self-analytical procedures constitute much of the program. The pilot experimental program has been reported by Knaus (1974) and is adaptable to any school system. The development of critical thinking skills and the application of the scientific method to self-understanding are the basic curriculum elements.

Lessons in rational-emotive education can also be used as a preventive and interventionist approach to emotional and behavior problems. Research indicates that, through these teaching procedures, students can become better equipped to cope with current and future problem situations that impede their personal progress.

MAN: A COURSE OF STUDY

A unique experimental program entitled Man: A Course of Study was designed by Bruner (1967) of Harvard University with instructional materials and films developed by Peter Dow and Lawrence Stenhouse. Program goals were to enable children between 9 and 13 years of age to (1) understand the nature of humanity and the biological ties that unite humans with other living creatures and (2) learn that people's behavior is shaped by their culture.

The initial project was supported by grants from the Ford Foundation and from the National Science Foundation in 1968. A basic premise underlying the entire program is that the cultivation of emotional issues in the classroom, whether by design or in response to the unpredictable, should be a means to the end of instructing children in subject matter; the resolution of emotional issues, when integral for learning, tends to deepen learning when relevant to educational objectives. The rationale for creating emotions in classrooms is to invite expression for the primary purpose of imbuing curricular issues with personal significance. It has been one of Bruner's major contributions to educational psychology that teachers are now beginning to cultivate the development of these emotional and imaginative skills in their students. The integration of feelings, fantasy, and cognitive material used in Man: A Course of Study is analyzed in some detail by Jones (1968).

Instructional lessons are provided for a period of 120 days within the context of a social studies course. Four major units are presented sequentially with a heavy reliance on film and group discussion. The first unit consists of a study of the life cycle of the Pacific salmon, which is then followed by a unit on the family structure of the herring gull. The third unit focuses on the complex social organization of baboons. The last unit is an in-depth consideration of the life of the Netselik Eskimo, including their language, tool making, social organization, childbearing, and world views and myths. Some criticism has been made of the vividly frank portrayal of Eskimo values, which are considerably different from those of most American children.

The training program for teachers intending to use this program provides a forum in which the basic ideas of the units are tested in workshop sessions; these basic ideas are embodied in part of the literature, *Seminars for Teachers,* which contains selected readings and activities designed to give insight to instructors. In 1972 Madeley College developed in-service training procedures for this program and tested them in several public schools.

Research findings are still very limited. Some reports show highly enthusiastic responses from both pupils and teachers. The program also demands team teaching and cooperative involvement of parents, which appears to be of considerable value. No data are yet available on the acquisition of specific skills and concepts by the children involved.

CONFLUENT EDUCATION

Confluent education is a term developed by Brown (1971) at the University of California, Santa Barbara, to describe the integration of affective and cognitive elements in learning. Brown developed an instructional model and suggested lessons that would help to merge emotions, attitudes, values, thoughts, and intellect.

With initial funding from the Ford Foundation, Brown brought a number of educators together to consider how education might better provide for the emotional, physical, and spiritual needs of pupils. In cooperation with Esalen Institute a number of experiential programs were tried and integrated into the emerging model. Emphasis was placed on merging affective education with cognitive and intellectual learning as part of the regular course of study. Some examples of various special study units in the existing curriculum are as follows:

Subject	Affective topics introduced
First-grade units	Body self-awareness, feeling rhythm, trusting others, living things, dealing with fear, imagination and language arts
Driver education	Anger, frustration, courtesy, and behavior change in driving
Remedial English	Courage, noncourage, and "being human" as portrayed in selected literature, films, and music
Ninth-grade social studies	The nature of humanity, self and self-discovery, emotional maturity
Tenth-grade English	The "human jungle" (good and evil) as presented through the book *Lord of the Flies* by William Golding
Special education units	Self-knowledge, varied styles of living, listening and communication, the use of drugs, loneliness and isolation, creativity and imagination training

The basic premise of Confluent Education is that the cognitive and affective domains of learning are in fact inseparable. A complete education is one in which intellectual and emotional growth develop together. The experimental program has included intensive use of experiential lessons and techniques for involving students in emotional-cognitive integration.

Brown has continued to work with the Confluent Education Demonstration Project in program and curriculum development and in teacher training. Pilot programs have been carried out in California, Pennsylvania, Massachusetts, and several places in Canada. A recent book describes many of the innovative instructional procedures used in these programs (Brown, 1975).

THE LOUISVILLE EXPERIMENT

An interesting experiment in humanistic education was conducted in an inner city setting at the Roosevelt Elementary School in Louisville, Kentucky, from 1972 to 1975. This is one of the few pilot studies with wide community involvement and parent participation (Dickerson et al., 1970).

The initial task was to create an effective neighborhood school board and an environment in which people would trust themselves to make their own decisions and to be able to succeed or fail and still feel accepted. A considerable amount of effort was expended on bringing parents and staff together to develop general goals and objectives.

A distinctive aspect of the program was that the local school board of parents worked directly with the teaching staff in interviewing and hiring teachers for the project. They also developed joint school workshops concerning goal implementation, curriculum, and teaching methodology, with emphasis on resolving the basic differences between behavioristic and humanistic approaches to education.

Students were finally allowed representation on the board and then participated in all decision-making processes. Children were grouped in an open, heterogeneous vertical grouping with continuous progress programs and no special education rooms. Parents were involved in classroom observation, conferences, and counseling of other parents. The school building was also used after school hours and during the summer months for innovative humanistic education programs.

Results indicated that curriculum success and failure in academic programs depended heavily on teachers making it relevant to the needs of the children. Staff evaluations were based on objective data submitted by each teacher, covering stated goals and objectives for children, parents, staff, and self in (1) academic growth, (2) social growth, and (3) personal growth (Foster and Back, 1974). The eminent psychologist Carl Rogers has made a film showing the Louisville experiment and discussing its implications for education.*

BEHAVIORAL SCIENCE EDUCATION PROJECTS

Some of the most extensive research in affective-humanistic education has been conducted by Long (1970). She began her initial pilot study with sixth-grade children in the Webster College Experimental School in St. Louis. The goal was to attempt to teach children something about themselves that was tied closely to real life and would also be good mental health education.

A course was constructed in behavioral science suitable for elementary school-

---

Humanistic Innovation in Education (50 minutes), available from the American Personnel and Guidance Association, 1607 New Hampshire Ave. N.W., Washington, D.C. 20009.

children. The main course content was people and their diverse behavior. Emphasis was on the educational process, using discussion, experiments, simulation games, story sessions, films, and field trips. Children showed great interest in designing and carrying through their own experiments; more than a dozen experiments were used, many of them done by pairs of students working together. Self-direction and self-initiated learning were reinforced as much as possible.

Results indicated that the discovery method was most successful and that the children experienced great joy in learning. Children were able to grasp difficult subject matter and to develop broad principles of behavior that one would have assumed were understandable only to college students of psychology. The initial pilot study was then generalized to the St. Louis Public Schools and also used by the Southwest St. Louis Community Mental Health Center.

Since then, Long has conducted a number of other studies and has also developed some curriculum materials for use in similar projects. Her materials include a number of games and lessons on self-awareness, emotions, problems, and other areas of human behavior. She has also described an extension of this model and a feasibility study for teacher training (Long, 1975).

Long's work has made a significant impact on community mental health programs. Many child guidance mental health clinics have been using her model and techniques for developing cooperative programs with the public schools. One of the most outstanding examples of such a collaboration is the Behavioral Science Education Project conducted by the Washtenaw County Community Mental Health Center of Ann Arbor, Michigan (Munger, 1975). The goal of this project is to encourage the development and dispersion of programs, methodologies, and materials that enable teachers and other school personnel to share with children and youth those concepts regarding human feelings and behavior that have been established by the behavioral sciences. The project acts as a resource information center that engages in various supportive activities in affective behavioral science education, including educational research, bibliography development, literature review, in-service training, materials preparation, evaluation, and consultation. The resource guides published by this project are of great practical value and are widely used throughout the country.

HUMAN DEVELOPMENT PROGRAM

Another pragmatic model for use with elementary school students is the Human Development Program, which was piloted by Harold Bessell, Aldo Palomares, and Geraldine Ball in San Diego, California (Bessell and Palomares, 1973). The program is a humanistic curriculum with sequentially developed objectives in the affective domain.

The Human Development Program is organized on age and grade levels, beginning with 4-year-old preschoolers and progressing through the third grade. Each of these levels uses strategies to involve groups of pupils to achieve stated objectives such as those on the following page.

Grade	Objectives
Preschool	Improved ability to sit still and express oneself; tolerance for individual differences
Kindergarten	Development of self-control and self-confidence; increased understanding of social interaction; increased verbal expression and listening skills
First grade	Ability to comfortably experience ambivalence; improvement of reality testing, self-confidence, effective meeting of needs; increased skill in making helpful suggestions
Second grade	Articulation of wide range of experiences in positive and negative feelings, thoughts, behavior; distinguishing between reality and fantasy; motivation to be responsible, productive, and kind
Third grade	Self-control as a matter of personal pride; verbal facility, skillful and tolerant listening; wise decision making and responsible, constructive leadership; courage in taking the initiative to build good social relationships

The methods and materials provide students with opportunities to deal with their own thoughts, feelings, and behavior in positive ways to produce increased self-awareness, self-understanding, and self-confidence. The primary educational process used is peer group discussion through what the authors term the magic circle. During these small group discussions, teachers and students follow guidelines presented in activity booklets available for each grade level; other activity guides are being prepared for use with junior and senior high school pupils. Special discussion guides are available for use with drug abuse participants and with the institutionalized.

Tentative research results indicate that, as students participate in these sessions, their ability to communicate effectively with both teachers and peers increases. They also become more aware of their feelings and tend to increase in self-respect. Although additional research should be conducted and data reported, it is apparent that the initial pilot program has proved of sufficient value to be expanded for use in other schools.

PSYCHOLOGICAL EDUCATION IN SECONDARY SCHOOLS

An extensive model for psychological education in secondary schools was presented in 1970 by Mosher and Sprinthall, who conducted their work and research at the Harvard School of Education. They concluded that schools do educate student's attitudes, self-concepts, and values through a hidden curriculum that effects total psychological development. In an indirect and unrecognized manner, schools affect how the student sees himself, his competencies, his worth, and his prospects as a human being.

They developed a humanistic psychological education program on an experimental basis. The program was established on the premise that self-knowledge enables the student to more fully realize his own potentialities and humanness and directly affects a person's way of behaving. The couse was offered as an elective to interested students. The intellectual focus for the core curriculum was personal history and self-study to answer the questions Who was I as a child? Who am I now? Who am I becoming?

A detailed list of 13 behavioral objectives was developed for instructional purposes (for example, to enable the individual to express feelings of his own). Lessons covered principles of human development, psychological theories, cultural differences, intelligence, personality, delinquency, etc. Educational processes included laboratory activities constituting approximately two thirds to three quarters of the total course experience for each student; labs involved film making, dance, drama, sensitivity training, peer counseling, and special projects. Discussion topics ranged from issues of relationships with authority figures to racial and ethnic differences, sex, social pressures, and parental relationships.

Initial field testing was conducted in Newton High School and then spread to other secondary schools. Evaluation procedures included the use of the Kohlberg Moral Dilemmas Test and other instruments. Systematic observations and written course evaluations by students were used, and in-depth interviews were conducted with a sample of the students involved in different aspects of the project. Tentative results were promising and led to the expansion of the program and research procedures.

PHILADELPHIA AFFECTIVE EDUCATION PROJECT

One of the first popular and objective reports on the importance of affective-humanistic education was made by Borton in a 1969 issue of the *Saturday Review*. In that article, Borton reviewed the Harvard research in psychological education and stressed the importance of developing practical programs to implement Alschuler's work on achievement motivation. Weinstein and Fantini (1970) organized an affective curriculum with a number of highly unusual lessons that compelled students to integrate their thoughts and feelings; many of the lessons were proposed in ways that could be used in regular classrooms as a new approach to traditional subject matter. Borton then joined with Norman Newberg to co-direct a pilot study of these programs in the school district of Philadelphia.

The Philadelphia Affective Education Project is perhaps the most extensive of its kind to have yet been conducted. The project has been developed gradually over a 10-year period, and considerable research data have now been made available. Its three major objectives have been the development of a positive self-concept, development of meaningful and satisfying relationships with others, and development of a sense of power or control over what happens to oneself. The curriculum content has been organized around psychological processes such as decision making that may be taught through social studies, English, or other subject matter. The major hypothesis was that there is a direct correlation between academic achievement and the ability to control one's personal environment, attitudes about self, relationships with other people. Specific lessons incorporated many of the previously researched techniques plus such things as creative art, poetry, role-playing and drama, meditation, and philosophical speculation (for example, What is worth living or dying for?).

Research results indicated that the affective education students had a dramatically different and more positive attitude toward their classes than did control students. There was a greater personal growth in the affective education students, particularly marked by fewer discipline problems and less absenteeism. Affective education students felt they were learning more cognitive skills, insights about self and others, and personal competence skills—even though there were no statistically significant differences in learning skills between the two groups (Gollub, 1971). The project continues to be modified and has served as a model for experimentation by many other public school programs.

SUMMARY

This chapter has reviewed a few of the most significant pilot studies in affective-humanistic education. Most of these have been innovative projects with distinctive curricular implications that have contributed much to the growing interest in this field of education.

Although all of these studies have suffered from the inevitable problems and limitations of applied field research, they have pointed the way for more thorough studies, which will undoubtedly be done in the future.

DISCUSSION QUESTIONS AND ACTIVITIES

1. Define "good human relations."
2. Describe your own achievement motivation. For what are you highly motivated? Have you ever learned how to increase your motivation?
3. To what extent do you agree or disagree with Glasser's contention that students must be helped to face the issue of right and wrong behavior?
4. Suggest a lesson activity that might help a pupil attain one of the 12 objectives of Self Enhancing Education.
5. Why is a Social Learning Curriculum of particular importance in the education of retarded children?
6. What kind of homework assignment can you envision as part of rational-emotive education?
7. Discuss some of the possible limitations of Man: A Course of Study.
8. What is Confluent Education?
9. Do you believe that parents should be involved in educational planning as reported in the Louisville experiment?
10. List two basic principles of human behavior that you think should be taught in an elementary school behavioral science project.
11. What is a "magic circle"?
12. Should the Kohlberg Moral Dilemmas Test or other similar instruments be used in psychological education in secondary schools?
13. What was unique about the Philadelphia Affective Education Project?

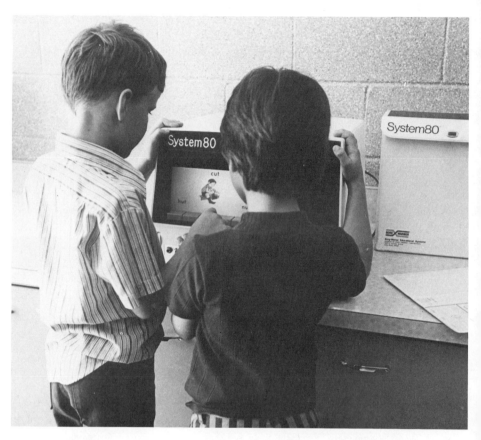

Numerous commercial curriculum models are being used in the public schools. (From Gearheart, B. R. *Learning disabilities: Educational strategies* [2nd ed.]. St. Louis: The C. V. Mosby Co., 1977.)

Education, to be successful, must not only inform but inspire.
T. S. KNOWLSON (1963)

CHAPTER 8

Commercial models

DURING THE 1970'S there has been a growing public interest in humanistic psychology and education. People are gradually becoming more aware of the importance of many different approaches to self-development. Numerous new personal and social development programs have been initiated within the schools and through other more informal approaches to affective education. Some of these have been created by commercial publishers and are usually attractive and even inspirational in part.

The practical philosophers have long admonished that education should be made "as attractive as sin." It now appears that this may indeed become a possibility. Many of the newer programs are so attractively designed and packaged that their high motivational value is immediately apparent. Eleven different and highly attractive commercial programs are presented in this chapter.

Of course, there are many other similar programs available, but space prevents their detailed description here. However, those presented have all been widely used in public school humanistic education programs and are representative of the best available. Most of these programs have also been used in nonschool affective education offerings through various community organizations and private growth groups or centers.

No attempt is made here to rate these programs in any way. Persons interested in current program revisions and prices should write directly to the firms indicated.

HUMAN VALUES SERIES

The Human Values Series is one of the first textbook series developed for affective education. Its authors are V. Clyde Arnspiger, W. Ray Rucker, and James A. Brill; the program is published by the Steck-Vaughn Company.*

---

*Box 2028, Austin, Tex. 78767.

Currently there are six textbooks for use in the first through the sixth grade. Teacher's manuals are available for each text. An accompanying values kit, values posters, and teaching pictures complete the program. The human values classification system on which the framework of this series is based is a result of extensive research at Yale University by Arnspiger, the senior author. Prepublication field testing of the program in experimental schools resulted in the selection of eight values around which instruction is based. These values are respect, rectitude, affection, wealth, well-being, power, skill, and enlightenment.

Each textbook consists of a series of short, age-graded, illustrated stories. The teacher's edition provides a comprehensive and simple plan for teaching about the human values presented in each story; the plan consists of a synopsis of the story, two major points to be developed, a value analysis of the story, and some suggestions for complementary assignments. Not only does the series teach students what values are, it helps them learn about ways of satisfying their own basic needs and wants without depriving others of similar values. The stories also help children obtain a better understanding of total human behavior; both characters and stories are set in multi-ethnic situations. Book titles are as follows:

About Me (grade 1)	*Seeking Values* (grade 4)
About You and Me (grade 2)	*Sharing Values* (grade 5)
About Values (grade 3)	*Think with Values* (grade 6)

The accompanying teacher posters help to introduce each value category to the students and to prepare them for thinking about the stories that are to follow. The Introducing Values Kit is made up of a set of overhead transparencies, 10 colorful picture posters, and six tape cassettes that help to make the beginning value exchanges in elementary classrooms fun and exciting.

The Human Value Series is a valuable contribution to affective education programs. It may be argued, however, that it deals more with basic human needs than values and might best be used as the basis for a more intensive humanistic education program to be developed by the teacher. This program also relies heavily on reading ability and therefore must be supplemented accordingly.

DIMENSIONS OF PERSONALITY

Dimensions of Personality is a graded mental health program for grades one through six developed by Walter J. Limbacher and published by Pflaum/Standard.* Through numerous classroom experiences and a systematic presentation of the principles of mental health, this course enables the child to develop insights into his behavior. Group-centered activities form the core of the program, which is presented through a variety of materials that nurture self-esteem and self-acceptance.

The program includes texts, workbooks, and activity sheets on each lesson presented. Textbook titles are as follows:

---

*2285 Arbor Blvd., Dayton, Ohio 45439.

Now I'm Ready (grade 1)   *I'm Not Alone* (grade 5)
I Can Do It (grade 2)   *Becoming Myself* (grade 6)
What about Me (grade 3)   *Search for Meaning* (junior high)
Here I Am (grade 4)   *Search for Values* (senior high)

On the adolescent levels, this program begins to deal with the critical problems of self-identity. Such questions as Why am I here? Where am I going? and How do I fit in? are all considered part of the young person's quest for meaning and purpose in life. The junior and senior high school–level programs utilize a variety of techniques and strategies to help students sort out their feelings about the world within and around them. Emphasis is placed on the development of personal value systems through the use of inquiry and discovery methods, self-reflection exercises, and peer interaction.

In these books there is an intensely personal appeal to the child as they offer him the opportunity to explore the familiar yet mysterious territory of himself. The pupil gradually discovers that, although he is an individual, he is not unique in problems of personal and social development. His common problems are shared by others, and his hopes, needs, fears, and dreams are recognized and respected for what they are. These books invite the learner to face himself realistically and to deal more openly with human concerns.

A number of learning activities precede each chapter presented. The child is led to experience an emotion or an affective state within the classroom and to deal with it as valuable subject matter itself. Students are allowed to express feelings without fear of teacher disapproval, and the questions and activities that follow lead them to self-understanding and the development of positive human relationships.

Most of the materials are attractively developed and could easily be incorporated into a regular class program. The activities, games, and learning experiences are highly stimulating to elementary children and are well covered in the teacher's manual. The emphasis is on group work and demands normal reading ability.

FOCUS ON SELF-DEVELOPMENT

The Focus on Self-Development program has been developed by the staff and consultants of Science Research Associates, Inc.* It emphasizes development of awareness of self, others, and the environment and is organized into three different kits or stages for use with elementary school pupils.

Stage One, Awareness, is for use with kindergarten through second grade and consists of 20 units covering self-concept development, awareness of the environment through the senses, socialization, sharing, and problem solving. The instructional materials include five filmstrips with records or cassettes, story records, photoboards, and pupil activity books. The program is developed in such a way that children can learn to relate openly and express themselves without fear of disapproval or of being different.

---

*259 E. Erie St., Chicago, Ill. 60611.

Stage Two, Responding, is for use with the second through fourth grades. Stories and activities encourage the child's response to his personal, social, emotional and intellectual life. Topics are expanded to include self-concepts, abilities, limitations, interests, concerns, communications, companionship, acceptance and rejection, and peer problems. Six filmstrips, records, photoboards, and activity workbooks are also provided for the stage.

Stage Three, Involvement, first presents the concept of involvement followed by units on causes of behavior, problem solving, self, emotions, experiences, choosing, responsibility, family and social relationships, rights, justice, and human conflict. Each unit encourages the pupil to examine his involvement with self, others, and the environment and to think about his values. Supplementary audiovisual materials provided are similar to those for stages one and two.

This program is well prepared and attractively packaged with a variety of approaches that stimulate thought and discussion. Discussion questions highlight important points; supplemental activities, artwork, role-playing, and other techniques promote pupil involvement. The program can be modified for individual as well as for group use.

TRANSACTIONAL ANALYSIS

Eric Berne (1964) is the father of the transactional analysis movement, which has now been adapted for use in the schools. In his clinical practice, Berne noticed that people tended to shift back and forth between different personality states according to the demands of interpersonal relations, or "transactions." From this observation he developed a model of personality consisting of three major ego states (systems of attitudes, feelings, and beliefs), which he termed Parent, Child, and Adult.

These three ego states are all learned from life experience. The Parent state consists of judgmental and authoritarian behaviors based on the perception of one's parents. The Child state consists of immature, impulsive, spontaneous, self-gratifying orientations and behaviors. The Adult state represents the rational objective elements in behavior and tends to mediate and responsibly integrate Parent and Child predispositions. A group learning program was developed to analyze the various interrelationships of these three ego states and to enable the person to develop a more balanced and wholesome personality.

Most transactional analysis programs consist of four parts: (1) structural analysis, studying one's own personality components and ego states, (2) transactional analysis proper, analysis of the kinds of transactions occurring between people and what can be expected from them behaviorally, (3) game analysis, study of the kinds of negative transactions that people use for ulterior purposes, and (4) script analysis, analysis of the life plans that we all act out unconsciously.

Many books, activity manuals, and audiovisual aids are now available for teaching transactional analysis to both children and adults. Alvyn Freed has developed program resources for use with both primary and elementary children.* Harris (1969) and James and Jongeward (1973) have authored books and manuals with exercises and learning activities suitable for use with adolescent groups.

Transactional analysis programs are being used with exceptional students as well as in regular programs. A typical example is the Project OK† of the Fresno Unified School District designed with federal funds to meet the needs of educable mentally retarded junior high school pupils. Although transactional analysis does require much verbal expression and group involvement, it has been found to be a practical cognitive approach to affective education, and production of new program materials will undoubtedly continue in the years to come.

DEVELOPING UNDERSTANDING OF SELF AND OTHERS

Developing Understanding of Self and Others (DUSO) is an unusually well-designed program for teaching kindergarten through fourth-grade children to understand themselves and other people; it was authored by Don Dinkmeyer and is published by American Guidance Service, Inc.‡

DUSO Kit D-1 is for use with kindergarten and lower primary pupils and has three major goals: learning more words for feelings; learning that feelings, goals, values, and behavior are dynamically related; and learning to talk more freely about feelings, goals, values, and behavior. The major study units are as follows:

Understanding and accepting self
Understanding feelings
Understanding others
Understanding independence
Understanding goals and purposeful behavior

Understanding mastery, competence, and resourcefulness
Understanding emotional maturity
Understanding choices and consequences

DUSO Kit D-2 is for use with upper primary and grade four children. The goals are extended to include an emphasis on value orientations and personal responsibility. Again, there are eight instructional units designed to enable the pupil to move toward self-identity, friendship, responsible interdependence, self-reliance, resourcefulness and purposefulness, competence, emotional stability, and responsible choice making.

Both of the kits include such attractive materials as colorful posters, picture storybooks, several animal puppets and props, and cassettes and records. A teacher's manual plus role-playing cards and puppet activity cards complete the program, which is packaged in a metal case. The units and activities themselves center around a series of fantasy experiences. Duso, the dolphin puppet, is the primary character and is very easy for children to identify with. The program is designed as an ongoing, sequentially presented form of affective education.

TA for Kids and *TA for Tots*, Jalmar Press, Department M, 391 Munroe St., Sacramento, Calif.
† James Corbo, coordinator, Department of Special Education, Fresno City School District, Fresno, Calif.
‡ Publishers' Building, Circle Pines, Minn.

This is one of the few programs with extensive field testing. It was developed over a 5-year period and began with a survey of teachers, counselors, and administrators to formulate and compile a set of social and emotional developmental areas that reflected the specific concerns and common problems of children. These developmental areas were then used as the unit themes around which the materials were prepared. Total field testing involved more than 5100 children of many different economic, racial, and ethnic groups in 175 classrooms in 17 states.

INSIDE/OUT

Inside/Out is an interdisciplinary series of 30 15-minute videocassette films portraying experiences common to young lives. It has been designed by health educators and learning specialists to help 8- to 10-year-olds understand and cope with their emotions. The series is produced by the National Instructional Television Center.*

The films deal in new and compelling ways with the social, emotional, and physical problems of children and are designed to help young people achieve and maintain well-being. Each of the 30 films considers a different set of feelings that the youngster may have toward himself or others concerning death, solitude, ridicule, divorce, sibling rivalries, moving, crushes, prejudice, personal limitations, and so on.

This series provides very interesting situational starters for discussions in which children can compare their feelings and reactions to those of children in the films and in their class. The films do not solve the problems but illuminate the concerns that youngsters have. Students gradually recognize that they are not alone and that the feelings or reactions that made them feel guilty or fearful are somewhat like those experienced by every other person of the same age. Film titles are as follows:

Because It's Fun	*Breakup*
Brothers and Sisters	*Bully*
But . . . Names Will Never Hurt?	*Buy and Buy*
Can I Help?	*But They Might Laugh*
Can Do/Can't Do	*Donna (Learning to Be Yourself)*
Getting Even	*Home Sweet Home*
How Do You Show	*I Dare You*
I Want To	*In My Memory*
Jeff's Company	*Just Joking*
Just One Place	*Living With Love*
Lost Is A Feeling	*Love, Susan*
Must I/May I	*A Sense of Joy*
Someone Special	*Strong Feelings*
Travelin' Shoes	*When Is Help*
Yes, I Can	*You Belong*

This program has a multicultural orientation and the films are not overly dramatic, but the language is realistic and familiar to elementary-age pupils; the pictures and music are also very appealing to children at this age level. The series can be

---

*Box A, Bloomington, Ind. 47401.

rented or purchased by school districts or institutions concerned. It has been shown by more than 200 television stations in more than 40 states and has become an integral part of many affective-humanistic education programs used by public and private schools throughout the country.

SELF INCORPORATED

Self Incorporated is a series of 15 15-minute color programs designed to help 11- to 13-year-olds cope with emotional, physical, and social problems that confront them; material is available on both film and videotape and is an extension of the Inside/Out series produced by the National Instructional Television Center.

Accompanying materials include a teacher's guide that contains questions and learning activities for each film lesson, a packet of background readings, a school/community awareness kit, and a teacher's in-service training kit. Each film is directed at a specific critical issue:

Trying Times (making decisions)
Who Wins (morality)
No Trespassing (privacy)
Getting Closer (boy-girl relationships)
Down and Back (failure and disappoint-
 ment)
Pressure Makes Perfect (pressure to
 achieve)
Two Sons (family communications)

The Clique (cliques)
Different Folks (sex role identification)
What's Wrong With Jonathan? (everyday
 pressures)
Family Matters (what is a family?)
My Friend? (ethnic/racial differences)
By Whose Rules (systems and self)
Changes (physiological changes)
Double Trouble (family adversity)

Self Incorporated was developed through a consortium of educational and broadcasting agencies in the United States and Canada. The films are well done, and the teacher's guide is well organized. The films can be purchased or rented, and preview prints are available without charge. The program should make a notable contribution to furthering humanistic education on the upper elementary level including the junior high school years.

TOWARD AFFECTIVE DEVELOPMENT

The Toward Affective Development (TAD) program has been designed by Henry Dupont, Ovitta Gardner, and David Brody for use with children in the third through sixth grades and is published by American Guidance Service, Inc.* It is an extension of the DUSO program for use with upper elementary grades.

Children's real life experiences—their feelings, interests, aspirations, and conflicts—are the content focus of TAD. Activities that stimulate these experiences are the core of the program. Students are encouraged to participate in each activity and then to verbalize their thoughts and feelings in the discussion that follows.

In Reaching In and Reaching Out, students are introduced to the three basic skills of social collaboration: listening to others, taking turns, and sharing ideas.

---

*Publisher's Building, Circle Pines, Minn.

The goal of Your Feelings and Mine is increasing students' awareness of feelings and of the ways feelings are communicated. Nonverbal communication and role-playing are used extensively.

Working Together helps students learn and practice the skills and attitudes that are basic to working together successfully. Cooperative group projects are emphasized as the major learning process.

The focus of Me: Today and Tomorrow is on helping students consider their individual characteristics, interests, and aspirations at the same time they are beginning to learn about career opportunities. Career-related activities provide pupils with options to experiment with various career identities.

In the final section, Feeling, Thinking, Doing, students develop skills to work on resolving interpersonal conflicts and in choosing the course of action that is best for them.

Supplemental instructional materials include filmstrips, cooperative games, illustrated career folders, tapes, feeling wheels, posters, and activity sheets. The program was field tested for 4 years with more than 2000 students, including black, Oriental, and American Indian children.

BECOMING

Becoming is a course in human relations for junior high school pupils authored by Chester Cromwell, William Ohs, Albert Roark, and Gene Stanford; it is published by the J. B. Lippincott Co.* in three different teaching modules. The Becoming course stimulates students to learn about themselves and their relationships with other people and to consider the kind of persons they would like to become.

Module I, Relating, focuses on learning to recognize and express one's feelings, increasing one's willingness to share thoughts and feelings with others, and developing skills of interpersonal communication. Learning activities cover self-awareness, accepting the feelings of others, distinguishing between thoughts and feelings, problems in communications, body language, and methods of assuring clear communication.

Module II, Interaction, gives participants an opportunity to learn how perceptions affect interpersonal relations, to acquire skills in working with others, and to develop the skills necessary for helping and supporting others. Lessons include role-playing for understanding opposing points of view, managing conflicts, using consensus in making group decisions, dealing with problems in helping people, and developing good listening skills.

The final module, Individuality, is divided into four parts: Stereotyping, Male and Female, Valuing, and Becoming. Questions and problems concerning the dignity and uniqueness of the individual, the roles of male and female, and the values that influence human behavior are all presented here. The last part, Becoming,

*Educational Publishing Division, E. Washington Square, Philadelphia, Pa. 19105.

encourages participants to identify personal changes that may have occurred during their learning experiences in this module and help the student to integrate and find personal meaning in what they have been doing.

All of the learning modules are attractively packaged and consist of audio cassettes, games, picture cards, puzzles, personal workbook logs, and teacher's manuals. The program can be used in part or as a whole and is one of the few designed for use with young adolescents.

TRANSCENDENTAL MEDITATION

In the last few years there has been increasing interest in a commercial meditation program developed by Maharishi Mahesh Yogi and named Transcendental Meditation (TM); it is made available to students on all levels of education through contractual arrangements with an authorized teaching center (*Fundamentals of Progress*, 1974).

TM is systematic and involves learning to relax and use a personal mantra for two 15-minute periods a day. Once learned, it can be practiced by the individual without requiring any special setting, preparation, or life-style, at any time or place, in a natural fashion. Rubottom (1972) has discussed the potential use of TM in the schools and suggests that meditation helps each person to free the creative forces within himself and thereby brings focus and meaning to life. The general goals of the TM program are as follows (*Fundamentals of Progress*, 1974):

- To develop the full potential of the individual
- To improve governmental achievements
- To realize the highest ideal of education
- To eliminate the age-old problem of crime and all behavior that brings unhappiness to the family of man
- To maximize the intelligent use of the environment
- To bring fulfillment to the economic aspirations of individuals and society
- To achieve the spiritual goals of mankind in this generation

These are indeed, humanistic goals of the highest kind and, although they may appear idealistic (and even unrealistic), they are being accomplished in part. Considerable research has now been conducted on the effects of meditation "to develop the full potential of the individual." Most of the research is supportive of the self-actualizing and health values of meditation (Bloomfield et al., 1975; LeShan, 1975).

Approximately 1 million persons have been taught TM in classes and courses operating out of 205 growth centers in the United States. Countless others have learned other forms of meditation in noncommercial courses and as part of broader humanistic education courses offered in schools and colleges throughout the country. In the future it can be expected that TM courses will expand their programs in cooperation with schools of all kinds. More likely, however, is the prospect that the public schools will develop eclectic meditation units consisting of an integration of the best techniques available and including breathing, relaxation, concentration, mantra, and body movement exercises.

VALUES ORIENTATION PROGRAMS

Argus Communications* is one of the major producers of value-oriented teaching materials that are designed to stimulate and motivate students to think for themselves about who they are and how they relate to their world. Three of their more widely used programs are described here.

Meeting Yourself Halfway

Meeting Yourself Halfway consists of 31 adventures in self-discovery in paperback form with accompanying spirit masters for duplication. The program is authored by Sidney Simon and is paced for individualized learning throughout the entire school year. The original book *Values Clarification* (Simon et al., 1972) also contains numerous practical strategies for use with students and is a good supplement to this program.

Making Sense of Our Lives

The Making Sense of Our Lives program is a life-centered approach to learning that brings connectiveness to the world of young people. It was designed by Merrill Harmin and consists of three separate units. Each unit contains a number of individual lessons that can be selected by the teacher according to classroom and pupil needs. The following are some illustrative lesson topics:

Friendship	Can You Laugh at Yourself?
Self-Confidence	Heroes
Prisons	Did I Do Wrong?
Should Life Center on the Past, Present or Future?	The Fury Within Us

The program can also be supplemented with filmstrips, cassettes, and colorful posters from the same company.

Lifeline

Five years of research and development through the Schools Council in the United Kingdom resulted in the Lifeline curriculum. The program was designed through a curriculum project based in the Department of Education, University of Oxford, England. The materials involve students in the process of making decisions, resolving conflicts, and learning to care. Materials include the following:

46 Sensitivity cards in full color	5 *Proving the Rule* booklets
71 Consequences cards in full color	6 *What Would You Have Done?* booklets
63 Points of View cards in full color	*Learning to Care—A Teacher's Guide*

The Lifeline program also has a 30-minute film for teacher orientation. Although the program was developed in England, it is now in widespread use throughout the United States and in a number of other countries.

---

*7440 Natchez Ave., Niles, Ill. 60648

DISCUSSION QUESTIONS AND ACTIVITIES

1. Critique the eight values covered in the Human Value Series.
2. What do you think might be included in a junior high school search for meaning program?
3. For what age groups was the Focus on Self-Development program created?
4. Give an illustration of each of the three ego states presented in transactional analysis.
5. What is the title of one of Alvyn Freed's transactional analysis programs for children?
6. Who is Duso?
7. Discuss some possible limitations that teachers might find in using the Inside/Out program by itself.
8. Which of these programs included American Indians in its field testing?
9. What is distinctive about the Individuality module of the Becoming program?
10. Discuss Rubottom's suggestion regarding the value of meditation programs.
11. Which program was developed in a foreign country? Research and critique another program developed in a foreign country.
12. Which program presented in this chapter contains a unique unit on career education? How might this be supplemented with other relevant activities?
13. Obtain a teaching unit from one of the programs described in this chapter and demonstrate it to your class or discussion group.

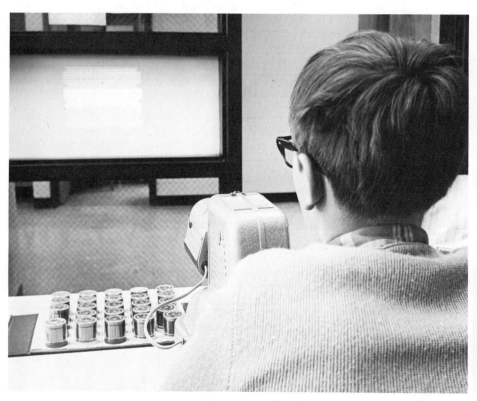
A resource materials library is part of most modern schools.

*While seeing to it that no ability is allowed to remain below
a minimum needed for ordinary living, we should . . . allow the
individual to make the most of what he can do best and what
gives him the most satisfaction.*

J. P. GUILFORD (1967, p. 476)

CHAPTER 9

Learning resource materials

ALTHOUGH EDUCATORS have long acknowledged the importance of providing
for individual differences, relatively little has been done about it until very recent
times. This may have been caused in part by a widespread belief that little could
be done by the schools to actually improve a child's intelligence or basic learning
abilities. This negative view has now been changed for the better. When the highly
respected psychologist Guilford published *The Nature of Human Intelligence* (1967)
and demonstrated that intelligence consists of many components—including social
intelligence—the trend toward individual programming and development of human
abilities was further enhanced.

Guilford argued that these abilities could be evaluated and developed through
distinctive practice exercises, and he stressed the importance of developing individual strengths, interests, and unique abilities. Stimulated by the work and implications of Piaget, Guilford, and others, commercial publishing firms began to create
special learning programs, kits, and resource materials. Only recently, however,
have many resource materials been created for special use in affective and humanistic
education programs.

Most of the learning resource materials available consist of multimedia aids such
as films, filmstrips, tapes, cassettes, records, booklets, posters, and charts that can be
selected by the teacher according to pupil needs and the demands of the overall
curriculum. It is, of course, impossible to list all of the resource materials available
for teacher selection. However, the materials described in this chapter are representative of the better ones now commercially available. Most teachers will find it
worthwhile to contact selected publishers for current information on materials of
interest to them.

PRIMARY RESOURCE MATERIALS (KINDERGARTEN TO GRADE 3)

I Am, I Can, I Will (Family Communications, Inc., Pittsburgh, Pa. 94002)
A multiresource package of 15 color videocassettes, 15 audio cassettes, and 5 children's books designed to facilitate conversation, closeness, and trust. Developed and produced by Fred Rogers of "Mister Rogers' Neighborhood."

The Early Childhood Social Science Series (Bowmar, Box 3623, Glendale, Calif. 91201)
A three-unit sound filmstrip program to help young children develop self-esteem, solve problems, clarify ideas, and search for meaning. Filmstrip titles are *Myself and Other People, My Family and Other Families,* and *Everyone Needs Many Things.*

Experiential Development Program (Benefic Press, 10300 W. Roosevelt Rd., Westchester, Ill. 60153)
For building basic social concepts and social readiness on the kindergarten level. Materials include activity books and pictures: You and Your Family, You and Your Friends, and You and Others.

Moods and Emotions (The Child's World, Inc., P.O. Box 681, Elgin, Ill.)
Material to introduce and expand the feelings and emotions that are common to all people and to help children understand the personal reactions to such emotions as love, loneliness, compassion, joy, thoughtfulness, anger, sadness, and frustration. Materials consist of eight large colored prints of children engaged in a variety of emotional experiences. The reverse side of each print presents specific lesson objectives, a participation story, activities, projects, and related resource materials.

The Character Education Curriculum (American Institute for Character Education, P.O. Box 12617, San Antonio, Tex. 78212)
Character-development affective education program for grades 1 to 5, consisting of systematic lessons and varied learning materials.

Kindle (Scholastic Early Childhood Center, 902 Sylvan Ave., Englewood Cliffs, N.J. 07632)
Three units: Who Am I? How Do I Learn? and Getting Along. Each unit contains five filmstrips and records or cassettes.

Project Me (Bowmar, Box 3623, Glendale, Calif. 91201)
Six different sound filmstrips covering happiness, sadness, anger, and fear. Emphasis is on understanding and recognizing basic emotions in facial and body movement cues.

On Stage: Wally, Bertha, and You (Encyclopedia Britannica Educational Corp., 425 N. Michigan Ave., Chicago, Ill. 60611)
An attractive puppetry kit and resource lessons for providing children with experiences that tend to build self-confidence in working within and before a group.

I Can (Scholastic Early Childhood Center, 902 Sylvan Ave., Englewood Cliffs, N.J. 07632)
Four filmstrips and records or cassettes promoting group cooperation, creating, sharing, and assuming responsibility.

Understanding Ourselves and Others (School Specialty Supply, Inc., 1504 Galena St., Aurora, Colo. 80010)
Three sets of large colored pictures: Moods and Emotions, Children of America, and Children Around the World. Discussion guides are printed on the back of each picture.

Ideas, Thoughts, and Feelings and *Getting to Know Myself* by Hap Palmer (Educational Activities, Inc., P.O. Box 393, Freeport, N.Y. 11520)
Two separate records that encourage young children to respond to the challenge of problem solving and independent thinking.

Mr. Rogers' Records (Columbia Records/CBS, Inc., 51 W. 52nd St., Brooklyn, N.Y.)
Five records to help young children understand and express their feelings in song and discussion: *Come On and Wake Up*, *Won't You Be My Friend?* *Let's Be Together Today*, *You Are Special*, and *A Place of Your Own*.

Guidance Stories (Educational Records Sales, 157 Chambers St., New York, N.Y. 10007)
Six filmstrips on common guidance problems of young children, such as honesty and fairness.

People in Action (Holt, Rinehart and Winston, Inc., Educational Materials Division, 383 Madison Ave., New York, N.Y. 10017)
Large black-and-white photographs that present intriguing problems to encourage inquiry at a simple level. The photographs provide opportunities for young pupils to define and explore alternative ways of solving difficulties and what the logical consequences might be.

Developing Your Personality (Educational Record Sales, 157 Chambers St., New York, N.Y. 10007)
Six filmstrips on friendships, promises, and making social judgments.

Basic Social Studies Discussion Pictures (Harper & Row, Publishers, 10 E. 53rd St., New York, N.Y. 10022)
An excellent series of large flip-over charts dealing with early childhood problem situations.

The Most Important Person (Encyclopedia Britannica Educational Corp., 425 N. Michigan Ave., Chicago, Ill. 60611)
A series of four short films on feelings, creative expression, attitudes, and personal identity.

Understanding Ourselves (BFA Educational Media, 11559 Santa Monica Blvd., Los Angeles, Calif. 90025)
A good film about self-concepts to stimulate group discussion.

Ripples (National Educational Television Film Service, Indiana University, Audio-Visual Center, Bloomington, Ind. 47401)
A series of 36 15-minute films designed to help 5- to 7-year-olds build human values, increase aesthetic sensitivity, understand themselves, and improve interpersonal relationships.

I Have Feelings by Terry Berger (Behavioral Publications, Inc., 2852 Broadway–Morningside Heights, New York, N.Y. 10025)
A nicely illustrated little book for reading with young children.

My Grandpa Died Today by Joan Fassler (Behavioral Publications, Inc., 2852 Broadway– Morningside Heights, New York, N.Y. 10025)
An excellent book designed to help children deal directly with their feelings about death.

For Beginning the School Day (Highlights for Children, 2300 W. Fifth Ave., Columbus, Ohio)
A fine collection of thoughts, poems, and stories for beginning the school day.

ELEMENTARY RESOURCE MATERIALS (GRADES 4 TO 6)

Mirrors (Educational Activities, Inc., P.O. Box 393, Freeport, N.Y. 11520)
A series of six filmstrips and records serving as stimulus material for group discussion. The purpose is to present a variety of people with different perceptions of problem experiences through which students may mirror feelings in their own lives. Emphasis is on seeing our own conflicts, growth and change, perceiving others, and resolving our problems. A unique

aspect of this material is its use of poems, myths, and stories from noted writers: John Updike, Langston Hughes, James Thurber, and others.

Values, Awareness, Responsibility (ACi Media, 35 W. 45th St. New York, N.Y. 10026)
Five different programs: Learning About Me, Learning About Others, It's OK for Me: It's OK for You, I Couldn't Care Less, Of Loneliness and Love. Each program consists of four sound filmstrips and teacher guides.

Teaching Children Values Through Unfinished Stories (Educational Activities, Inc., P.O. Box 393, Freeport, N.Y. 11520)
A series of filmstrips, stories, and records covering such values as responsibility, love, courage, and justice that involve the pupil in considering appropriate courses of action or ways of behaving.

Secrets by Maxwell Maltz (W. Weitsman Leadership Associates, 2801 Ponce de Leon Blvd., Suite 820, Coral Gables, Fla. 33134)
A series of six very personal tapes for direct use with elementary-aged children for the purpose of helping them to improve their self-image. All tapes are directed to the child on such topics as You're Something Special. This is an excellent set of tapes to use in personal guidance and individualized instruction.

This Is You (Educational Record Sales, 157 Chambers St., New York, N.Y. 10007)
Eight filmstrips covering the human senses and basic biology. Good for units on sensory awareness and perception.

Learning About Values Discovery Kit (American Education Publications, 245 Long Hill Rd., Middletown, Conn. 06457)
A series of values photo posters, story cards, vocabulary charts, and guidebook to help children begin to understand personal values.

Wit and Wisdom (Teachers Aids Co., 1609 W. 29th St., Davenport, Iowa 52804)
A set of 160 famous quotations printed on colored 9 × 12 inch cards. An excellent way to supply a class with a thought for the day.

Meditations for the Modern Classroom (Educational Record Sales, 157 Chambers St., New York, N.Y. 10007)
Two records of inspirational readings useful in transcendental and meditational study units. Each reading can also be used separately as a basis for group discussion.

Brotherhood by Norman Rockwell (Curtis Publishing Co.)
A large attractive poster designed as part of the My Weekly Reader Holiday Poster Series. The poster is frequently used for initiating discussions on concepts of universal brotherhood and the family of man.

Affective Posters (Argus Communications, 7440 Natchez Ave., Niles, Ill. 60648)
Argus Communications produces dozens of colorful and well-designed humanistic posters with meaningful phrases. Nature photographs, cartoons, and modern art forms are all used. These posters are suitable for use on both elementary and secondary levels as well as with adults.

Understanding Others (BFA Educational Media, 11559 Santa Monica Blvd., Los Angeles, Calif. 90025)
A good film to introduce the study of feelings in other people.

Guidance Films (Churchill Films, 622 N. Robertson Blvd., Los Angeles, Calif. 90069)
A series of attractive short films on fears, drugs, friendship, and personal handicaps.

The Right Thing to Do (BFA Educational Media, 11559 Santa Monica Blvd., Los Angeles, Calif. 90025)

A short but excellent film covering social rules and moral dilemmas facing children. Ends with open discussion questions for affective education study groups.

Involvance Poems (Ann Arbor Publishers, 611 Church, Ann Arbor, Mich.)
A little book of poems about personal involvement in problem situations.

Unfinished Stories for Pupils (National Education Association, 1201 16th St. N.W., Washington, D.C. 20036)
A widely used collection of open-ended discussion stories published over the years by the NEA. Stories are available for different age groups with varied problems.

Seven Stories for Growth by Daniel Sugarman and Rolaine Hochstein (Pitman Publishing Corp., 6 E. 43rd St., New York, N.Y. 10017)
A book of interesting stories that involve children in common dilemmas and guide them to consider alternative possible solutions and the values involved.

Ideals (Ideal Publishing Co., 11315 Watertown Plank Rd., Milwaukee, Wis. 53226)
An ongoing series of magazine-sized booklets that contain poems, short stories, and inspirational material for use with persons of all ages. The colorful and attractive designs are highly motivational.

SECONDARY RESOURCE MATERIALS (GRADES 7 TO 12)

Emotions and Social Attitudes (Creative Visuals Co., Box 1911, Big Spring, Tex. 79720)
A set of 44 colored overhead transparencies with a teacher's guide for use with adolescents. Some of the transparencies have two or three overlays, all directly related to the development of healthy emotions and attitudes. A unique set of resource materials.

Achievement Motivation Materials (Educational Ventures, Inc., 209 Court St., Middletown, Conn. 06457)
A workbook entitled *Who Am I?* plus activity sheets, games, and materials for high school students to help them clarify self-images, to establish personal standards of excellence, and to experience support and recognition from classmates and teachers.

National Forum Developmental Guidance Series (American Guidance Service, Publishers' Building, Circle Pines, Minn.)
A series of textbooks, charts, and guides: Seeing Ourselves, About Growing Up, Planning My Future, Being Teenagers, Discovering Myself, and Toward Adult Living.

Turner Career Guidance Series (Follett Corp., 1010 W. Washington Blvd., Chicago, Ill. 60607)
Booklets on guidance and occupational concerns of young adolescents. A good resource for career-education units.

The Great Lives Series (Encyclopedia Britannica Educational Corp., 425 N. Michigan Ave., Chicago, Ill. 60611)
Thirty-five small books on the lives of great individuals: Marion Anderson, Mark Twain, Dag Hammarskjold, and others. Good inspirational literature for young people.

Accent-Social Contact by B. Dare and E. Wolfe (Follett Corp., 1010 W. Washington Blvd., Chicago, Ill. 60607)
A series of booklets covering typical adolescent concerns such as social acceptance, responsibility, and maturity.

Going Places With Your Personality: A Guide to Successful Living by Charles Kahn, Robert Tong, and Wing Jew (Fearon Publishers, 6 Davis Dr., Belmont, Calif. 94002)
A workbook that uses information, observation, and discussion to help students develop desirable attitudes and habits with a strong emphasis on interpersonal relations.

Getting It Together Is Life Itself by Sol Gordon (Educational Activities, Inc., P.O. Box 393, Freeport, N.Y. 11520)
   A sound filmstrip on youth drug problems that promotes thoughtful discussion and possible solutions.

Your Own Thing—The Contemporary Reading Series (Leswing Communications, Inc., San Francisco, Calif.)
   A series of six books and a teacher's manual written for junior and senior high school students with reading problems. The stories are excellent for moral problem solving and value orientation lessons.

It's Your Life (Benefic Press, 10300 W. Roosevelt Rd., Westchester, Ill. 60153)
   A unique work and activity book covering self-awareness, goals, and values. Good material for group discussion and follow-up role-playing sessions.

A Better You (Benefic Press, 10300 W. Roosevelt Rd., Westchester, Ill. 60153)
   Six records on friendship and personality development most suitable for the junior high school pupil.

The Nature of Human Nature by Ashley Montague (Educational Record Sales, 157 Chambers St., New York, N.Y. 10007)
   Ten records that serve as a forum for discussion of the many facets of our culture including love, morality, aggression, and cultural evolution.

Words to Live By (Educational Record Sales, 157 Chambers St., New York, N.Y. 10007)
   An album of outstanding poetry for meditation and group discussion.

Meditation by Demetri Kannellakos et al. (Big Sur Recordings, 2015 Bridgeway, Sausalito, Calif. 94965)
   A tape explaining meditation as a psychophysiological experience and its implications for wholesome living.

Buddhism and Meditation by C. T. Rinpoche (Big Sur Recordings, 2015 Bridgeway, Sausalito, Calif. 94965)
   A fascinating tape on meditation by the head of an ancient Tibetan monastic order.

Issues in American Democracy (Educational Record Sales, 157 Chambers St., New York, N.Y. 10007)
   Two records on controversial issues in fundamental American political values.

Self-Actualization by Robert Valett (Argus Communications, 7440 Natchez Ave., Niles, Ill. 60648)
   A personal workbook and guide to happiness and self-determination. Lessons and exercises covering self-understanding, purpose, love, will, work, self-control, tension reduction, self-confidence, self-renewal, and others.

Guidance Series Booklets (Science Research Associates, Inc., 259 E. Erie St., Chicago, Ill. 60611)
   A set of 45 guidance booklets covering numerous educational, vocational, and personal-social concerns of youth.

Family Development Series (Steck-Vaughn Co., P.O. Box 2028, Austin, Tex. 78767)
   Ten high-interest and easy-reading books on problems of personal, family, and community living. Emphasis is on practical problem solving strategies. Also suitable for use with compensatory education adult groups.

I Am Loveable and Capable by Sidney Simon (Argus Communications, 7440 Natchez Ave., Niles, Ill. 60648)
   A small pamphlet with accompanying filmstrip demonstrating that personal affirmations are the beginning point for successful living.

Why Am I Afraid to Tell You Who I Am? by John Powell (Argus Communications, 7440 Natchez Ave., Niles, Ill. 60648)
This book stresses the importance of truth in developing positive interpersonal relationships and communication.

Personal Adjustment by Carl Rogers (Human Development Institute, Instructional Dynamics, Inc., 166 E. Superior St., Chicago, Ill. 60611)
A warm and intimate series of 10 tapes covering such important topics as the lonely person, the generation gap, the place of feeling, and the struggle to become a person.

Problem Solvers (Churchill Films, 622 N. Robertson Blvd., Los Angeles, Calif. 90069)
An interesting 20-minute film on how a designer, an inventor, an astronomy student, and a truck troubleshooter examine and solve problems.

Games People Play by Eric Berne (Time-Life Films, Time and Life Building, Rockefeller Center, New York, N.Y. 10020)
Two 30-minute films on the theory and the practice of transactional analysis.

Searching for Values (Learning Corp. of America, 711 Fifth Ave., New York, N.Y. 10022)
A series of 15 short films on the individual's search for meaningful relationships. The films lead to open-ended and provocative discussions.

A Thousand Suns (Arthur Barr Productions, Inc., P.O. Box 7-C, Pasadena, Calif. 91104)
A film that puts the ethic of consumption into a human perspective and presents ecological and spiritual problems of existence.

The City and The Self (Time-Life Films, Time and Life Building, Rockefeller Center, New York, N.Y. 10020)
An award-winning film probing the impact of city life on human feelings and future development.

Peak Experiences (Center for the Health Sciences, Film Services, University of California, Los Angeles, Calif. 90024)
A beautiful film on a variety of peak experiences enjoyed by unique persons.

Where All Things Belong (Essentia, 50 Sonora Way, Corte Madera, Calif. 94925)
An inspirational film on the place of people in nature and the joy of rebirth.

DISCUSSION QUESTIONS AND ACTIVITIES

1. Define "social intelligence."
2. Who is Mr. Rogers?
3. Which of these resource materials relies heavily on the use of puppets?
4. Select an emotional picture from a magazine or news story and suggest how it might be used as a learning resource aid.
5. What is one of the major advantages of using filmstrips in affective education?
6. List one or two resource materials that help pupils to consider the consequences of their behavior.
7. How is *Mirrors* unique?
8. Write two quotations or proverbs that might be included in the *Wit and Wisdom* materials.
9. Which company produces colorful contemporary posters for use in affective-humanistic education programs?
10. What resource material might be helpful in a unit on drug education?
11. List two affective education workbooks for possible use with adolescents.
12. If possible, preview one of the resource films listed in this chapter and outline how it might be used as part of a lesson you would teach in humanistic education.

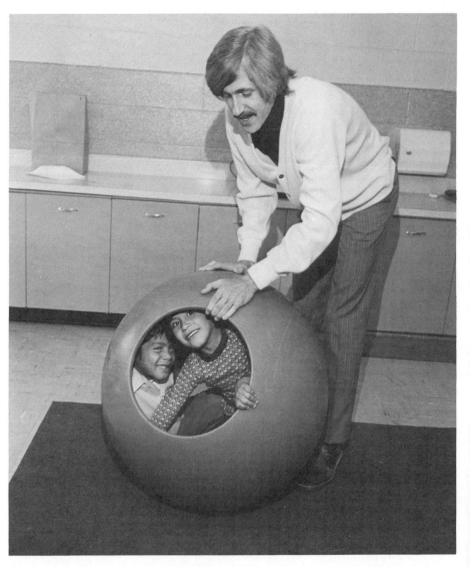

We learn from our experience and actions. (From Gearheart, B. R. *Learning disabilities: Educational strategies* [2nd ed.]. St. Louis: The C. V. Mosby Co., 1977.)

Nothing great was ever achieved without enthusiasm.
                    RALPH WALDO EMERSON (1847)

CHAPTER 10

Experiential activities

BECAUSE THERE IS no single affective-humanistic education program adequate for all persons of different needs, ages, and grade levels, it is necessary that the teacher select appropriate supplemental activities and learning experiences. To be effective, these activities must evoke mutual enthusiasm and involvement of both pupils and teachers. There are a number of special experiential learning activities that are commonly used in humanistic education programs on all levels. These include personal human involvement programs, expressive art and music, humor, inspirational literature, self-evaluation techniques, social skills games, and interpersonal growth activities. Several of these are presented here to illustrate how such experiential activities can further stimulate total human growth and enthusiasm for learning. The general description of each activity is presented first and is then followed by sample lessons.

HUMAN INVOLVEMENT PROGRAMS

To be effective, humanistic education must provide for real life experiences outside of the classroom. The world of the young, the middle aged, and the old is one that children need to be exposed to through field trips and actual involvement with people in varied situations. Trips to hospitals, slums, homes for the aged, and institutions for the mentally ill and handicapped should be as much a part of school excursions as the more traditional ventures to museums and parks. Through such activity, it is possible to plan projects with people, for example, volunteer assistance to the elderly and the hospitalized. Opportunities to become involved with other ethnic groups through home, community, church, and other visits put vitality into the classroom discussion of human relations. Most children and classes are fully capable of planning their own involvement and field trip programs if encouraged to do so.

Recent innovations in career-education and applied social studies courses are also increasingly involving students in more meaningful community learning experiences.

149

For example, the County Alliance for Career Education and Industry Education Councils of Los Angeles represent more than 100 groups in business, industry, government, and labor unions and sponsor practical work experience, observation, and work-study activities. The New Orleans Center for the Creative Arts is providing opportunities for highly talented students in the visual and performing arts. Cleveland, Ohio, schools have started a job development program that includes extensive field trips and interviews with employers (McCormack, 1976).

DEVELOPING PERSONAL GOALS AND ASPIRATIONS

Think of three things: whence you came, where you are going, and to whom you must account.

ANONYMOUS

Starting point

When Paul Brown saw the Trainees Wanted sign in front of Mr. Thompson's construction firm, he really felt excited. "Maybe this is my chance for a good job," he thought. He had always liked to build things and the idea of a construction job turned him on.

He was glad to find Mr. Thompson in his office and willing to talk to him. Paul had known Mr. Thompson from the time his firm had supported Paul's baseball team with new uniforms. "What kind of job do you want?" said Mr. Thompson. "We have several openings for fellows interested in electrical work, carpentry, drafting, and even plumbing, but you have to make a choice as to where you want to start and what you would really like to do."

Paul had really not thought about it much. Now he felt it was important to select a trainee job that he could really get interested in. "How should I answer Mr. Thompson's questions?" he wondered.

1. What should Paul do?
2. If Paul cannot decide where to start, what would you suggest he do?
3. Why is it important for Paul to make up his mind?
4. Complete these sentences:

I wish _____.

Ten years from now _____.

Someday I would like to _____.

The place for me to start is _____.

The most important thing in life for me is _____.

Tomorrow I _____.

My goal is _____.

From Valett, R. *Getting it all together—A guide for personality development and problem solving.* San Rafael, Calif.: Academic Therapy Publications, 1974.

The practical aspects and values of community involvement programs are frequently reported in the news media. In Riverton, Wyoming, a ninth-grade course in social economics involves the students in setting up a company, deciding on a product to produce, selling stock, producing and marketing the product, and using advertising and sales techniques (McCormack, 1976). In the Clinton High School at Clinton, Iowa, students in an interdisciplinary program have built 27 homes over a 28-year period; the homes are designed, constructed, painted, decorated, maintained, and managed by students and then sold to local citizens (Mayhugh, 1975). In Sanger, California, senior students in a Marriage and the Family course must simulate a marriage, go out and find an apartment, buy furniture, groceries, insurance, and clothing, plan for children, and otherwise budget their "income" of $750.00 a

---

ACCEPTING HELP

He is my friend who helps me and not he who pities me.
ANONYMOUS

Where to turn

Since she had found out that she was pregnant, Nancy had been very upset. Much of her time had been spent alone in her room crying and sleeping; she felt like a real wreck. It was almost impossible for her to believe that she was going to have a baby at her age. The last thing she had ever wanted was to be a mother at 17!

The thing that disturbed her most, however, was that Mike had not called her or asked her out since she told him he was going to be a father. And that was 2 whole weeks ago! Suddenly, she felt so alone and rejected that she cried out, "I need to be with someone and talk to them."

Then Nancy thought, "What shall I do about the baby? Wow, what am I going to do about Mike and myself? I wish someone could help me!"

1. How do you think Nancy might be helped?
2. Who might help her?
3. What could a friend do to help Nancy?
4. Complete these sentences:

My friends _____.

Love is _____.

I need help with _____.

It is hard to decide _____.

Right now _____.

The thing for me to do is _____.

From Valett, R. *Getting it all together—A guide for personality development and problem solving.* San Rafael, Calif.: Academic Therapy Publications, 1974.

month; this real life–simulation class and its community involvement assignments are enthusiastically supported by pupils and parents alike (Keeler, 1975).

Numerous books, workbooks, and other educational materials are available for use with experiential activities such as those described. Workbooks usually help to develop cognitive skills such as reading, writing, and thinking and allow them to be integrated in a meaningful way with the more direct experiential activity. For example, the preceding two stories are taken from the workbook *Getting It All Together—A Guide for Personality Development and Problem Solving* (Valett, 1974). The first story, "Starting Point," is typical of those used to supplement work-experience, involvement, and career-education programs. The second story, "Where To Turn," is typical of those used in family life, sex education, and practical child development programs.

EXPRESSIVE ART, DRAMA, AND MUSIC

Many forms of art, drama, music, and poetry lend themselves to an understanding of human feelings and aspirations. Most students are capable of finding and sharing meaningful poems, photographs, pictures, and musical scores. These can then become the basis for class discussion and individual projects.

One widely available form of expressive music that lends itself well to affective education is popular records. When such records are played and the lyrics carefully considered, they can have a dramatic impact on the total program. Many powerful messages are readily available through selected songs. In one special education class at Washington Union High School in Easton, California, contemporary music is used to teach reading, writing, and responsible behavior (Drummond, 1973). The following records were selected for use in this program because their central theme is the development of responsible behavior in adolescents; the lyrics were used for initial group discussion and then as the basis for written assignments and alternative problem-solving projects.

- *That Was The Night The Lights Went Out in Georgia* (Vicki Lawrence)
- *Bad Bad Leroy Brown* (Jim Croce)
- *Werewolf* (Five Man Electrical Band)
- *I Shot the Sheriff* (Eric Clapton)
- *Back Stabbers* (O'Jays)
- *Freddie's Dead* (Curtis Mayfield)
- *Living For The City* (Stevie Wonder)
- *Don't Burn Down the Bridge* (Gladys Knight and the Pips)
- *Bridge Over Troubled Water* (Jackson Five)
- *People Make the World Go Round* (Jackson Five)
- *Who Made the Man* (Stapel Singers)
- *He Ain't Heavy, He's My Brother* (Osmond Brothers)

Other inspirational records widely used in affective education programs include Johnny Mathis' *Life Is a Song Worth Singing*, Mama Cass' *Don't Let the Good Life Pass You By*, John Lennon's *Oh My Love*, Joni Mitchell's *All I Want*, Joan Baez's *Ghetto*, and Carole King's *Beautiful*.

Poetry has long been used as an effective medium by individuals and in classes and groups of all kinds. It is currently being widely used in public schools and also in correctional institutions, drug rehabilitation programs, hospitals, private growth centers, etc. Lerner (1975) has recently discussed its therapeutic value and has given the following examples. The first poem was written by a 17-year-old girl who had attempted suicide twice:

> I can always do away with me
> That's no trick as all can see.
> My struggle is just to be
> A person who likes me.

A young inmate of a correctional institution wrote the following:

> Love is
> Absorbed
> Into the senses
> Like a giant dry sponge.

Poetry, drama, role-playing, and other expressive forms can also be integrated into special lessons. The All in the Family experiential learning activities presented below are illustrative of such combined forms of expression.

ALL IN THE FAMILY

Objective: To be able to express personal feelings about family relationships through the use of drama and role-playing

Procedure: Write down a frustrating experience you have had in trying to express yourself and be better understood within your own family.

Activities

1. Select some classmates to help you act out this frustrating experience.
2. Coach each person on how you want them to role-play your brother, sister, father, mother, or other relatives involved.
3. Role-play the scene before the class, acting yourself as naturally and as honestly as you can.
4. When you have finished, ask the class to identify the feelings and emotions and problems involved.
5. Request another group to act out a possible solution (or alternative way of acting) to the frustration and problems presented.
6. Discuss your own feelings about alternative ways of acting that you would like to experience.
7. Write a brief poem expressing your All In The Family frustrations and alternatives.

HUMOR

People express themselves through varied forms of humor such as jokes and cartoons. Children and adolescents alike enjoy telling, reading, and listening to humorous episodes. It is well known that cartoons can be powerful shapers of human behavior, as is evidenced by their use in political campaigns, editorials, and adult comics. It is also possible to select cartoon strips for specific instructional purposes. For example, the "Peanuts" characters can be used to stimulate a study of character and personality traits by presenting pictures of the strip and personality traits for discussion as follows:

- Charlie Brown: A friendly, stable, persevering individual who always bounces back in the face of adversity?
- Woodstock: A bird representing joy, love, and affection?
- Schroeder: The typical introvert dedicated to aesthetic values?
- Peppermint Patty: The extroverted joiner, organizer, and tomboy?
- Snoopy: The person who lives in his own world of fantasy, usually concerned with power or status as portrayed by the Red Baron and others?
- Thibault: The individual who is constantly in trouble because of his aggressive behavior?
- Linus: The person showing immaturity and a constant concern with basic physical security as represented by overdependence on his blanket?
- Lucy: The bossy person struggling to become a person in her own right but often making others feel inadequate?

Some students also enjoy making their own cartoon strips or posters that convey messages of importance to them. Others write their own jokes or stories, which can be used as part of any good creative program. Because humor offers a socially acceptable means of expressing negative and positive feelings and emotions, it should be used much more widely in educational programs.

HELPFUL ADVICE?

Objective: To use humor in expressing and understanding feelings
Procedure: Study the cartoon above and think of some humorous advice that the doctor might be giving his patient.
Activities
1. Write in the doctor's words.
2. Write in the patient's words.

3. Show your cartoon to others and discuss the humorous situation you had in mind.
4. Look at and discuss the cartoons made by other pupils.
5. Select the three most humorous cartoons that appeal to you and explain your choice.
6. Select and bring to class two real cartoons that you judge to be very funny.
7. Discuss what makes a situation humorous or funny.

LAUGH A BIT!

Objective: To share and enjoy a good joke or humorous situation
Procedure: Read the following jokes.

Nothing so needs reforming as other people's habits.

MARK TWAIN

"Do you have trouble hearing?" asked the teacher of a boy who
sat dreamily at his desk.
"No, ma'am," replied the boy. "I have trouble listening."

ANONYMOUS

To find out a girl's faults, praise her to her girl friends.

BENJAMIN FRANKLIN

"My father is an Elk, Lion, Moose, and Eagle," boasted the boy.
"Oh yeah! Do they have him in a circus?" asked another boy.

ANONYMOUS

Activities
1. Take turns telling the jokes to each other.
2. Which one did you enjoy the most? Why?
3. Find and tell a favorite joke or story to the class. Why did you select this joke?
4. Discuss why humor is so important in life.

INSPIRATIONAL LITERATURE

The use of selected books and readings in understanding human feelings and emotions is a valuable part of most humanistic education programs. Children can and do relate to the characters they read about, and inspirational stories can help them to develop personal insight and approaches to their own problems.

Any school library contains numerous books that could be used in such a program. Public libraries and the availability of paperbacks at popular prices make it possible to develop a practical reading list without great difficulty. Stories of cultural heroes, outstanding sports figures, religious and social leaders, etc. should all be readily available. So, too, should the classics of poetry, myths, fairy tales, the Bible, and selected prose such as Gibran's *The Prophet,* Hesse's *Siddhartha,* and other novels.

Public bookstores also contain many popular new books of inspirational value that can be easily adapted for educational purposes. Some of the more recent books being used in adolescent and adult programs are listed below.

Allen, J. *As a man thinketh.* Mt. Vernon, N.Y.: Peter Pauper Press, 1969.
Allport, G. *Becoming.* New Haven: Yale University Press, 1955.

Anderson, M., and Savary, L. *Passages: A guide for pilgrims of the mind.* New York: Harper & Row, Publishers, 1973.

Assagioli, R. *Psychosynthesis.* New York: The Viking Press, Inc., 1965.

Brennecke, J., and Amick, R., *The struggle for significance.* Beverly Hills, Calif.: Glencoe Press, 1971.

Huxley, A. *The perennial philosophy.* London: Fontana, 1958.

James, W. *The varieties of religious experience.* New York: The New American Library, Inc., 1958.

Jung, C. *Man and his symbols.* New York: Doubleday & Co., Inc., 1964.

Kennedy, E. *The heart of loving.* Niles, Ill.: Argus Communications, 1973.

Krishnamurti, J. *Think on these things.* New York: Harper & Row, Publishers, 1964.

Lair, J. *I ain't much baby—but I'm all I've got.* New York: Fawcett-World library, 1972.

Lembro, J. *Help yourself.* Niles, Ill.: Argus Communications, 1974.

LeShan, E. *The wonderful crisis of middle age.* New York: David McKay Co., Inc., 1973.

May, R. *Man's search for himself.* London: George Allen & Unwin, Ltd., 1953.

McFee, T. *Love and other painful joys.* Philadelphia: Dorrance & Co., Inc., 1970.

Newman, M., and Berkowitz, B. *How to be your own best friend.* New York: Ballantine Books, Inc., 1971.

Pirsig, R. *Zen and the art of motorcycle maintenance: An inquiry into values.* New York: William Morrow & Co., Inc., 1974.

Sagon, C. *The cosmic connection: An extraterrestrial perspective.* New York: Doubleday & & Co., Inc., 1973.

Tournier, P. *A place for you.* New York: Alfred A. Knopf, Inc., 1959.

Valett, R. *Self actualization.* Niles, Ill.: Argus Communications, 1974.

Van Dusen, W. *The natural depth in man: A searcher's guide for exploring the secret spaces of our inner worlds.* New York: Harper & Row, Publishers, 1972.

MY WISH

Objective: To wish for something and to discuss it with friends

Procedure: Write your name. Close your eyes and make a wish; wish for something that is important to you, that you would really like to have come true.

Activities

1. In the area above your name, draw or color a picture of your wish or a part of your wish.
2. Explain your wish to a group of your friends. Answer any questions they might have about your wish.
3. Listen carefully to what your friends wished and talk with them about their wishes.
4. Tape your picture of your wish on the wall where you can see it and think about it for a week. Place it next to pictures of other wishes.
5. After a week, discuss your wishes again with your friends. Would you change your wish? If so, how and why?
6. Read an inspirational book, magazine, or news story about someone who helped to make their wishes come true. Share the story with your class.

SELF-AWARENESS AND EVALUATION

Since most humanistic education programs attempt to develop self-awareness, insight, and self-understanding, many learning activities should be provided in these areas. Self-concept inventories, procedures, biofeedback, stories, autobiographies, and related exercises are all widely used. The following are some example of these:

Interest finders

My three wishes are _____ .

I like to spend my time at _____ .

My hobby is _____ .

Self-description ratings (extremes)

I feel sad most of the time.   ___ ___ ___ ___ ___   I feel happy most of the time.

I am smart.   ___ ___ ___ ___ ___   I am stupid.

I have many friends.   ___ ___ ___ ___ ___   I have few friends.

Like me–unlike me ratings

	Like me	Unlike me
I never worry about anything.	_____	_____
I'm proud of my school work.	_____	_____
I'm a failure.	_____	_____

Social affiliations

Who is your best friend? _____

Who would you most like to be like? _____

Which student in your class does everyone like? _____

Biofeedback apparatus

A number of high school science experiments using biofeedback brain wave analyzers have been designed and used by King (1975) and others. This curriculum teaches students to observe their own brain wave activity, to become aware of left and right brain functions, and to develop their own abilities and talents. Some of the more interesting comments from students participating in these self-awareness experiments were as follows:

- It's theta when I'm mad.
  It's beta when I add.
  Therefore, I can't add when I'm mad.

- Theta keeps time with music.

- I can make the lights go out
  and turn off the sound.
  I just space out and the voltage
  goes down.

The use of biofeedback experiments and apparatus will continue to increase in both humanistic education and related biological science curriculums. They will, however, most likely be used along with many other self-awareness and evaluation activities such as those that follow.

MAKING SELF-JUDGMENTS

Observe all men; thyself most.
BENJAMIN FRANKLIN

Playback

As Steve watched the playback film of the last basketball game, he couldn't believe his eyes. Was it actually him making all of those mistakes? After all, he was the first-string forward with an outstanding record. And, although his team had lost the game by only 3 points, he tried hard to win.

The last quarter was unbelievable. As he saw himself make foul after foul, he recalled the coach's words to "get hold of" himself. And then he saw himself denying his fifth foul and swearing that the officials had made a mistake. But there he was on the film, holding his man tightly with his own two arms. Why couldn't he even remember that he had actually done it?

1. Why do you think Steven could not remember committing his fifth foul?
2. What does it mean to "get hold of yourself?"
3. What might Steve learn from watching the playback film?
4. Complete these sentences:

What I like most about myself is _____.

I am best in _____.

The biggest mistake in my life was _____.

What I dislike most about myself is _____.

My talents are _____.

What I really enjoy is _____.

I am _____.

From Valett, R. *Getting it all together—A guide for personality development and problem solving.* San Rafael, Calif.: Academic Therapy Publications, 1974.

WHO AM I?

Objective: To be able to establish emotional contact with another person in a short period of time

Procedure: Use a regular 8½ × 11 inch sheet of paper. (1) Print the words "Who Am I?" in the center of the paper. (2) Print your name under these words. (3) In the upper right-hand corner, print the names of two persons, other than family members, who have been most influential in your life. (4) In the lower right-hand corner, write the year that has been the happiest for you. (5) In the lower left-hand corner, write the year that has been the most unhappy or traumatic for you. (6) In the upper left-hand corner, write your personal goal aspiration.

POSITIVE AND NEGATIVE SELF-CONCEPTS

Procedure: Describe several of your positive and negative self-concepts below:

Concept	Self-descriptions	
	Positive	Negative
Love (lovable—unlovable)		
Ability (capable—not capable)		
Care (caring—not caring)		

The best thing about me is _____.

The worst thing about me is _____.

Activities

1. Pin the completed paper in the center of your shirt or blouse.
2. Walk around the room and quickly read to yourself what other people have written about themselves.
3. Select a partner and spend 15 minutes listening to his interpretation of what he has written. Ask him questions that will help you get to know him better.
4. Now tell your partner about yourself for 15 minutes.
5. Remove the paper, turn it over, and write your feelings about this experience on the back.
6. Discuss what you have written with the group.

MY BODY PUZZLE

Objective: To become aware of your feelings about your body

Procedure: Lie down on a large piece of butcher paper. Have a friend draw your body outline on the paper.

Activities

1. Draw in your other body parts (eyes, nose, hair, etc.).
2. Color your body parts and your clothes.
3. Use scissors to cut the picture into several large puzzle pieces.

4. Mix the pieces and put them back together.
5. Write a description of your body parts and your appearance.
6. Which part of your body do you like the most?
7. Which part of your body are you most concerned about? Why?
8. What are some of the things that people do to improve their feelings about their bodies?
9. How do you feel about changing or improving your own body?

MAKING A PLAN

What is the use of running when you are not on the right road?

ANONYMOUS

Independence

For several months Terry had been puzzled about what she should do after graduation. Now she had decided that, whatever she was going to do, she wanted to do without interference from her parents or relatives. She felt she had never had enough freedom and the thought of doing her own things in her own way really excited her.

"I am definitely going to move into my own apartment as soon as possible," said Terry to herself. Then she began to dream about how the apartment might look and what she could do with a place all to herself. As she was dreaming about what her new life might be like, she resolved to move within the next few weeks.

Then she stopped and thought, "How can I do it in just a few weeks? What must I do to make it all possible?" There were so many questions and things to think about that she felt overwhelmed and almost began to cry.

1. What was Terry's goal?
2. Do you think she was taking the proper action and "on the right road" to achieve her goal?
3. If you were Terry, how might you plan to achieve your goal?
4. Check one of the goals listed below and then outline a possible plan for accomplishing this goal:

   Buying a car _____

   Taking a vacation _____

   Getting married _____
5. Complete these sentences:

   If I had a magic wand I would _____.

   There are many ways to _____.

   My life is _____.

   In order to _____.

   I really plan to _____.

From Valett, R. *Getting it all together—A guide for personality development and problem solving*. San Rafael, Calif.: Academic Therapy Publications, 1974.

MIRROR, MIRROR ON THE WALL

Objective: To be able to verbally express personal feelings about ourselves
Procedure: Look into a full-length hanging wall mirror at yourself quietly for 3 minutes. Study yourself carefully. Turn on a tape recorder for the following activities.

Activities

1. Describe your physical self in detail. Be sure to describe your major body characteristics and impressions.
2. Describe the kind of person you feel yourself to be at this time. Include your strengths and weaknesses.
3. Describe your interests, hopes, and aspirations in some detail.
4. Describe how you think you may look 10 years from now.
5. Turn the recorder off. Play the tape back and listen carefully to your self-description.
6. Write a brief paragraph evaluating your own self-description.

SELF-ASSERTION CARDS

Procedure: Using different colored felt pens, print the words listed below on 3 × 5 inch cards.

Activate	Evolve	Hope	Plan	Serve
Aspire	Faith	Imagine	Play	Spirit
Becoming	Feel	Improve	Praise	Smile
Beautify	Forgive	Joy	Pray	Transcend
Care	Fun	Laugh	Purpose	Understand
Celebrate	Freedom	Live	Realize	Value
Cheer	Glory	Love	Relax	Welcome
Cooperate	Goal	Meditate	Reason	Will
Create	Grow	Nurture	Renew	Wish
Dream	Happiness	Peace	Risk	Work
Exercise	Help			

Words are powerful symbols that stimulate our thoughts and actions. If we perceive things positively and think about their meanings, they can contribute to our own self-actualization.

The cards can be used in several different ways. Perhaps the most effective is to select one card a week and place it in a prominent place such as on the refrigerator door, bedroom mirror, or bulletin board as a frequent reminder to think positively.

Another way is to pull one card from the deck each day and make a positive verbal statement to oneself about that card. For example, if the word "risk" is pulled, the person might say, "Today I will risk doing something a bit different." The cards can also be used in a class or discussion group in much the same way.

Activities

1. Pass the cards around in your group and decorate them with different colors making them as attractive as possible.
2. Select a positive word card and everyone in the group take turns making positive self-assertions using that word.
3. Discuss the positive self-assertions made in the group and ask the person to elaborate on them.

MY SELF-CONCEPTS AND TRANSACTIONS

Objective: To be able to describe the kind of person you think you are
Procedure: Select a current photograph of yourself that you like. Study it carefully and write self-descriptions as follows.

SELECTING POSITIVE ALTERNATIVES

A wise man changes his mind, a fool never.

ANONYMOUS

Stereo

John had worked and saved for a long time to buy the components for his new stereo hi-fi set. Now he finally had everything he needed for a fine music system. Eagerly, he began to assemble and test the components. Then he heard the sound and realized he was not getting any stereophonic effect.

Quickly, he checked his connections to make sure they were secure, but again there was no stereo sound. Now he was feeling frustrated as he disconnected the set and started over. He knew he was doing the job right as he put it back together again exactly as before. But when the stereo still failed to come on, he began to feel angry and then he banged it hard with his fist. "That might do it," he thought as he prepared to test it once more.

1. What was John's problem?
2. What else might John have done to attempt to get stereo sound?
3. How does being stubborn interfere with problem solving?
4. Complete these sentences:

Life could be better if _____.

The choices people make _____.

I have tried _____.

What the world needs now _____.

If I could start again _____.

Success to me means _____.

Another way of dealing with my problem is _____.

From Valett, R. *Getting it all together—A guide for personality development and problem solving.* San Rafael, Calif.: Academic Therapy Publications, 1974.

Activities

1. Physical self: Describe your present body build, size, poise, general appearance, health, and strength.
2. Social self: Describe your social personality, interests, status, social acceptance, interpersonal relations, and significant social achievements.
3. Psychological self: Describe your real feelings about your strengths and weaknesses, your disposition and temperament, will, motivations, life interests, and values.
4. Ideal self: Describe goals, aspirations, ideals, achievement orientations, and the kind of person you would like to become.
5. Self-transactions: Draw arrows between the statements on the next page and the ego state or personality function projecting such a statement.

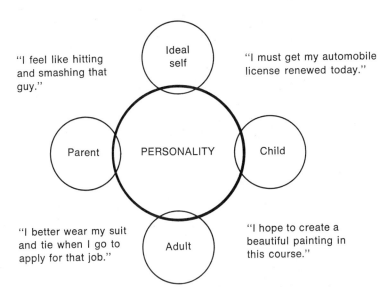

"I feel like hitting and smashing that guy."

"I must get my automobile license renewed today."

"I better wear my suit and tie when I go to apply for that job."

"I hope to create a beautiful painting in this course."

EDUCATIONAL GAMES

Many educational games have been created for teaching social skills and improving human relationships. Some of these have been devised as part of new affective education curriculums. Others are commercially produced and available in most toy and department stores. Examples of these are presented here.

Black Attaché Case game

The Black Attaché Case game is actually a learning program for secondary students that was originally developed in St. Croix, Virgin Islands, and described by Miceli (1969). The program consists of sessions during which students can ask questions of an imaginary computer in an attaché case placed on the table. Students then select the questions that are most worthwhile to them for study and follow-up with writing and other projects. Samples from one session are Why are grown-ups always angry at teenagers? What should we do about Vietnam? How would you describe fear? and Describe the flight of a seagull. The technique involves focusing on affective concerns so that the student himself becomes the subject of study.

Social-personal simulation games

A number of games have now been developed to teach social and personal skills and also to further cognitive development. Traditional games such as checkers and chess have long been used in some classrooms, although chess is the only one that has been widely used in social studies, science, and math curriculums. As games are simulations of life experiences, they involve the player in a learning situation that may generalize to the real world in which he finds himself. Two practical presentations on the use of games in school are by Coleman (1967) and Carlson (1969). Some of the new games being used in social learning curriculums are The Disaster

Game, Life, Career, Personality, Game of Democracy, and The Dating Game. *Psychology Today* magazine is also producing a series of games such as Blacks and Whites and Body Talk that should be considered for secondary level programs. The following are other games being used widely in humanistic education programs:

> *The Ungame* (Aud-Vid, Inc., P.O. Box 965, Garden Grove, Calif. 92642)
> Designed to enhance affective communication.
>
> *Touring* (Parker Brothers, Box 900, Salem, Mass. 01970)
> A game of planning and cooperation.
>
> *Come To My House* (Milton Bradley Co., Springfield, Mass. 01101)
> For teaching cooperative play to primary children.
>
> *Driver Ed* (Sears Roebuck Co.)
> Teamwork learning of driving rules and skills.
>
> *The Cities Game* (Dynamic Design Industries, 1433 N. Central Park, Anaheim, Calif. 92802)
> Stimulates cooperation in urban planning activities.
>
> *Happiness* (Milton Bradley Co., Springfield, Mass. 01101)
> A game dealing with emotions and feelings.
>
> *Compatibility* (Reiss Games, Inc., New York, N.Y.)
> A game of mutual decision making for high school students.
>
> *Feel Wheel* (Dynamic Design Industries, 1433 N. Central Park, Anaheim, Calif. 92802)
> A game that allows the players to express feelings toward specific persons and to learn to identify feelings.
>
> *Helping Hands* (Pennant Educational Materials, 4680 Alvarado Canyon Rd., San Diego, Calif. 92120)
> A game that provides opportunities for teachers to introduce value discussions.

INTERPERSONAL GROWTH ACTIVITIES

During the 1940's Lewin, a social psychologist at the Massachusetts Institute of Technology, began to develop a series of small group discussion methods and experiential activities for furthering interpersonal communication. These techniques, called T-group methods, were successfully used in business, scientific laboratories, and by the military services to help minimize tensions and enable persons to deal more honestly and openly with their feelings; since then, the National Training Laboratories was formed, with headquarters in Arlington, Virginia, and has trained thousands of educators and other group facilitators in these methods. Gradually, most of these group techniques have been modified or adapted for use in many affective education programs.

Several books have outlined and illustrated various experiential group activities suitable for use in humanistic education programs. Peso (1972) has developed a human movement program and accompanying exercises for expressing unconscious feelings and interpersonal problems. Zunin (1972) described a number of unique "contact experiences" that are useful in helping persons to improve their personal interactions and effectiveness. Castillo (1974) has collected specific experiential lessons for use in the schools; they deal with sensory awareness, imagination, communication, emotional expression, and other interpersonal concerns. More recently, I have published a program, *Self-Realization Training* (Valett, 1976), that includes numerous experiential group activities to promote self-awareness, acceptance, expression, endurance, responsibility, commitment, renewal, and self-transcendence. The following experiential activities are illustrative of those that can be used to facilitate interpersonal growth.

GROUP PROBLEM SOLVING

Objective: To be able to arrive at several possible solutions to personal problems through the use of group discussion

Procedure: Join a discussion group of 10 or 12 other class members. Write on a 3 × 5 inch card a brief description of a problem you have that you feel you need help with. Place all cards facedown on the table.

Activities

1. The teacher turns up the top card and requests that the pupil concerned read and explain the problem to the group.
2. Everyone in the discussion group listens carefully and then takes turns asking a question of the person concerned. The question should be one that will help clarify the problem.
3. Everyone writes one positive suggestion for dealing with the problem on a 3 × 5 inch card. Each person then reads and explains his suggestion and, when all suggestions have been made, the cards are given to the pupil concerned to consider.
4. The pupil concerned selects three cards containing the suggestions that are felt to be most helpful. The reasons why these are felt to be most helpful are then discussed with the group.
5. The pupil concerned writes a brief story entitled "Group Suggestions That May Help Me Deal With My Problem."

IMAGES OF CLAY

Objective: To express feelings about yourself; to explore your self-image with other people

Procedure: Divide the class into groups of four or five. Use regular modeling clay or permaplast to make an image of yourself.

Activities

1. Show your clay image to other members of your group. Discuss your image and how accurately you feel it portrays how you look.
2. Ask other group members to evaluate your image and your remarks about it.
3. Discuss the self-concept you have that cannot be portrayed in clay.
4. Take turns with each member of the group presenting his image. Listen carefully to each description and participate in evaluating each image.
5. How well do you feel the group listened to your self-description? How well do you feel they really understood you?
6. In what way was the group helpful to each other in exploring and evaluating self-concepts?
7. Pair off with another group member and continue the discussion in more detail.

SOCIAL ACCEPTANCE

There are three things extremely hard: steel, a diamond, and to know thyself.

BENJAMIN FRANKLIN

Lost friends

Tim felt lonely. He had just called several friends to plan something for Friday night, but everyone was busy with something else. Now that he stopped to think about it, he remembered that none of the gang had called him for a week or so. He had even gone to the school dance all by himself and no one had talked to him.

"I'm definitely being ignored and getting the cold treatment from the guys," Tim said to himself. Then he thought about Sam, who had always been his best friend, and he began to wonder why he had not heard from him. "If Sam doesn't call me soon, something must be wrong," he pondered. Then Tim thought, "I wonder why they don't want me around?"

1. What was Tim's concern?
2. What might Tim do to solve his problem?
3. Describe several problems that friends of yours have had.
4. What is the most important problem concerning you at this time?
5. Complete these sentences:

What really bugs me is _____.

Sometimes I worry about _____.

I get upset when _____.

I am afraid of _____.

My life is complicated by _____.

From Valett, R. *Getting it all together—A guide for personality development and problem solving.* San Rafael, Calif.: Academic Therapy Publications, 1974.

WHAT OTHERS DO FOR ME

Objective: To think about and consider what members of your family do for you
Procedure: Use butcher paper to make a 3-foot square. Draw solid black lines to make nine 1-foot squares. Print in the names of different family members (mother, father, older brother, older sister, younger brother, younger sister, grandmother, grandfather, aunt, or uncle).

Activities

1. Join a group of five or six class members and take off your shoes.
2. Take turns stepping into a square of your choice and describing to the others what you feel that person does for you.
3. Before stepping out of the square, describe something you do for that person.
4. Take several turns so you can describe at least three different family members.
5. Write a story entitled "What My Family Does for Me."

ACKNOWLEDGING SOCIAL JUDGMENTS

Be civil to all; sociable to many; familiar with few; friend to one; enemy to none.

BENJAMIN FRANKLIN

Shakes

She felt like she was going to die. The cramps and thirst were so bad that she was thrashing about on the bed out of control. Then Mary Hunter started seeing the bugs again; she screamed as they began moving toward her. Although she desperately needed a drink, she somehow knew that her husband and the doctor were right in keeping her in her room.

Since that last automobile accident happened while she was drunk, everyone knew that something had to be done. Mary also wanted to help herself, but she felt so powerless to do anything about her drinking. She wondered if her friends really cared for her or if they only wanted to see her put away where she wouldn't bother them anymore.

1. Where was Mary Hunter?
2. How did she get there?
3. What are several things that might happen to her?
4. Do you feel that other people are right in judging Mary's behavior and what might be best for her?
5. Complete these sentences:

Other people feel that I _____.

My job is _____.

I feel that society _____.

My father _____.

The best advice I ever received was _____.

Social responsibility is _____.

My conscience _____.

From Valett, R. *Getting it all together—A guide for personality development and problem solving.* San Rafael, Calif.: Academic Therapy Publications, 1974.

TRIP TO MARS

Objective: To consider the desirable qualities and characteristics of close friends and companions

Procedure: Imagine that you are about to leave on a space trip to the planet Mars where you will live for the rest of your life. You may take five other people that you do not yet know with you to live there. Think carefully for a few minutes about the kind of people you would want to take with you.

Activities

1. Draw or color a picture of the five people you would take with you.
2. Describe their ages, sex, and physical characteristics.

3. What kinds of interests and skills would you like them to have?
4. Describe their personalities and other qualities.
5. What do you feel would be the most important thing about the people you select to go with you?

GOOD STROKES

Objective: To become more aware of the importance of saying something nice about another person.

Procedure: Form a group of 10 or 12 persons. Everyone writes his name on a small card and places it in a pile. The teacher or group leader then shuffles the cards, selects one, and reads the name. The name card is then pinned on the person, who sits in the middle of the group to receive "good strokes."

Activities

1. Each group member writes something that he likes about the person selected on a 3 × 5 inch card.
2. Pupils take turns briefly reading their cards and telling the person what they like about him.
3. After speaking to the person receiving the "good strokes," each pupil pins his card on the person's shirt or blouse.
4. The person being "stroked" listens carefully but does not reply to the strokes.
5. After all "good stroke" cards have been pinned on him, the selected person removes the cards and copies them on a sheet entitled "Good Strokes From Other People."

DISCUSSION QUESTIONS AND ACTIVITIES

1. List three local places (hospitals, institutions, etc.) that might be suitable for humanistic field trips. What might be the goal of each trip?
2. What might be some of the difficulties in duplicating the Clinton, Iowa, model in other communities?
3. To what extent should pregnancy, abortion, and marriage problems be included in affective-humanistic education programs?
4. Select one of the records listed in the discussion of expressive music in this chapter, write out the lyrics, and discuss how they might be used in a lesson.
5. Read a favorite poem to the class or discussion group and suggest how it might be used as part of a humanistic education learning unit.
6. List a joke book appropriate for use with selected pupils. Present one of the jokes and explain what the objective might be in using it.
7. What other book or books would you add to those listed as "inspirational" literature?
8. Arrange with your instructor to demonstrate and critique the use of some biofeedback apparatus to your class.
9. Complete one of the self-awareness and evaluation activities listed and discuss it with your class.
10. What is a self-transaction?
11. List another educational game for use in affective education and describe the objectives involved.
12. Discuss the purpose of T-group techniques.

A person's behavior is modified by new experiences.

The child can internalize the moral values of his parents and
culture and make them his own as he comes to relate these values
to a comprehended social order and to his own goals as a social
self . . . the fundamental factor causing such a structuring
of a moral order is social participation and role taking.

LAWRENCE KOHLBERG (1964, p. 395)

CHAPTER 11

Humanistic behavior modification

THE GOALS, OBJECTIVES, units, learning activities, and model programs for humanistic education presented in this book can be used in either regular or special education programs for affective and humanistic development. The common elements in most of these lessons and activities are group discussion, social participation, and role-playing.

Because of its very nature, affective development requires interpersonal experience and involvement. Accordingly, both regular and special classroom programs should provide for extensive group participation, discussion, and self-regulation. This chapter will present several techniques that have proved useful in the development of classroom management systems in which the emphasis has been on social and intrinsic reinforcement as the primary motivation for affective development.

The child with a behavior disorder characterized by inattentiveness, distractibility, hyperactivity, and lack of self-control usually has great difficulty in learning. Children with neurological perceptual problems, mental retardation, emotional disturbance, and specific learning dysfunctions often present such behavior problems; however, these behaviors are occasionally manifested in regular classrooms and have been encountered by most experienced teachers. If such behavior is allowed to continue, the child experiences increasing failure in learning that, together with growing frustration and social maladjustment, may seriously interfere with the educational program of the entire class. In such situations it is obvious that some system of positive intervention must be instituted if the entire learning situation is not to be jeopardized.

Every teacher has some system of classroom and pupil control that supposedly enhances effective learning. In most cases an interested teacher with a flexible curriculum, well-organized lesson plans, and a realistic marking system is sufficient to provide the structure, motivation, and reward essential to learning. Children with chronic behavior disorders, however, need more than these basic essentials. First and foremost, they require a teacher capable of love and understanding, who is concerned about doing more to help the child learn. Of equal importance is the ability to define the pupil's educational needs; develop specific learning programs with realistic goals; set consistent limits; provide direction, training, and guidance; and encourage gradual and continued success through reinforcement systems of praise and rewards.

Such a humanistic approach to behavior modification has been illustrated in some detail by Rousseau's (1956/1762) description of the education of Emile. Rousseau suggested the use of firm guidance, minimal verbalization, emphasis on imitation and modeling, and many experiential lessons in which the pupil could practice "active benevolence through keeping occupied with doing all the good deeds within his power." Jung (1964, p. 254) also stressed the importance of helping the child to develop individual meaning and a sense of power over his life that would contribute to the further evolution of civilized people. The goal of making individuals *aware* so that they can help mold themselves and exercise a greater control over their own lives has been receiving increasing attention by educators. The applied research of London (1971), Mahoney and Thoresen (1974), Wilson and Davison (1975), and Valett (1974), among others, has demonstrated the feasibility of a humanistic behavior modification approach and accompanying technology. But educators are increasingly concerned with the problem of student discipline and control, and punishment remains the "correctional" method most often used. Recently, the New York Civil Liberties Union has complained that students all over the country are being punished and harassed for refusal to conform to relatively minor matters of personal taste (Haney and Zimbardo, 1975). The need is obviously great for furthering rational, humanistic, and effective means of behavior modification in the schools.

BASIC PRINCIPLES

For learning to occur the pupil must be motivated to attend, concentrate, and respond to appropriate stimuli; continued interest and motivation are dependent on some measure of success and reward for effort expended. For many children with behavior problems the fundamental difficulty has been the lack of motivation resulting from repeated failure and uninteresting lessons. For example, the pupil who is continually given work beyond his basic skills or ability seldom experiences success sufficient to motivate him to keep working. Obviously, a strong and well-organized system of rewards is essential if we wish to keep children interested in learning.

Most children who have been reared in a home and community environment in which their primary needs of physical care, love, and attention have been adequately provided for have been taught to respond to such secondary reinforcers as encouragement and recognition. These pupils are more capable of self-control and deferring immediate gratification of their inclinations. Other pupils, however, must be taught to attend, respond, cooperate, and gradually acquire self-control and responsible behavior.

It is now well accepted that children can be taught appropriate responses through conditioning procedures that are sure to reinforce or reward the specific behavior that is desired. What is necessary is the development of a reinforcement system around the appropriate responses that have been clearly identified. Furthermore, to be educationally effective the technique must provide for immediate primary or token rewards to the single pupil and must also encourage total classroom or peer group support of the individual and the group learning situation.

Azrin and Lindsley (1956) were among the first to demonstrate experimentally that a system for the reinforcement of cooperation between children was feasible. Since then, Lindsley (1963) has analyzed the terms and conditions necessary for a social reinforcement system, and Hewitt (1968) has defined the levels of educational tasks that can be programmed in a reinforcement system. Hewett (1966) has also demonstrated the effectiveness of a reward system in shaping the behavior of educationally handicapped pupils. *Newsweek* magazine has also focused public attention on the value of reward systems for keeping dropouts in school and in transforming low-achieving pupils into honor students ("Golden Grades," 1966).

Over the last few years, extensive research has been conducted on more specific social and intrinsic reinforcement systems. In a recent article, Levine and Fasnacht (1974) reviewed the research on token economies and material rewards and concluded that their use may actually reduce the frequency of those behaviors that already have intrinsic value to the person. Numerous other studies have supported the importance of developing intrinsic and social reinforcers over token and primary food rewards.

Highly effective social reinforcing peer group techniques such as "good behavior" games have been researched and developed by Barrish et al. (1969) and Harris and Sherman (1973). Other techniques using peer tutors and peer managers have been studied by Hart et al. (1968), Solomon and Wahler (1973), and Greenwood et al. (1974). The social reinforcement value of peer imitation, role-playing, and modeling is vividly illustrated in articles by Csapo (1972), Surratt et al. (1969), and Clark et al. (1975). The pragmatic use of group discussion methods and "citizens councils" as social reinforcers has been described by Valett (1966) and Stiavelli and Shirley (1968).

However, the most humanistic approach to behavior modification is the development of self or intrinsic reinforcement systems designed to develop self-control, self-determination, and self-management. A report in Benjamin Franklin's *Autobiography* demonstrated the feasibility of self-recording techniques in reducing personally defined undesirable behaviors. The value of self-recording techniques with elementary schoolchildren was researched by Milligan (1970), and similar self-management programs involving self-recording and self-reinforcing procedures have been studied and demonstrated by Lovitt (1973), Ballard and Glynn (1975), and many others. An excellent summary of the research on self-monitoring and behavior change has been presented by Kazdin (1974). The rapidly expanding use of self-control possibilities for use with exceptional children has been summarized by Kurtz and Neisworth (1976).

On the basis of these and other studies, several simple principles have emerged that can and should be used in any practical system concerned with modifying pupil behavior and improving learning. These can be briefly stated as follows:

- Pupils must be educationally programmed according to their level of development and achievement.
- Material to be learned must be systematically organized and able to elicit response and success from the pupil.
- Success in learning (desirable behavior) should be immediately rewarded. If necessary, primary reinforcement (food, praise, etc.) should be used.
- Immediate primary food or material reinforcers should be used only as part of a broader system involving social and intrinsic reinforcers.
- Rewards should be attainable after a reasonable period of effort (lessons should not be too long and should be designed to be broken down into smaller units with subsequent reinforcement as necessary).
- The pupil must be able to understand the desired behavior change, the rewards involved, and the operation of the total system. The system should be clear, available (written out), and as concretely illustrated as possible.
- Token systems should be designed to include self-recording and peer group management procedures.
- Self-reinforcement and regulation should be the goal of all humanistic behavior modification programs.

SOCIAL REINFORCEMENT TECHNIQUES

Within the educational setting, social tolerance is basic to the operation of any reinforcement system; that is, the pupil must be capable of being physically present to become part of the system. Not all children with behavior disorders can be tolerated in the public school setting. If a student's behavior is inimical to the welfare of the class or school, it may be essential to limit him to a shorter school day or, in extreme cases, to exempt him from attendance.

Most children with behavior disorders can learn to control themselves for given periods of time by reduction of attendance to a half day, a period or two, or whatever amount of time that self-control can be maintained. Sometimes such children are further aided by a mild tranquilizing medication that, together with a limited day, may make some school attendance possible. Over a period of time, most children come to prefer the stimulation of their peer group, and therefore school attendance itself becomes a strong social reinforcer.

As long as the child is part of the class, he is a member of a social system that can be managed to control his behavior. Primary reinforcers such as candies, raisins, sugared cereals, and peanuts have been found to be effective in eliciting responses and stimulating basic motivation; these rewards, however, should always be accompanied by verbal praise ("very good," "good boy," etc.) and occasional physical reinforcers such as pats on the head and back and hugging.

Tokens such as poker chips may also be used as immediate reinforcers if they are exchangeable later for food, simple toys, or social privileges. Marks for correct responses (C) can also be strong reinforcers if they, too, lead to extrinsic rewards. Tokens and check marks can also be used by the pupil to gain access to classroom activity corners such as listening centers for records and tapes, science puzzle centers, library reading centers, or arts and crafts centers. Some reinforcement systems provide for the further encouragement of good marks through awarding stars, which are exchangeable for tangible goals.

Perhaps one of the more effective social reinforcers is earned eligibility to student citizens councils, where recognition pins, special privileges, and honors are available. Of course, formal grades or report card marks can also serve as reinforcers if they are awarded relative to the pupil's ability and achievement; however, for most children with behavior disorders, report card marks are usually too removed and abstract to be effective by themselves in motivating pupil behavior.

One model social reinforcement technique applicable to elementary classes and programs for the mentally retarded or educationally handicapped is presented here. It can be modified according to the age of the pupils and the nature of their learning and behavior problems. This approach integrates both primary and secondary reinforcers and is based on the careful programming and constant evaluation of pupil behavior. The Weekly Work and Reward Record (p. 176) is retained by the pupil and serves to constantly remind him of his progress and attainment at any given time. The model is applied in the following way.

As pupils arrive at their desks, they find their individual work packets with basic assignments for the day. Specific lessons, work sheets, page references, etc. for arithmetic, reading, writing, and special training (such as visual-motor exercises) are there. The children take their first assignment and, on demonstrating that they are ready to work, are rewarded by the teacher, who hands them a poker chip. Following completion of the assignment, the child's work is immediately evaluated, and he is rewarded with a chip for each assignment completed and with another chip if the assignment was accurately done with the overwhelming majority of the items correct. The teacher also marks the child's Work and Reward Record with C following presentation of the chip.

The teacher marks each individual assignment item C if correctly done; wrong answers are not checked in any way and should become the basis for individual work with the child to enable him to understand and correct his errors and then obtain a C mark. On satisfactory completion and correction of an assignment or two (dependent on the pupil), the child is further rewarded by the teacher by being allowed to go to an activity corner of his choice for a period of time. The pupil follows a regular daily schedule of individual and class activities so that he comes to anticipate the general behavioral requirements to be made of him.

Weekly Work and Reward Record

Pupil's Name_____ Class_____ Week_____

I. Regular Assignments	Mon.	Tues.	Wed.	Thurs.	Fri.	Total
Ready to work						
Self-control and good behavior—a.m.						
Self-control and good behavior—p.m.						
Helping others						
Arts and crafts						
Physical education and games (2)						
Music and special training (2)						
Arithmetic (2)						
Reading (2)						
Writing (2)						
TOTAL CHIPS EARNED:						

II. **BLUE STAR AWARD**
15 chips = 1 blue star ☆☆☆☆☆

III. **GOLD STAR AWARD**

5 blue stars = 1 Gold Star Surprise ☆

Date awarded _____

IV. **CITIZENS COUNCIL AWARD**

Elected to Citizens Council on _____
Completed one week on Citizens Council
and awarded pin on _____

V. **CITIZENS HONOR AWARD**

earned on _____ for four
continuous weeks on Citizens Council

Under this particular system it is possible for the child to earn 15 chips during a normal school day. One chip is awarded for completion of each assignment in writing, reading, arithmetic, music, special training, and physical education and games; another chip is awarded for accuracy of work in each of these areas. One chip is awarded after the lunch period to students displaying readiness to work, self-control, and good behavior during the morning class; another chip is awarded near the end of the day to students exhibiting self-control and good behavior during the afternoon. Another chip is awarded for helping others as the occasion demands.

At the end of the school day, the teacher schedules a council meeting at which the day's work records are reviewed, problems are discussed, and chips are exchanged for candy, peanuts, or other food items. The number of chips earned is then totaled by each pupil in the daily column. When 15 chips have been earned, a Blue Star Award is gummed on the record sheet. Some children may easily earn a blue star each day; it may take 2 or more days for other children to earn this award. When five blue stars have been earned, the pupil is presented with the Gold Star Award, which is affixed to his record and the date indicated.

On Friday afternoons the council meeting is extended to include an award party. First, each pupil counts the total number of chips he has earned during the week, and an equal number of food items is placed in the class party dish. These food rewards are then shared equally by the class as a whole. During this party, pupils who have earned the Gold Star Award are allowed to select a special award from the Gold Star Surprise Box; the surprise box usually contains small trinkets such as plastic cars, whistles, balloons, and other simple inexpensive toys.

Children who have earned the gold stars are eligible for membership on the Citizens Council. After 1 week on the Citizens Council the pupil is presented with a C pin, which he is encouraged to wear during class. If the pupil fails to continue to earn at least four blue stars weekly or breaks any special conduct code established by the council, he may then be voted off the council and must earn his way back. Occasional privileges such as acting as a messenger or game leader, tutoring peers, and free time are awarded to council members. After 4 continuous weeks on the Citizens Council, pupils are automatically given the Citizens Honor Award. This may consist of such special privileges as athletic passes, theater tickets, bowling, unusual field trips, luncheon out, and related social activities.

A number of other systematic social reinforcement techniques and programs have also been designed for classroom application. A series of special responsibility charts developed by Childs (1974) helps to record daily pupil progress in acquiring desirable personal and social traits of responsible persons. Behavior record forms, tabulation methods, task cards, daily and weekly performance reports, and school integration records for direct use by teachers are presented in *Effective Teaching—A Guide to Diagnostic-Prescriptive Task Analysis* (Valett, 1970). A similar methodology has been developed by Goodwin and Coates (1976) for the practical application of behavior analysis techniques in the classroom. Several commercial firms are even beginning to market behavior modification kits and packages that stress social reinforcers for use in classroom management; one such example is the *Behavior Improvement Program* (Buckalter et al., 1975) recently produced by Science Research Associates, which can be used in both regular and special classrooms.

SOCIAL IDENTIFICATION AND MODELING TECHNIQUES

Several social identification and modeling techniques have been devised for use in modifying children's behavior. Essentially, these rely on the power of identification with influential peer models and cultural heroes of one type or another. The "hero" is a person such as another child or even a selected adult who has successfully coped with a problem situation of concern to the pupil; therefore the model's behavior may be perceived as a desirable alternative form of acting. Direct imitation, practice, and emulation with accompanying social reinforcement and praise are used. Parents and other family members, friends, selected classmates or other peers, mythological story characters such as Davy Crockett, Snow White, and Superman, and current sports figures are the persons most often studied and imitated. Successful modeling programs and techniques have been demonstrated by Bandura (1969), Sarason (1975), and Meichenbaum and Cameron (1974).

An example of commonly used modeling techniques in the classroom is presented in Chapter 4; 12-year-old Martha was taught to imitate Jane's participatory behavior. A prescriptive modeling lesson using videotape with a socially maladjusted adolescent boy has also been detailed and illustrated (Valett, 1974). Systematic approaches for teaching parents to be good models and to use social reinforcement techniques have been developed by Patterson and Gullion (1968), Smith and Smith (1966), and Valett (1969).

As a brief illustration of effective parent modeling, let us consider the case of 5-year-old Ann.

Ann: During her preschool years Ann had developed very little expressive vocabulary and limited self-care skills such as being able to dress herself. As she approached school age her parents became increasingly concerned and finally sought professional help, which resulted in their involvement in a humanistic behavior modification program within their own home. The program began with both parents systematically recording Ann's verbal expressions and the self-help skills of most concern to them. Then the parents selected several target behaviors such as words to be learned, simple sentences to be taught, and self-help skills to be acquired. Parent modeling and immediate reinforcement of desirable behaviors began to produce almost dramatic progress. For instance, Ann's father would model making her bed, dressing, brushing her teeth; etc.; then guide her through the same process; and take photographs of her completing the assigned tasks. These pictures were then mounted on a large wall chart next to daily tabulation columns and served as a systematic self-teaching guide and simple recording method. After seven detailed charts and numerous modeling sessions over a 6-month period, Ann had achieved the immediate behavioral goals set for her.

Story characters of all kinds have been used as a cognitive approach to modeling. Selected experiences or behaviors from stories and folk characters such as Tom Sawyer have long been read in class, discussed, role-played, and otherwise used as models for considering possible alternative courses of action. An interesting approach to the similar use of fairy tales has recently been proposed by Bettelheim (1976) because myth and fairy tales stimulate the imagination, clarify emotions, give recognition to common personal difficulties, and suggest solutions to the problems of children while promoting the development of self-confidence; Bettelheim demonstrates that the fairy tale is future oriented and can provide guidance for the child in terms that both his conscious and unconscious mind can understand.

The sequential steps to be followed for modifying behavior through the use of systematic modeling techniques can be summarized as follows:

1. The teacher uses videotape, film, tape, and other media to vividly collect and portray desirable and undesirable baseline pupil behaviors. The pupil needs to see and understand what his behavior actually consists of at the beginning of the modeling program.
2. The teacher models and imitates the behavior desired and verbally describes it and the tasks involved while actually demonstrating it to the pupil.
3. The teacher again models the behavior, but the pupil verbalizes the entire task and action sequence.
4. The pupil imitates the teacher's demonstration while the teacher verbally instructs and directs the task behavior.
5. The pupil does the task on his own and verbally directs himself aloud.
6. The pupil repeats the task again while directing himself with whispered verbal instructions.
7. The pupil models the task with covert verbal self-direction.
8. The pupil records each successful task behavior on a personal record chart and reinforces himself with overt and covert praise.
9. The pupil models and overtly describes the task to another pupil with similar needs.
10. The pupil teaches his peer to follow the instruction, to record progress, and to reinforce himself.

SELF-REGULATION AND CONTROL TECHNIQUES

Since Benjamin Franklin started using personal growth charts and diaries to regulate and control his own behavior, numerous other techniques and technological aids have been developed. These include the use of automatic behavior counters and recorders, conditioning and biofeedback apparatus, biorhythm calculators, social contract systems, and special exercise and behavioral programs such as relaxation, self-actualization, and assertiveness training.

The many uses of biofeedback apparatus in the classroom have been discussed by Mulholland (1973), who has shown that such equipment can enable the person to reduce anxiety and develop more pleasant states of being that facilitate learning, remembering, and retrieval. Research has shown that biofeedback techniques can enable the student to control brain waves and very specific psychophysiological responses. For example, Green et al. (1971) have presented a program, "Psychophysiological Training for Creativity," that involves conscious production of theta brain waves (a rhythm of 4 to 8 cycles per second) to produce a reverie-imagery state, permitting both the conscious and unconscious mind to propose creative solutions to problem solving. At the other extreme, Sterman has demonstrated the use of bio-feedback self-control training for epileptic and hyperkinetic children (Trotler, 1973). Kurtz and Neisworth (1976) have recently reviewed a variety of self-control strategies used with exceptional pupils; they include cue regulation, self-reinforcement, and self-observation techniques. Although it is impossible to illustrate all or most of the self-regulation and control techniques currently in use in the schools, a few of the more simple and common ones are presented here.

The Weekly Work and Reward Record (p. 176) is most effective when the pupil himself tabulates the number of chips he has earned for each assignment. Whatever system is being used, the goal must be to enable the learner to observe and monitor his own behavior and gradually to select his own goals and to record and regulate his own rate of learning. In addition to peer group pressure to retain membership on a Citizens Council once it is earned, most pupils need to develop intrinsic awareness and concern about their own specific behaviors.

Self-concern and regulation can usually be developed by techniques that help the pupil to focus on his desirable and/or undesirable behaviors. One such technique is to have the pupil observe and record the behavior of another person. The Pupil Observation Record (p. 181) can be used for this purpose. By observing, recording, and discussing the behavior of his peers, the pupil becomes more aware of what others may be concerned about. He also becomes more accepting of other persons recording and discussing his own behavior, and this awareness in and of itself often leads to immediate change.

Another self-regulation technique found to be helpful is the Weekly Citizenship Evaluation Report (p. 182). This report has many uses, including the following:

- Evaluation of a pupil by the Class Council
- Evaluation of a pupil by a class team or work group
- Self-evaluation by the pupil concerned

The form is most frequently used at the end of a week. In the form shown on p. 182 George rated his own behavior as average to very good and specified his areas of concern. We can see that he felt he did very well by cooperating with his classmates in producing the Mexico mural. He also felt very good about helping Joan do her arithmetic. His teamwork project was helping to run the projector, which he also rated good. Of special concern for self-regulation was "not yelling in class," which he rated as good (the reliability of which can be quickly checked by the observing teacher). His total points earned (35) can then be exchanged according to a contingency system developed by George and his teacher. The fact that he noted that he felt he was getting better at not yelling "so much" is a very important part of George's self-regulation program. Most pupils who make daily or weekly self-evaluations such as this and who keep their records for future comparison make gradual progress toward their behavioral goals.

PUPIL OBSERVATION RECORD

Instructions: This record is to be used when a pupil is observing and recording the behavior of another pupil. Carefully observe one or two pupils in your room. First write down their names and the time you begin to observe them. Then write a brief description of what they are actually doing as you watch them. Check any of the desirable or undesirable behaviors displayed by the pupils. If you are observing a specific behavior not listed, write it in the space provided.

Pupil(s) Observed	Time Observed	Verbal Description of Behavior	Desirable Behaviors				Undesirable Behaviors				Other Specific Behavior
			Working hard on assignment	Cooperating with group	Correcting mistakes and errors	Helping another child learn	Not working on assignment	Talking	Walking around	Not listening to teacher	
Name:											
Name:											

Comments (What did the pupil observed do very well? How might he improve?): _____

These behaviors were observed by _____

Date of observation _____

WEEKLY CITIZENSHIP EVALUATION
by: Class Council or (Self-Evaluation)

(Student) or Team Evaluated: _George Lucas_   For Week of: _March 5-9_

Desirable Behaviors	Points Awarded by Council				
	Poor	Fair	Av.	Good	Very Good
	(1)	(2)	(3)	(4)	(5)
Pays attention and works hard				X	
Completed learning assignments				X	
Made progress and corrected errors			X		
Sportsmanship in games and athletics			X		
Cooperated with classroom team on joint learning projects *(Mexico Mural)*					X
Courteous and polite to all			X		
Helped another child learn *(I helped Joan do arithmetic)*					X
Contributed to team work project *(I helped run the projector)*				X	
Other: *Not yelling in class*				X	
Total 35			9	16	10

Comments:

I'm getting better at not yelling so much.

PROGRAM EVALUATION TECHNIQUES

Humanistic behavior modification programs that utilize class councils, discussion groups, modeling, and self-regulation techniques often produce very insightful pupils. Many teachers use these procedures to involve their pupils in suggesting improvements in the entire program itself. This is most frequently done by requesting individual pupils and the class as a whole to consider specific questions such as How can we improve our council meetings and discussions? How can we improve our classroom? How can we improve our reading, writing, arithmetic? How can we learn to observe and regulate our own behaviors more effectively? Some actual responses to these questions received from an elementary school pupil discussion group were as follows:

- Require everyone to record their own behaviors.
- Give 15-minute breaks to council members to help other children who need help.
- Change the room arrangement so an area can be set aside for the three younger children to move and make "quiet noises" without disturbing others.
- Change the use of the citizenship cards by putting rewards on them when the child was good rather than marking them when he was bad or made mistakes.
- Have everyone suggest their own rewards.
- Make individual changes in our daily schedule so that we won't have the same things every day and will have more time for art, science, cooking, and making things.
- Use the videotape more often so that we can actually see our mistakes and when we are correcting ourselves.
- Let me come in at lunchtime to work on my arithmetic; I want to learn multiplication faster.
- Let us use English books like they do in other classes. ("Oh, are Language and English the same? Well, you *show* us how to use the Roberts English books and we'll understand.")
- Let the council members lead the older children to lunch first so that the younger ones can see how responsible we can be.
- Set aside a regular time every day for silent thought, meditation, and quiet relaxation.
- Let us run our own class more often, like you did the times you had a substitute.

TEACHER SELF-EVALUATION

The teacher who is truly concerned with developing an effective educational program will not hesitate to evaluate his own performance as well. Where attempts are being made to provide for individualized instruction and continuous progress toward behavioral goals and objectives, teacher self-evaluation should be used frequently.

There are many program self-evaluation procedures available to interested teachers. Most of them attempt to modify or improve pupil behavior and performance through the development of more effective teaching strategies. The self-evaluation model illustrated on pp. 184 and 185 specifies 14 key teaching strategies in the five areas of *l*ove and concern, *e*valuate and assess, *a*ssign and record, *r*einforce

MODIFYING PUPIL BEHAVIOR THROUGH EFFECTIVE TEACHING

Model "LEARN"

Teaching Strategies	All of the time	Usually	Sometimes	Occasionally	Not yet
LOVE and Concern:					
1. Do you demonstrate your care and concern for individual pupils by discussing their special needs, interests, and problems with them? . . .					
2. Do you attempt to encourage your pupils to help determine their own learning objectives and activities?					
EVALUATE and Assess:					
3. Do you diagnostically evaluate each pupil's current performance and achievement prior to the selection of individual educational objectives? .					
4. Do you involve the pupil in making self-evaluations and judgments of his own behavior and achievement?					
5. Do you critically evaluate your own attitude and curricular expectations of individual pupils to determine if they are positive and realistic? .					
ASSIGN and Record:					
6. Do you assign priority learning tasks and lessons that are *clearly understood* by the pupil?					
7. Do you maintain a room learning environment which is arranged and structured to permit pupils to work on varied assignments? . . .					
8. Do you use an individual record system that enables the pupil to record his rate of progress toward specific objectives?					

Teaching Strategies (continued)	All of the time	Usually	Sometimes	Occasionally	Not yet
REINFORCE and Reward:					
9. Do you use a token or point system in reinforcing progress toward individual and group learning objectives?					
10. Do you involve the class and class teams or groups in directly encouraging and rewarding desirable achievement and behavior? . . .					
11. Do you request your pupils to help determine their own consequences and rewards?					
NEGOTIATE and Contract:					
12. Do you involve your pupils in the determination of class rules, social regulations and learning contracts?					
13. Do you provide opportunities for your pupils to critique your curriculum and teaching methods, and to help plan and develop new learning opportunitities?					
14. Do you provide your pupils with a class council or other means whereby they may judge, reward, penalize, and control their own behavior? .					

Select one of the above strategies that you would like to implement as soon as possible and describe how this might be done:

and reward, and *n*egotiate and contract. These strategies have been found to be essential ones for teachers concerned with the development of a humanistic behavior modification program.

All of these strategies have been discussed in detail throughout this book and emphasize pupil involvement and social reinforcement. The teacher should carefully read each of the 14 strategies and then rate himself by placing a mark in the column that best describes the teacher's current performance. Qualifications may be written alongside the rating or placed on the back of the reproduced form for later use and reference. Following the self-evaluation, it is recommended that the interested teacher circle one strategy area in the model that is of most concern and that should receive priority for improvement. Some possible means of improvement and implementation should be written on the bottom of the form, which then might serve as a basis for further follow-up such as consultation or in-service training.

HUMANISTIC IMPLICATIONS

The behavior modification techniques presented in this chapter can be used to aid the teacher concerned with developing desirable behaviors in his pupils. Good teaching strategies and the principles of reinforcement can be humanistically applied with the emphasis on peer group involvement, modeling, self-regulation, and ongoing teacher evaluation of the entire program.

These techniques are most effective when clearly understood by the pupils and their parents. Teachers can obtain further reinforcement of desirable behavior by involving parents and other colleagues through occasional conferences that help them become more aware of the pupil's needs and objectives, the nature of the total program, and how they might lend support to the unique reinforcement system being used. As Wilson and Davison (1975, p. 59) have pointed out, "behavior therapy is far from being inconsistent with a humanistic philosophy. On the contrary, it is probably the most effective means of promoting personal freedom and individualism because it enhances the individual's freedom of choice."

Since the publication of *Behavior Modification in Education* (Thoresen, 1973) as the yearbook of the National Society for the Study of Education, we have seen a rapid growth in the application of more humanistic behavioral principles in educational programs of all kinds. Through the use of such techniques, persons begin to experience success and derive pleasure from increased achievement and self-control. In the years to come it can be expected that humanistic behavior modification principles will be increasingly and effectively used in educational programs for regular and exceptional students alike.

DISCUSSION QUESTIONS AND ACTIVITIES

1. Discuss the behavioral characteristics of "hyperactive" children.
2. What are the essential characteristics of effective teachers who work with children with chronic behavior disorders?
3. To what extent do you feel a "sense of power" over your own life?
4. Make a list of primary, token, social, and intrinsic reinforcers.
5. Read one of the research studies cited in this chapter and present a critique of it to your class or group.
6. What is the goal of humanistic behavior modification programs?
7. What are the most effective motivational factors in your life?
8. How might you modify the system awarding 15 chips a day for regular assignments (p. 177)?
9. Select a desirable behavior for a child to model and explain the rationale and reason involved.
10. Describe some group and other social reinforcers that could be used to ensure effective modeling.
11. Select a fairy tale that could be read, discussed, and role-played as a model for problem solving with elementary aged children.
12. Discuss the feasibility of educational programs that are designed to teach epileptic children self-control.
13. What are some of the problems that might be encountered in using the Pupil Observation Record (p. 181)?
14. Which of the strategies listed on pp. 184 and 185 do you think might be the most difficult to implement in a regular classroom?

People must learn to live together with mutual help and respect.

The new learning society will have transformed its values in such a way that learning, fulfillment, and becoming human will become its aims with all institutions directed to this end.

ROBERT HUTCHINS (1965, p. 11)

CHAPTER 12

The humanistic community

THERE IS COMMON AGREEMENT that our country is in the midst of social changes so profound that they are affecting the entire world. This, of course, is not an especially new occurrence, as our history is one of revolutionary change and constant development toward the humanistic ideals proclaimed in the Declaration of Independence and the Bill of Rights. Over the past few years, however, the technological advances of our society combined with national concern over population control and environmental pollution, the demand to extend civil rights to all groups (including women), and growing unemployment have caused the populace, especially the young, to reassess our goals and priorities and our entire life-style. In time, these factors alone would have been sufficient to produce a crisis of self-evaluation and redirection, but the additional tragedy of the Indochina War has made it increasingly clear that our entire social structure is subject to stresses that are relatively unique in our nation's history.

It is also apparent that no segment or institution in our society is going to escape careful scrutiny and critical analysis resulting in changes of a truly revolutionary nature either through the enactment of legislation or as a result of the peaceful evolution of policies. Another likely possibility is that such changes will be brought about as a result of the increasing use of protest, demonstrations, legal confrontations, and outright violence on the part of many individuals and special interest groups.

As our educational system is inextricably bound to the existing social-legal structure through policies and codes stemming from federal, state, and local boards of education, there can be no doubt that education and educators are being caught up in this social revolution. One needs only to follow the newspapers and the various professional education journals to become aware of the extent to which education is being subjected to conflicting demands and resulting stresses. My major concern at this point is to discuss the role and obligations of educators who now realize that they are indeed a part of this psychoeducational revolution. I wish to stress here that the proposed education and development of the learner take place within a particular system (usually a local district school) and that it is usually assumed that all educators will work "within the system" and the community of which it is a part.

However, many communities, schools, and educators have failed in their tasks. They have failed to produce meaningful behavioral changes in the children that they serve. This is, of course, a gross generalization, but I will attempt here to state a case for self-indictment in that we have seldom done those things that we now know are fundamental in producing more effective behavior on the part of children. The reason for this is that much confusion has existed and still exists, first, as to what kind of behavioral changes we are attempting to bring about in students and, second, as to our own priorities in how we are to proceed—especially how we are to proceed within the unique system of which we find ourselves a part. With this assertion, it should be clear that we must be intimately involved in the determination of behavioral and teaching objectives and the structure of the entire learning system by which these objectives are to be realized. It is here, for instance, that most educators have failed, because they have not given adequate time to the consideration of the learner's goals and educational tasks and to the development of those components in the environmental system by which these goals and tasks might be realized.

The problem most often presented by this dilemma is that the educator must be aware of desirable educational goals and curricular expectations and philosophy, and these are subjects in which traditional training programs have been somewhat inadequate. Because educational goals are derived from social, personal, and cultural expectations and developmental growth levels, the teacher must feel at home in judging which goals satisfy the requirements in both areas. Of basic concern is the awareness that human values and development are inextricably related. It should also be apparent that some values can be judged as more psychologically sound than others; few educators, for instance, would value violence and aggressiveness over cooperation and love. Accordingly, a good place to start is for individual learning objectives and the system's objectives to be analyzed to determine if they are compatible and to decide which ones are to receive priority emphasis. This is not an insurmountable task; enough psychological evidence now exists that we can distinguish between conflicting values and objectives and select those that further human survival and psychological wholeness.

THE QUEST FOR VALUES

What, then, are some of these human values that should be used in the development of educational programs and especially in work with those children suffering from social or personal behavior deviations within the school system? The work of many psychologists—Jung, Freud, Murphy, Allport, Rogers, Maslow, and others—has contributed to our knowledge of what constitutes psychological wholeness and the kinds of behaviors that should be fostered within any sound cultural-educational system. A few of the principles that can be derived from this extensive work are as follows:

- Psychological wholeness (or "happiness") is essentially a self-transcendent state of rational altruism.
- The process of becoming individuated or self-actualized requires meaningful involvement, personal commitment, and work.
- Self-actualization can only be achieved when basic needs, such as food and love, are gratified.
- The life instincts or drives for actualization, creativity, etc. can best be furthered under organizational and political systems of social democracy.
- Self-domination, ego control, and instinctual sublimation are essential for psychosocial integration and must be learned by the individual.

These principles can become guidelines for instructional purposes within our schools and community organizations. They can serve as the basis for program development whereby educators and other specialists design total systems enabling the child to grow and develop toward psychological wholeness. This can be accomplished by specifying operational definitions of desirable behaviors to be learned, such as cooperation and self-control, and then designing the educational structure so that appropriate educational experiences will evoke and reinforce those behaviors.

Education is being caught in the midst of conflicting cultural and social demands that negatively affect the entire system and its functioning components. Teachers can remain "neutral" and thereby professionally impotent, leaving other forces and groups to determine educational goals and policy that will adversely affect professional practice and the children we serve, or we can become actively involved both professionally and politically in the process of self-determination through the formulation of "more desirable" goals, objectives, standards, and systems of accountability. In a stimulating article, Slater (1970) stated that he did not "believe our society can long continue on its old premises without destroying itself and everything else." He went on to discuss many of the value conflicts (such as property rights over human rights, technological requirements over human needs, competition over cooperation, and violence over sexuality) that confront our society and are beginning to divide many groups (for example, young and old) therein. It is apparent that these central value issues must be of educational concern and more fully covered in the curriculum. It is also apparent that many of our young people are caught up in intense value conflicts while others are living in a "value vacuum" in which immediate self-gratification is the only guiding principle for their behavior.

There should, in fact, be no qualms about educators becoming involved in helping their students to develop meaningful personal and social values for living. After all, it has now been many years since Krathwohl et al. presented their taxonomy of educational goals and classified valuing at the pinnacle of the affective domain. In that taxonomy the importance of teaching persons how to organize their value systems was strongly emphasized. Several means of evaluating the extent to which one's value system had been developed were also illustrated. For instance, the following are three test items used as models for such evaluation (Krathwohl et al., 1964, p. 139):

- Weighs alternative social policies and practices against the standards of the public welfare rather than the advantage of specialized and narrow interest groups.
- Develops techniques for controlling aggression in culturally acceptable patterns.
- Has the tendency to act with consideration of others and their ultimate welfare.

Since then a good number of value orientation, value clarification, and value organization curriculums have been developed for school use. Some of these stress the importance of social and community values. For example, Casteel and Stahl's (1975) workbook for high school students entitled *Values Clarification in the Classroom: A Primer* contains a series of excellent lessons covering topics such as war, abortion, political honesty, crime, justice, labor problems, genetic counseling, school achievement, and loyalty.

Similar value orientation programs have been started in the elementary schools. In their book *Toward More Humanistic Instruction*, Zahorik and Brubaker (1972) present some interesting case studies of elementary school classes involved in studying such real community problems as poverty, population control, pollution, unemployment, trouble in the schools, and intolerance. Learning methods used with both elementary and secondary pupils included interviews, letters to the editor, simulation games, door-to-door polling of community residents, and pupil participation on local radio and television "talk shows." One simulation game on unemployment required pupil involvement in the following:

- Identifying feelings the technologically unemployed may have, such as feelings of frustration and failure
- Recognizing that technological unemployment occurs regardless of the efforts of the individual who has been displaced
- Considering possible alternative approaches to technological unemployment and what the unemployed may actually do about it

It is interesting to consider how many school programs throughout the country have been deliberately organized over the last few years to teach such affective skills as value organization and how they have measured their success. According to the Gallup poll's latest annual report on American education, 79 percent of the people surveyed favored "instruction in the schools that would deal with morals and moral behavior." Growing public support for moral, value, or character education is evident by the slow but steady growth of school systems that are just beginning to offer such programs. *Newsweek* magazine has recently reported the development of several new programs in Tacoma, Pittsburgh, Minneapolis, San Antonio, Irvine (Calif.), and Brookline and Cambridge (Mass.); according to the report, Lawrence Kohlberg's Stages of Moral Development model is being used as a feasible structure for offering this kind of education in the public schools (Woodward and Lord,

1976). Some special education programs have also been designed to teach selected social and affective objectives such as these, but they are markedly few in number.

The question might justifiably be raised as to whether or not our school boards and administrators are consciously aware of the degree of public concern and support for providing social, moral, and value education for all children; we might also ask to what extent school board members and administrators are committed to doing something about providing such education in our schools.

In my experience, teaching such skills has only been a secondary concern of educators and the systems in which they work, with very little direct time or attention devoted to teaching such things as value analysis, value organization, value characterization, and concomitant motivational sets towards cooperation, altruism, and love. Could it be that part of the national divisiveness we are now experiencing is due to the failure or reluctance of the educational system to develop socially desirable behaviors in children? Has "the system" gone overboard, for instance, in stressing individuality and personal freedom at the expense of the common good? In his later years Jung became increasingly concerned about this problem and pointed out that a danger exists that the production of unadapted individualists with ruthless egos may be the result; Jung's reflections are worthy of serious consideration by all of us who work with children:

> The more "scientific" our education attempts to be, the more it orients itself by general precepts and thus suppresses the individual development of the child. One of these general precepts states: "The individuality of the child should be taken into account and protected."
>
> This principle, praiseworthy in itself, is reduced to absurdity in practice if the numerous peculiarities of the child are not adjusted to the values of the collectivity. . . . It is very likely that too general an application of the principle will produce unadapted individualists rather than individuals capable of adaptation. The former are ruled by a ruthless ego, but the latter recognize the existence of factors which are equal if not superior to their own will.*

Let us consider this matter a bit further. Is it not true that much of our work has to do with children (and adults) who are ruled by a "ruthless ego"? Do we not see many children early in their school lives who lack self-control, are impulsively self-gratifying, and seemingly unconcerned or even unaware of the collective welfare? Have we not assumed that much of this deviant behavior stems inherently from the individual child and, accordingly, have we not failed to adequately examine the school and social system for etiological factors? Are not most of us aware of the peculiarities of many educational systems, which actually evoke (or teach) maladaptive and egocentric behaviors? And is it not true that, even when we have recognized that the root of many of the problems resides in the system rather than in the child,

---

*From Jung, C. Civilization in transition. Vol. 10 of *The collected works of C. G. Jung* (2nd ed.) (H. Read, M. Fordham, and G. Adler, Eds.; R. F. C. Hull, Trans.; Bollingen Series XX). Princeton, N.J.: Princeton University Press, © 1970. Reprinted by permission of Princeton University Press.

we have turned away from any active involvement or commitment to intervene and change the system?

Recently, many young people have been advocating the social reorganization philosophy of Marcuse, with its emphasis on the radical implementation of humanistic values. Seldom, however, do they acknowledge Marcuse's adage that life is a struggle with oneself and the environment. The substance of life is unpleasure, not pleasure, and its goal is meaningful labor whose fruits may result in a moment of relaxation or happiness. And as for freedom, or anarchy as some would profess, Marcuse (1970, p. 11) agrees with Freud that the basic condition of life in civilized society is the suppression and sublimation of the primal instincts, and he acknowledges that freedom is established "in the self-discipline and self-renunciation of individuals who have learned that their inalienable freedom is subject to duties not the least of which is the suppression of instinctual drives."

ENCOURAGING HUMAN ASPIRATIONS

Most human behavior can best be understood as an attempt to realize human aspirations. When personal aspirations are highly realistic and clearly defined, we have achievement orientation and integrated, purposeful behavior. When human aspirations are ill defined, lacking, or absent, we find shiftless and meaningless behavior with social and personal disorganization. And when rational, integrated, purposive strivings toward human aspirations are thwarted or prevented, individual behavior becomes socially and self-destructive.

By human aspirations I mean those distinctive goals, dreams, ideals, and images that have acquired symbolic meaning for us. They are symbolic and forceful in their own right as a result of the way we have associated words and concepts with sensory and affective experiences; these symbols seem to have a compelling, magnetic effect on our actions and predispositions. Although it is true that humanity is driven by such basic needs as hunger and sex, we are primarily a species given to the formulation of aspirations through unique abstract language systems. When clearly formulated, human aspirations tend to produce symbolic systems, which result in the creation and application of tools, practices, structures, and techniques that enhance the possibility of self-realization. For example, personal vocational aspirations— wanting to become a nurse, a salesman, a military conqueror, a doctor, an artist, a teacher—all result in the development and use of practices to accomplish that end. In a similar sense, social aspirations also compel and channel behavior in that given direction. Therefore, if we aspire as a social system to reach the moon or to "purify" the true church, we respond with the creation of scientific tools and techniques or with the appropriate inquisitional practices.

In short, the individual tends to do what he aspires to do. The essential problem in understanding a human being as a unique organism is in comprehending his wants and desires and the program that he has designed to provide for them. This is a major function of education, for education is intrinsically concerned with the continued development of human behavior in accord with the direction provided by cultural aspirations. Thus the educational system as established by the community projects the societal goals and local norms and then transmits human practices and techniques to the new generation. Education tends to shape, mold, and change the behavior of the learner in proportion to the availability of tools, the clarity of goals and aspirations, and the flexibility of the system to respond to needed change and evolution. Lacking these qualities, the educational system and the culture itself may die or be replaced by a more "healthy" system that has continued to change and evolve with the varied demands made on it.

The major task, then, of all who work within the schools is to help develop desirable human behavior. And the problem confronting the educator is essentially threefold:

- First, to define and formulate the specific behavior to be developed or changed in that given individual, subculture, or community. This involves the clarification of teacher, parent, pupil, and *system goals and aspirations* and the specific task expectation.
- Second, to work with fellow teachers to help design the total system, establish the practices, and develop the curriculum structure necessary to permit the realization of these educational aspirations.
- Third, to help evaluate the effectiveness of the learning system (including the broader "educational community" itself), the progress of the individual learner toward his goal realization, and the way that this system can continue to evolve most smoothly.

SOME HUMANISTIC COMPONENTS

A number of essential components of the system require careful design by the humanistic educator. Skinner has aptly pointed out that the task that falls to the cultural designer is to accelerate the development of practices that bring all the consequences of behavior into play. Insofar as the educator is or will become a cultural designer, I believe we can readily delineate a number of critical practices over which he can exert significant control. The following are some of these practices that we might design:

- Development of content and structure of affective education programs
- Development of alternative educational systems for those with learning problems
- Design of new systems for enhancing social cooperation
- Creation of new individualized learning systems and programs
- Creation of improved communication and in-service training systems for psychologists and teachers working together in the schools
- Systematic development and improvement of positive reinforcement programs and the teaching of love

Let us consider the last of these in some detail, since many teachers have already been designing reinforcement systems for a number of years. At the same time we have been increasingly aware of the many problems involved, among which is the danger of a mechanistic application of the basic principles of learning that may be antagonistic to human development. As an example, we have known that the use of primary reinforcers such as food and trinkets is usually of limited value with young children. The effective system must, of course, be designed to enhance token and symbolic reinforcers and eventually to transcend these to the point of intrinsic self-reinforcement. As we know, the learner who is involved in selecting and designing his own program has something of value to aspire to that is even more effective with the use of self-pacing and self-rewarding practices. In the classical sense, then, the teacher is concerned with the development of the human qualities of wisdom and temperance as critical elements in human behavior. The history of education has demonstrated what the philosophers from Plato on have emphasized, that the youth who "has the seed of these qualities implanted in him and is himself inspired, when he comes to maturity desires to beget and generate" (Plato, 1968). Certainly the adolescent who has learned self-control and temperance at an early age (perhaps as a result of a careful design) and who is self-selective and reinforcing is wise beyond his years. With such qualities of character, an individual finds it easier to realize his aspirations. It should also be recognized, of course, that these are qualities of character that must be acquired or learned if we are to become capable of loving and living with our fellow human beings.

Reinforcement systems, then, are programs that may be designed by the educator to further individual happiness through the realization of personal and social aspirations. The interdependence of cooperative personal and social reinforcement systems is not always apparent but is nevertheless basic to any such design. Hence the educator must struggle with the mechanics of structuring a system whereby love of self (egocentrism) and love of others (altruism) are balanced so that both personal and social realization can occur. Basically, then, social reinforcement is concerned with the application of the pleasure principle and the variegations of what we have traditionally referred to as love. The design of more adequate systems to provide both love and social cooperation is a central task for the educator and psychologist concerned with shaping human behavior. This is further emphasized if we accept mutual love between people as the "fundamental law of human existence." This was well formulated by Tolstoy (1963, p. 317) who also pointed out the result of its mismanagement:

> People cannot be treated without love, just as one cannot handle bees
> without care. Such is the nature of bees, if they are carelessly handled by
> a person, they hurt both themselves and him.

These observations can be summarized by proposing that the primary task of the educator concerned with affective-humanistic education should be to formulate designs to enhance altruistic behavior among people. Current reinforcement principles and technology make this a feasible aspiration that can shape our professional practice. In the past our educational systems and our professional practices have not been effectively designed to this end; consequently, many pupils have failed to realize both self- and social expectations and have even responded at times with destructive asocial and antisocial behavior. Other pupils who have been frustrated by the gross inadequacies of the system have regressed to states of anxiety, despair, or withdrawal; developed significant learning disabilities; or have even dropped out of the system itself. In short, our educational system has been primarily designed to impart cognitive skills with an undue emphasis on the acquisition of academic subject matter.

We are now becoming aware that the development of the affective and humanistic potentialities of the learner are of at least equal importance to cognitive studies. Such a change in emphasis is revolutionary and requires major adaptations in our professional aspirations and self-concepts if we are to succeed. The prime objective of all educational systems should be to meet the individual needs and aspirations of the learner so that self-realization of his uniquely human potentiality becomes at least a possibility. The design of more effective system components that teach children to relate meaningfully, to predict the consequences of their actions, to solve life problems, and to adapt to continual technological and social change is essential. This has been expressed quite simply by Toffler (1971, p. 397), the perceptive author of *Future Shock*, who projects the central task of education as expanding people's adaptive capacities. Such an instructional program must be geared to the developmental level of pupils and involve training of the emotional and aesthetic faculties as well as the intellect, since problems of humanity are never solved through an intellectual approach alone. Specific educational programs should be designed to enhance our understanding and capability in dealing with critical problems of family living, social and sexual adaptivity, political and socioeconomic involvement, and religious and spiritual development (Valett, 1963). Over the years I have become even more convinced that these should be the priority targets for the design of an effective educational system. Unless the present and coming generations become more proficient in the application of their basic learning abilities in successfully coping with the critical problems of their time, all else will be to no avail.

POLITICAL CONCERNS

There are many broader aspects of the educator's role as a designer of more effective learning systems. For example, an awareness that extreme protein deficiency caused by malnutrition in infancy commonly results in mental retardation should involve the teacher in more effective socioeconomic interventions on a preventive basis. This might result in the development of school-based early childhood programs including nutritional guidance to families, an extended school lunch and breakfast program, parent education, and even direct medical and dental care to children (such as has long been provided schoolchildren in New Zealand, for example). A similar illustration is presented in the implications of the current work of Mercer (1971) on adaptive behavior; her report of high correlations between socioeconomic variables (such as the amount of living space within the home, whether a family is buying or owns their home, and the mother's educational aspirations for her children) and the degree of adaptive behavior displayed by the child should certainly have some bearing on our professional practice. It is quite apparent that unemployment and poverty are the root cause of many of our socio-economic problems—including educational ones. Some time ago Galbraith (1969, p. 294) clearly pointed out that in order to eliminate poverty efficiently we must invest more than proportionately in the children of poor communities:

> . . . it is there that high quality schools, strong health services, and special provisions for nutrition and recreation are most needed to compensate for the very low investment that poor families are able to make in their own offspring.

Although some steps have been taken toward this end, it is apparent that in most communities there is much that needs to be done to reduce unemployment and to take major steps toward a significant reduction in poverty and its degrading effects on life and learning.

The effective educator must also be a designer and proposer of *alternative* educational systems and programs. If it is obvious, for instance, that current programs are ineffective and resulting in a significantly high dropout rate on the secondary level, what alternatives could be proposed? Would it be possible, for instance, that a community-based work-study program with little or no attempt at integration into the existing "regular" education program could become a feasible alternative? For that matter, would a work-study or outdoor education–conservation program with earlier school leaving age be a feasible alternative for many "regular" students on the verge of dropping out of the system? And what about alternative approaches to the punitive and restrictive grade-marking system such as proposed by individualized instruction, supplementary education, and continuous progress programs?

Many possibilities for changing the system are presented to us daily. Years ago Lenin presented the question What is to be done? as the starting point for considering revolutionary changes. The question remains valid as a guideline today, but, as Skinner (1971) has pointed out, "if we wish to make the social environment as free as possible of aversive stimuli we do not need to destroy that environment or escape from it—*we need to redesign it*" (italics mine). There is already considerable evidence that educators are becoming actively involved in the political process in order to redesign the social-educational-economic system of which we are all a part. Many teachers, for instance, are working with John Gardner and Common Cause for purposes of political and congressional reform. In California

a unique coalition of educators and politicians calling itself Self Determination—
A Personal Political Network* has been organized around three basic premises
(*Second Report*, 1975):

- That our personal lives and our social/political lives are highly inter-dependent
- That people have the right and capacity for exercising more power in determining their own lives and the future of society
- That technical skills and information, and supportive relationships, are vital to empowering persons to take more control in their lives

Self Determination proposes that people work together to promote their own personal growth by bringing about humanistic social changes in the society in which they live through actual involvement in politics; one member of this organization is John Vasconcellos, a legislator who has already become well known for his humanistic approach to politics. Among other things, Vasconcellos has sponsored State Assembly Bill 4481, which protects mental patients from being involuntarily forced to accept certain kinds of treatment. Another example of a humanistic approach to politics is Governor Jerry Brown, who frequently consults with such educators as Paul Ehrlich on population problems, Stewart Brand on ecological concerns, and Ivan Illich on the redesign of medical and educational delivery systems (Skelton, 1976).

The process of questioning, evaluating, planning, and redesigning the educational system may be a painful endeavor, but it is certainly an essential one for professional educators. We can no longer avoid confronting the issues presented by ineffective educational systems, and we might well consider the advice of Jung (1966): "If ever there was a time when self-reflection was the absolutely necessary and only right thing, it is now, in our present catastrophic epoch." The need for change and more effective adaptation is readily apparent, and we should be capable of responding accordingly. Only our limited imagination and ingenuity restrict the formulation of alternative responses to such pressing social and educational problems.

IMPLICATIONS FOR TEACHING

What are some of the implications of all this for teaching? First of all it is clear that the teacher must be intrinsically involved in the overall design of the instructional program. This has perhaps been best accomplished within the United States by private residential schools and camps and semiprivate enterprises that have exerted considerable control over both instructional design and program. On the international level both Israel and the Soviet Union have reported successful programs in character education, including the inculcation of specific value characterizations. For instance, Bronfenbrenner of Cornell University has for some years

---

*P.O. Box 126, Santa Clara, Calif. 95052.

closely followed the Soviet system of character education. In his book entitled *Two Worlds of Childhood: U.S. and U.S.S.R.*, he has described the effectiveness of techniques for teaching cooperation within the Soviet school and concludes that honesty, friendliness, self-reliance, and cooperation are a regular part of the Russian curriculum. It is also disconcerting to read the results of studies concerning children's readiness to engage in cheating or in denying responsibility for property damage (Bronfenbrenner, 1970) and to find that:

> Soviet children acted to support the values of adult society to a much greater extent than either Swiss or American children did. They seemed much less willing to entertain the idea of committing anti-social acts. In addition the Soviet children relied on themselves, rather than on adults to discipline the wrongdoers.

It is well known that the twenties and thirties in the United States were a period of much study and concern with character education. Among others, the work of Hartshorne and May on character organization and Havighurst and Taba's studies on adolescent character and personality, together with the many test references on character education in the *Mental Measurements Yearbook,* attest to long-term interest on the part of professionals in this country. It appears, however, that little of the research has been utilized in the development of lesson materials for classroom use. My concern in pointing out some of these specifics is to emphasize that a great deal of information is already available that can serve as a basis for the development of a program to teach social and personal skills, including value orientations. I have used this one area of education to stress the many ways that specialists should be involved with teachers in the design and implementation of an instructional system that includes the selection of priority affective objectives.

It has also been previously indicated that children with chronic learning and behavior disorders first require a teacher capable of love and understanding and concerned about doing more to help the child learn. Of equal importance is the teacher's ability to define the pupil's educational needs, develop specific learning prescriptions with realistic goals, set consistent limits, provide direction, training, and guidance, and encourage gradual and continued success through reinforcement systems of praise and rewards. To acquire such skills teachers need continued in-service training and support. One approach in meeting this need is through the organization of "program study groups." Through such provisions, teachers can be brought together on a voluntary basis to study and design such innovative programs as supplemental education, continuous progress systems, behavior modification systems in the classroom, teacher evaluation and programming of learning disabilities, experiential civics and government studies, moral and character education, and other humanistic-affective education programs.

But above all, persons must become more responsible citizens who begin to actualize their care and concern about humanizing education and the society in which we live and work. We must begin to demonstrate our belief that education should prepare people not just to earn a living but to live a more fruitful and meaningful life—a joyous, creative, sensitive, contributing, and humane life. In the words of Pirsig (1974, p. 297), "the place to improve the world is first in one's own heart and head and hands, and then to work outward from there." Rogers (1974) has also emphasized the importance of exercising one's personal will and sense of responsibility in effecting desirable educational change:

> I cannot help but conclude by saying that we have the theoretical knowl-
> edge, the practical methods, and the day-by-day skills with which to radi-
> cally change our whole educational system. We know how to bring together,
> in one experience, the intellectual learning, the range of personal emotions,
> and the basic physiological impact, which constitute significant learning by
> the whole person. Do we have the will, the determination, to utilize that
> know-how to humanize our educational institutions? That is the question we
> all must answer.*

There are many indications that humanity may be on the verge of another epochal breakthrough to new and better ways of living. By our aspirations and actions we do participate in the actual transformation of our society and its institutions to a more humanistic community of educated and wholesome persons.

CONCLUSION

In his penetrating critique of the public schools, *Crisis in the Classroom*, Silberman (1970, p. 196) concluded that "what is most wrong with American education is its failure to develop sensitive, autonomous, thinking, humane individuals." In this book we have considered why this is so and what might be done to rectify the situation. I hope that the reader will have acquired an understanding and feeling of the importance of humanistic education.

Only with such a new emphasis can we design an educational system that will make it possible for children to become more successful in their struggle with life. Years ago Wells (1920) wrote in his *Outline of History* that "human history becomes more and more a race between education and catastrophe." During this past century mankind has developed power and weapon systems that have literally been misused to the point where we have neared catastrophe and even annihilation. What humanity needs now is a new education that will enable each person to live a joyous and fruitful life rather than cringing in fear of his self-destructive tendencies.

This is all possible if we are committed to bringing it about. Such a commitment, however, involves a determination to teach our children to know themselves, to become altruistic, and to place human values and aspirations above gross materialism. Affective education can be instrumental in the attainment of such goals.

---

*From Rogers, C. *Education*, 1974, 95(2), 113-114.

The concerned teacher will contribute to this development by helping the learner to formulate his aspirations, to anticipate the future, to modify his behavior, and thereby to shape his own destiny.

The eminent historian Will Durant (1935) once defined progress as the extent to which man gains control over his environment. I would suggest that this might be altered to include control over environment *and self.* If the purpose of education is to further such progress and to help shape the environment in accord with human aspirations, then our programs and systems must be designed to that end. I hope that such an education will become a reality in the not too distant future.

DISCUSSION QUESTIONS AND ACTIVITIES

1. List several local and national social issues that have been of real concern to you.
2. Describe some specific values and characteristics of your community and how they have affected the local educational system.
3. How might a school unconsciously promote the development of aggressive behaviors instead of more socially desirable cooperative behaviors?
4. Critique the principles of psychological wholeness presented on p. 191.
5. What other social value conflicts would you add to those listed by Slater?
6. Consider the following item for evaluating a pupil's level of value organization:

   Weighs alternative social policies and practices against the standard of the public welfare rather than the advantage of specialized and narrow interest groups.

   How might a teacher determine to what extent this behavior had been acquired?
7. Suggest several other community problems that might be added to those suggested by Casteel, Stahl, Zahorik, and Brubaker.
8. Poll your class to determine how many fellow students favor "instruction in the schools that would deal with morals and moral behavior." Discuss the results with your class.
9. Define "collective welfare." To what extent should this value concept be taught within the public schools?
10. What are your own personal aspirations? Share them with a fellow student.
11. Describe some community you know or have heard about that has "died" or deteriorated due to lack of aspiration, goals, or flexibility. How might this have been prevented?
12. What might your high school have done to further reinforce and teach the value concept of mutual love between people.
13. Discuss the effects of poverty on education and individual learning.
14. How might you go about promoting your own personal growth by bringing about humanistic social changes in your community?
15. Discuss the contrasting behavior of school children in the U.S. and U.S.S.R. as reported by Bronfenbrenner.
16. What is your personal answer to Roger's question presented on p. 201?

In-service training is a necessity for professional growth.

Let such teach others who themselves excel.
ALEXANDER POPE

CHAPTER 13

Professional training

WHAT ARE THE ESSENTIAL qualities and skills required of the humanistic educator or therapist? How and where do teachers and others concerned with humanistic education acquire the necessary skills and competencies involved? Can these qualities and skills really be acquired through professional training? These are the basic questions to be considered in the final chapter of this book.

PERSONAL QUALITIES

There *are* certain personal qualities and skills required of those persons who would become humanistic educators. The first and foremost qualification is that this kind of educator must excel as a balanced and wholesome person in his own right. Koestler (1967) has pointed out that most human beings have developed an evolutionary emotional imbalance resulting from the lack of integration between our visceral brain and our cerebral cortex; this imbalance has resulted in the unique tendency of many persons to drive themselves to exhaustion, to become dependent on alcohol and narcotics, to become emotionally disturbed, to commit suicide, and even to wage massive war found in no other animal species. A new humanistic education is needed to develop integration and balance within the growing person—and the facilitator of such a process must, to a considerable extent, exemplify the desirable qualities to be emulated by others. As Krathwohl et al. (1964, p. 139) have stated, the teacher will attempt in many overt ways to model and demonstrate the ideal qualities and behaviors desired, but "since the values of our society are not completely consistent (e.g., competition vs. cooperation), the task of the teacher is markedly complicated."

Yet research and experience have both disclosed that these desirable teacher behaviors and tasks, although surely complicated, can be learned and enhanced through professional training and practice. In the past, most humanistic educators have acquired the necessary skills and knowledge through a series of slow, hap-

205

hazard, and often painful experiences. This has recently been dramatically presented in a case description of Sam, a seventh-grade teacher who over the years gradually "stumbled and fumbled his way into a real concern for his students as people, with their interests, values, and sense of right and wrong" (Charles, 1976, p. 3). However, we have known for some time now that humanistic skills, knowledge, and practices can be systematically learned and need not be left entirely to the chance events of time and experience.

An early study by Aspy (1965) disclosed that deliberate positive facilitative teacher attitudes produced happier students and significantly greater gains in third-grade reading achievement. Rogers (1969) proposed that significant learning really takes place when the subject matter is perceived by the student as relevant to his own needs; Rogers then suggested that the effective teacher is one who serves as a facilitator by minimizing threats and by involving pupils in self-initiated learning and evaluation.

The hypothesis that facilitative learning would result in increased independence, creativity, self-reliance, and achievement has been subjected to experimental study. Aspy (1969) found that teachers who offered empathy, positive regard, and congruence produced significantly superior cognitive growth in their pupils. In a series of studies conducted by the National Consortium for Humanizing Education, Aspy (1972) developed a technology for demonstrating how teachers could learn to acquire these facilitative skills; interestingly, elementary teachers proved to be more amenable to training than secondary teachers (elementary teachers were also more skillful in interpersonal relations).

Other studies by Luria, Meichenbaum, and Cameron have demonstrated the importance of talking to oneself for developing inner direction and self-determination of desirable behaviors (Meichenbaum and Cameron, 1974). Teachers who wish to develop positive facilitative behaviors begin to do so by first expressing the desire to do so and by reinforcing this positive intention through continued subvocal self-direction of their own professional behaviors. In another study, Aspy and Roebuck (1974) showed that pupil use of higher cognitive processes such as problem solving and thinking aloud (rational verbalization) is apparently a kind of interpersonal risk that is done more often when the learner is sure he is valued and held in high positive regard by the teacher; teachers can then be trained to improve such facilitation skills as giving more response to student's ideas, lecturing less often, and promoting student initiated behavior. In a recent review of the research, Rossiter (1976) summarized the essential orientation of the humanistic educator as concern with the whole person, involvement with pupils, self-awareness and commitment to personal dignity and freedom, and nondogmatic approach to learning.

TRAINING MODELS

Several professional training models that stress the acquisition of teacher facilitation skills and interpersonal relations have now been developed. Four of these will be considered here. The educational experiences, techniques, and methodologies used in all of these models are now being utilized widely in college and universities and in ongoing in-service and continuation training programs.

Freedom to Learn model

The Freedom to Learn model is based on Roger's (1969, pp. 325 to 342) proposal that teachers should be personal facilitators. One of the most interesting applications of this model took place at Immaculate Heart College in Southern California. An experimental project in self-directed change was designed to involve the college, several high schools, and a number of elementary schools. The project provided for the use of intensive T-groups, encounter groups, and human relations workshops as the basic tool for educational change and development. These group experiences were offered to school administrators, teachers, parents, and students alike (Rogers, 1974).

Participants' evaluations and feedback reports received from elementary and secondary teachers indicated that the in-service "facilitator-encounter workshops" had dramatic effects on changing instructional techniques. The use of such group procedures with high school students also resulted in positive attitudinal changes of students toward self, fellow students, and teachers and a new openness to learning.

Objective evaluation of the new self-directed group facilitative program at Immaculate Heart College showed increased student interest and participation in classes and in initiating constructive change and innovations in teaching. Students in education were also beginning to help initiate, design, and direct their own professional training programs.

Teacher Effectiveness Training

Building on the work of Rogers, Aspy, and others, Gordon has developed a systematic Teacher Effectiveness Training program. Methods and skills are taught through workshop groups that significantly improve teacher-pupil communication skills. For example, teachers are introduced to a series of problem-solving strategies that enable them to arrive at solutions that meet teacher needs as well as pupil needs.

Teacher Effectiveness Training activities include both theory and practice. The basic concepts of self-esteem, personal responsibility, and "active listening" are stressed through experiential lessons. For instance, teachers role-play involvement sessions with students in which they learn to attend and listen actively to what students are actually concerned about. Acquiring active listening skills enables the teacher to relate more effectively to the student and work out mutually agreeable compromises for most problem situations. The program also includes other conflict resolution strategies and classroom management techniques helpful to teachers.

In his film *Teacher Effectiveness Training,** Gordon illustrates and explains the concepts of "active listening," the no-lose method of resolving conflicts, and

---

*Media Five, 1011 N. Cole Ave., Hollywood, Calif. 90038

"I" messages; public school teachers who have successfully used these techniques in the classroom also share their experiences on film. This model has been described in detail by Gordon (1974) in his book.

Schools Without Failure

The Schools Without Failure model was developed by Glasser (1969) and utilizes reality therapy principles and techniques. This model shows teachers how to conduct different kinds of classroom meetings and discussion groups that tend to facilitate learning and solve interpersonal problems. Teachers are trained to become effective group facilitators, to become meaningfully involved with pupils, and to place responsibility on the child for learning constructive behavior.

A number of teacher training films are now available to help educators implement this model in the schools. The following films (available from Media Five) all present Glasser in a variety of classroom settings that help to illustrate the principles and techniques involved.

> *Glasser On Schools* (19 minutes)
> *Schools Without Failure* (46 minutes)
> *A Success-Oriented Classroom* (28 minutes)
> *Why Class Meetings* (28 minutes)
> *The Reality of Success* (28 minutes)

• • •

The Freedom to Learn, Teacher Effectiveness Training, and Schools Without Failure models all stress the importance of developing professional facilitation skills and interpersonal techniques. Few educators would doubt the importance of facilitating continuing progress and self-directed learning, conducting classroom discussion groups, and acquiring active listening skills. Teachers also need to learn how to talk more effectively with their students, and several professional training techniques have been developed to help improve verbal communication between teachers and students.

One such method is called Interaction Analysis and was created by Flanders (Amidon and Flanders, 1963). This training technique enables teachers to observe and analyze their own verbal interactions with pupils. Subsequently, the effective teacher learns to talk less, involve students more, and become more accepting, clarifying, and encouraging in verbal exchanges with students. Another similar approach to improving verbal interactions has been described by Ginott as "congruent communication," which he defines as harmonious and authentic communications in which the words expressed fit the feeling involved. Ginott's (1972) book *Teacher and Child* contains numerous anecdotal verbal interchanges between teachers and pupils that have proved very useful in professional training programs.

Considerable research indicates that these facilitation and communication skills can be acquired through systematic professional training and practice. Obviously, these are desirable skills for all educators and should be developed in part through college or university courses and laboratory experiences. Unfortunately, however, very few teacher training institutions have required course offerings in professional facilitation and communication skills (by whatever names they might be called). Usually, concerned teachers must take elective counseling, special education, or psychology classes if they wish to acquire these particular competencies. Ideally, personal involvement in some human relations laboratory experience or interpersonal growth group should be required of all teaching aspirants.

Affective curriculum models

Humanistic education demands that the teacher be an effective person and facilitator of learning. The three models just presented are, in essence, different kinds of communication models. The teacher who has acquired these essential communication skills can apply them in any educational setting. Earlier in this book it was stated that such techniques have been successfully employed by mathematics and foreign language instructors as well as by other subject matter specialists, regular grade school teachers, and by special educators of all kinds. In short, humanistic skills and techniques can and should be employed in all forms of traditional education.

These facilitation and communication skills must also be used as an integral part of affective curriculum models in which the teacher actually uses his own personality to teach carefully selected affective lessons. Affective curriculum models emphasize emotive and humanistic content and subject matter that is to be directly taught to the pupil. The teacher therefore must also be knowledgeable of and trained in these newly developing curricular offerings. This requires that teachers learn about and personally experience lessons from such varied programs as DUSO, TA, TM, and the many others previously presented in this book.

Professional training in affective curriculum models is now being offered by many colleges and universities and through extension courses and workshops. In most cases such classes are labeled Humanistic Education, Social and Affective Education, or Affective-Humanistic Education. Invariably, such courses involve extended laboratory and field experiences in which the new curriculum can be demonstrated and experimented with. There are, of course, many new affective curriculums being developed throughout the country. One of the newest is the Human Behavior Curriculum Project funded by the National Science Foundation. This project consists of 30 teams of high school teachers, students, and psychologists in different parts of the country who are designing 2- to 3-week instructional modules for use in secondary schools. A *Module Design Handbook* is being distributed from the project office at Carleton College in Northfield, Minnesota. Eventually, several major curriculum models like this will be available to interested educators.

However, with the rapid growth of affective and humanistic education, it cannot be expected that aspiring educators will be trained in all or even most of these emerging curriculum models. But professional training programs will undoubtedly offer their trainees increasing exposure to curriculum principles and representative curriculum models and will require some proficiency in their use. In the future, then, professional training will focus on the development of facilitative skills and their application in affective curriculums.

FORMAL TRAINING PROGRAMS

Formal training in humanistic education is now offered in many institutions of higher learning. A few of these are briefly described here along with their distinctive offerings. For current and more detailed information the reader should write directly to the institution concerned.

University of California, Santa Barbara

With funding from the Ford Foundation, Brown began a pilot project to explore ways to adapt approaches in the affective domain to the school curriculum. After attending extensive workshops at Esalen Institute, educators participating in the project began to develop a theoretical foundation and a number of techniques that they then termed Confluent Education, which refers to the integration of the affective and cognitive elements in learning (Brown, 1971). Following extensive field application in cooperating public schools, this model has been further developed and is now being used in the professional training program of the School of Education at the University of California, Santa Barbara.

The essence of this program has recently been described by Phillips (1975). The goal is to produce humanistic educators who are nonmanipulative persons and who have the critical capacity to make choices that expand human consciousness and to project meaning into the world. A three-pronged approach to training is used and includes the following:

- Modeling the type of educational environment it seeks to create in the schools (demonstrating cognitive respect, participation, and nonmanipulation of pupils)
- Involvement of students in a critical examination of their own thoughts, feelings, and actions as educators (active participation in personal and group growth experiences)
- The development of "social literacy," or critical consciousness of the social context of which the school system is a part (including ways to influence, redesign, and change the system itself)

This is one of the very few models with an extensive theoretical rationale and an empirical base of field experience. It has already made a significant contribution to teacher education and it can be expected to be even more influential in the years ahead.

Boston University

Representative of the newer interdisciplinary eclectic approaches to professional training is the program at Boston University. This program in humanistic education gives sustained attention to the special problems of how to derive concepts more cogently from experience, how to ground experience more adequately on a theoretical base, how to test theory more systematically in field settings, how to examine seriously the social, political, and ethical assumptions and implications of experiential learning, and how to understand better the nature of the experience itself (*Humanistic Education,* 1975).

Located in the School of Education and coordinated through the Department of Humanistic and Behavioral Studies, this program offers both undergraduate and graduate training. Component areas of study include Meaning and Context of Humanistic Education, Authority and Power, Values and Evaluation, Change, Consultation, Research, Self, Human Relations, Creativity, and Curriculum and Design.

The undergraduate major includes such unique course offerings as Introduction to Humanistic Education, Existentialism and Education, Humanistic Analysis of Educational Programs, Education and Moral Development, and Practicum in Humanistic and Behavioral Studies. Many advanced graduate classes are also offered on both the master's and doctoral levels. Program graduates become teachers; administrators; counselors and teachers in prisons, hospitals and other institutions; and private humanistic therapists.

California State University, Fresno

Professional training in affective-humanistic education is also being incorporated in specialist programs for teaching exceptional persons. Many exceptional individuals have affective and behavioral problems (as well as other learning disabilities); it is important that special teachers be prepared to deal with these problems.

The California State University, Fresno, program is typical of those institutions offering graduate specialist training in this field. Students who already have a basic teaching credential may proceed to earn a Learning Handicapped Specialist Credential and a Master of Arts in Special Education degree. Graduate classes are all conducted as seminars with accompanying laboratory and field experience and are offered in the following developmental sequence:

Introduction to Exceptional Children	Language and Cognitive Abilities
Introduction to Learning Disabilities	Behavior Modification in the Schools
Individualized and Prescriptive Instruction	Counseling Exceptional Children and Parents
Motor, Sensory, and Perceptual Abilities	Vocational-Career Education
Evaluation of Exceptional Children	Social and Affective Education

This program is also competency based. For example, Social and Affective Education is a seminar and laboratory course on the development and remediation of social and affective skills and abilities and also includes model programs for normal children and prescriptive interventions for those with social and personal behavior disorders. Students must make oral and written critiques of current humanistic research and model programs. They must then demonstrate and critique selected affective education programs to the class. A major competency requires actual involvement with a person who has an affective problem and requires prescriptive teaching or therapy and a case presentation to the class. The final competency is a traditional one of designing and completing an indepenent research paper or project relevant to social and affective education. Students must also participate in an ongoing experiential laboratory designed to enhance their own awareness of the self-actualization process.

Humanistic Psychology Institute

The Humanistic Psychology Institute (HPI) is a private graduate school that offers advanced training at the doctoral level in humanistic psychology and education. It is an educational extension of the Association for Humanistic Psychology. Founded in 1970, the HPI is a university without walls offering an interdisciplinary program; each student's course of study and projects are individually designed and implemented. The admission procedures attempt to select only those students who are best able to conduct self-directed study and whose project proposals appear to be of definite benefit to humankind.*

The HPI faculty has included such distinguished humanists as Richard Farson, Stanley Krippner, George Leonard, Sam Keen, and various visiting professors such as Moshe Feldenkrais of Israel. Although some intensive advanced seminars and workshops are conducted by the institute, most of the training occurs through carefully designed field projects and faculty supervision. So far, several hundred research fellows have been enrolled, all of whom have pursued innovative and humanly beneficial research intended for publication or replication.

Other formal training programs

It is, of course, impossible to list and describe most of the formal training programs now being offered in humanistic education. However, the following are some representative institutions that have programs with a special emphasis:

The University of Massachusetts (Amherst, Mass.)
Located in the School of Education, this program is directed by Sidney Simon and has a heavy emphasis on values education.

Center for Life Long Learning, Hunter College (New York, N.Y.)
This center emphasizes ongoing workshops and institutes in humanistic education for practicing teachers.

School of Special Education and Rehabilitation, University of Northern Colorado (Greeley Colo.)
A major center for preparing special educators, it also has a humanistic emphasis.

Department of Counseling and Guidance, Eastern Michigan University (Ypsilanti, Mich.)
An interdisciplinary program in humanistic counseling and guidance.

Sonoma State College (Sonoma, Calif.)
One of the few colleges offering an undergraduate major in humanistic psychology and psychic studies.

---

*For more information contact Hank Basayne, Executive Officer, Humanistic Psychology Institute, Box 42340, San Francisco, Calif. 94101.

Antioch College/Cold Mountain Institute (Vancouver, B.C.)

   An experimental Master of Arts program in humanistic education and psychology located on Granville Island in natural surroundings.

University of Connecticut (Storrs, Conn.)

   The National Institutes of Mental Health have developed a cooperative teacher training program at this institution, which has resulted in the production of innovative curriculum materials in humanistic education.

College of Human Learning and Development, Governors State University (Park Forest South, Ill.)

   This institution has developed an extensive laboratory experience as part of its teacher education program. The Humanistic Teaching Skills Laboratory is an innovative and successful approach to experiential learning.

Continuing education

   An increasing emphasis is being placed on continuing and in-service education for professionals of all kinds. This may take the form of required attendance at workshops and other in-service training offerings within the school system itself, or it may require participation in elective extension courses and other approved professional growth experiences. Such continuing education is being widely offered in actual field settings by numerous colleges and universities and by private consulting organizations as well.

   Continuing education differs from the more traditional formal education in that degrees or professional credentials are usually not made available through this means. However, promotional credit, relicensing, and salary advancement training are all commonly acquired in this way. Some of the major continuing education and in-service training offerings in humanistic education are presented here.

University of California Extension, Santa Cruz

   Most state university extension programs now offer a wide variety of training opportunities in humanistic education. One such example is the University of California Extension at Santa Cruz. The course announcements for the Winter and Spring of 1976 contain the following courses and workshops:

Creative Dreaming
Altered States of Awareness
Accepting the Challenge of Intimacy
Songs of Love
Awareness and Integration Through
   Movement and Art
The Healing Process
Touch and Psychotherapy with Children
Touch and Enrichment in Our Lives
A Workshop on Assertive Behavior
Transactional Analysis of Life Scripts
Change and Crisis in Adult Life
Managing Anxiety
A Workshop on Human Potentialities
The Single Woman's Search for Self

Coping Effectively with Difficult People
Raising Self-Esteem in Children
Conflict Resolution
A Biofeedback Workshop for
   Professionals
Energy Within
Advanced Values Clarification Workshop
Teaching Human Sexuality
A Workshop in Confluent Education
Synergic Education: Teaching for Both
   Sides of the Mind
Teacher Effectiveness Training
   Workshop
Individualized and Personalized Learning
Caring About Hyperactive Children

Association for Humanistic Psychology

The Association for Humanistic Psychology is a worldwide network formed in 1962 for the development of the human sciences in ways that recognize our distinctively human qualities and that work toward fulfilling the innate capacities of people and society. The association transcends the usual academic boundaries to include a broad spectrum of disciplines and approaches to human experience and behavior (*What is AHP?* 1975). Continuing education programs are provided through regional conferences and workshops and during the annual national meeting which provides numerous training opportunities. The association publishes the quarterly *Journal of Humanistic Psychology* and monthly *Newsletter*. In addition the Education Network brings together members interested in humanistic education. The Network is responsible for editing the Education section of the AHP *Newsletter;* distributes educational materials and papers; sponsors workshops, conferences, and special courses; and compiles a list of humanistic schools.

American Educational Research Association

The American Educational Research Association is a special interest group of professional educators formed in 1971 with the purpose of promoting and disseminating applied research in affective education.* In cooperation with the West Virginia College Institute it publishes a quarterly newsletter, *The Affect Tree,* that informs teachers about current research projects, models, programs, books, educational materials, and professional issues in humanistic education. In addition it sponsors the publication of special books and reports such as *Activities and Exercises for Affective Education,* a frequently revised practical handbook for use by teachers.

Esalen Institute

Esalen Institute is a center to explore the trends in education, religion, philosophy, and the physical and behavioral sciences that emphasize the potentialities and values of human existence. Its activities consist of seminars and workshops, residential programs, consulting, and research (*Esalen Catalog,* 1976). Esalen is certified as a nonprofit educational institution and is the first major "growth center" in the world to offer humanistic training for educators of all kinds.

Training programs and opportunities are available in two locations. Weekend workshops and evening courses are available at the San Francisco center. Workshops and extended week-long and residential programs are held at the Big Sur center. Through the years many major figures in education and psychology have given workshops at Esalen; among these are Aldous Huxley, Gerald Heard, Alan Watts, Arnold Toynbee, Ken Kesey, S. I. Hayakawa, Linus Pauling, Paul Tillich, Norman O. Brown, Rollo May, Bishop James Pike, Carl Rogers, B. F. Skinner, Carlos Casta-

---

*For more information contact Kent Beeler of the American Education Research Association, 13 Boone Hall, Eastern Michigan University, Ypsilanti, Mich. 48197.

neda, and Abraham Maslow. A sample of the course offerings in the January-March 1976 *Esalen Catalog* illustrates the diversity of humanistic learning opportunities available at this center:

Dance as Meditation	Growth Through Risk Taking
A Psychosynthesis Workshop	Exploring Self-Acceptance
Biofeedback and Altered States of	Schizophrenia as the Visionary Mind
Consciousness	Feldenkrais and Massage
Psychic Liberation	The Gestalt Process
Self-Experience	Leadership Training
Centering	Introducing Humanology
The Wisdom of the Body	Bioenergetics
Yoga for Modern Living	On Friendship
Energy	Paths of Transformation
Interpersonal Sensing	

In addition, Esalen conducts special summer workshops on topics of current interest to educators (Confluent Education, open schools, futuristic education, etc.). It also publishes a variety of books and materials useful for teachers interested in affective-humanistic education. Esalen will continue to be a major center for the development of human potential, and its programs can be expected to make significant contributions to the transformation toward a more humanistic society.

Center for Studies of the Person

The Center for Studies of the Person is one of the major private humanistic research centers in the United States. It was founded for the purpose of promoting interdisciplinary humanistic studies, and its staff consists of noted humanists such as Carl Rogers. Most of the research is conducted by visiting fellows who retreat to the center at La Jolla, California, for study and contemplation for several months at a time. The program is entirely individualized and is open for advanced graduate study to carefully selected applicants. Typically, professors, therapists, and researchers use their fellowship time to write and produce scholarly books and materials of value in furthering humanistic education and psychology.

Erhard Seminars Training

Erhard Seminars Training (est) was developed by Werner Erhard. The purpose of the training is to transform the participant's ability to experience living "so that his or her problems clear up in the process of life itself" (*What is the Purpose*, 1974). The training sessions usually take place over 2 consecutive weekends and consist of basic theory, intensive personal confrontation, group encounter, and sharing experiences. As a result of such intensive personal involvement, participants develop increased self-awareness and self-acceptance, which is hoped to make them more contented and effective human beings.

Special est seminars are held for educators and other professionals. It has been widely used as a specific program of in-service personal growth training by business firms, correctional and medical institutions, and schools of all kinds. Some of the

California school systems using est training for teachers are Laguna Honda in San Francisco, Oakland, Cupertino, and Castro Valley (Divoky, 1975). The training has also been modified for direct use with children and youth as another form of affective education. The children's training takes 4 days and includes body awareness exercises, participation games and songs, individual sharing, and discussion. Teenagers can participate in 10-day summer workshops in special settings such as Squaw Valley, California.

Although est training is expensive, it does provide a relatively quick and intensive personal immersion in humanistic education for those educators who desire such an experience in preparation for teaching others. By itself, however, it is inadequate as a complete form of professional training because of its very limited theoretical framework, lack of curriculum content, and inadequate exposure to other models and research results.

Designing local training programs

Most professional in-service training programs for teachers are conducted by local school districts. Programs are usually developed by committees of representative teachers, administrators, and other educators who come together to design a program suitable to their own needs. Such training is frequently conducted in the form of ongoing workshops and practical follow-up sessions in local classrooms with fellow educators as instructors. An outstanding example of this kind of training is the in-service Teacher Preparation for Affective Education program conducted by the School District of Philadelphia (Levin, 1972); in this program it was found that experienced classroom teachers mastered affective skills such as gaming, role-playing, fantasizing, physicalizing, improvising, grouping, and other experiential techniques more successfully than student teachers or new teachers.

A multitude of in-service training material in affective-humanistic education is now available. In addition to materials and curricular programs presented in this book, audiovisual resources make it possible to offer teachers very specific training within their own school or home. For example, the production of cassette tapes for in-service training offers almost unlimited flexibility and choice of material; one such company, Sigma Information, Inc., has a Behavioral Sciences Tape Library* for professionals. The following offerings are included:

Self-Actualization	Affective-Humanistic Education
Diagnosis and Treatment of Minimal	An Affective School Counseling Program
Brain Dysfunction	The Affective Development of Children
Children with Learning Disabilities	and Teachers in School
Behavior Modification in the Classroom	

In addition hardly a month goes by without the publication of new resource guides such as the *Humanistic Education Sourcebook* (Read and Simon, 1975), which

---

*A comprehensive catalog of cassettes is available from Sigma Information, Inc., 240 Grand Ave., Leona, N.J. 07601.

PROFESSIONAL COURSE/WORKSHOP EVALUATION

Course title: _____

Date and time given: _____
What were the objectives of this course?

To what extent were the objectives accomplished?

What did you like best about this course?

What did you like least about this course?

Please comment on the effectiveness of the following:
    Class discussions and presentations

    Laboratory experiences

    Books and materials used

    Projects and assignments

    Tests or exams

    The instructor

Please suggest how this course could be improved for future students.

Comments:

Do not sign your name

can be used as a discussion base for local in-service training. Ideally, professional training should consist of a combination of formal preparation in colleges and universities, selected continuing education workshops, and ongoing in-service programs specifically designed for local needs. However, whatever form it may take, all professional training experiences should involve careful evaluation by the participants to determine feasibility and how the program could be improved; a typical evaluation form used for such a purpose is presented on p. 217.

SUMMARY

In this chapter we have reviewed the major issues and approaches in the professional training of humanistic educators. These included the desirable personal qualities of the teacher, current training models, formal programs offered by colleges and universities, and several different kinds of continuing education. Professional training in humanistic education is still in its infancy, but already many new and innovative approaches have been tried and developed and are now being made available. In the years to come this will continue to be one of the most rapidly expanding areas of teacher education.

This book has been concerned with introducing the basic principles, methods, and models of humanistic education. It has stressed the importance of actualizing human potentialities for growth and creativity, of self-awareness and self-determination, and of student-centered teaching and learning. The role of the humanistic educator has been presented as a facilitator of this growth process through the modeling of acceptance and respect for the thoughts and feelings of others and by designing new ways of helping them to become more capable and worthy persons. Through such means it is possible to create a more supportive humanistic educational and social system that will help children learn more effectively and that will benefit all humanity.

DISCUSSION QUESTIONS AND ACTIVITIES

1. Think of an effective humanistic teacher you have known and describe his outstanding personal qualities.
2. List several conflicting values of our society that make it difficult for teachers to decide what and how they should model for their students.
3. Describe the major "facilitative" behaviors desired of humanistic educators.
4. Role-play a facilitating teacher and a nonfacilitating teacher presenting a lesson.
5. Design your own ideal professional training program and discuss it with your class.
6. What is "active listening"? Demonstrate it with your discussion group.
7. Lead a simulated classroom discussion group concerned with clarifying and solving interpersonal problems of sixth-grade pupils.
8. Select several interchanges from Ginott's *Teacher and Child;* role-play them and discuss alternative verbal interactions that might be possible.
9. Assume you are a member of a professional humanistic curriculum project team designing instructional modules and lessons. What kind of module or lessons would you be most interested in designing?
10. Present an oral critique of one of the formal professional training programs presented in this chapter.
11. What are the three major ways of acquiring continuing education?
12. Describe a continuing education program being offered in your geographical area in which you might be interested in participating.
13. Critique the use of est with schoolchildren.
14. What are some of the advantages of designing a local in-service training program for teachers interested in humanistic education?
15. How interested are you in becoming a humanistic educator?

References

CHAPTER 1

Bloomfield, H., Cain, M., Jaffe, D., and Kory, R. *TM—Discovering inner energy and overcoming stress.* New York: Dell Publishing Co., Inc., 1975.

Gollub, W. *Summary of research 1970-1971: Affective education project.* Philadelphia: The School District of Philadelphia, Pa., 1971.

Harris, T. *I'm OK—You're OK: A practical guide to transactional analysis.* New York: Harper & Row Publishers, 1969.

Inside Out—A guide for teachers. Bloomington, Ind.: National Instructional Television Center, 1972.

Maslow, A. H. Toward a humanistic biology. *American Psychologist*, 1969, *24*, 732.

McCurdy, J. Experiment in education—A school that parents built. *Los Angeles Times*, November 28, 1975, pp. 1-2.

Meichenbaum, D., and Cameron, R. The clinical potential of modifying what clients say to themselves. In M. Mahoney and C. Thoresen (Eds.), *Self-control: Power to the person.* Monterey, Calif.: Brooks/Cole Publishing Co., 1974.

Project Alpha. Niles, Mich.: Niles Community Schools, 1974.

Valett, R. Task analysis and the development of social behavior: Peri. In *Learning disabilities—Diagnostic prescriptive instruments.* Belmont, Calif.: Fearon Publishers, 1973.

Williams, H. D. Experiment in self-directed Education. *School and Society*, 1930, *31*, 715-718.

CHAPTER 2

Bloom, B. S. (Ed.). *Taxonomy of education objectives: Handbook 1, cognitive domain.* New York: Longmans, Green & Co., Inc., 1956.

Goodlad, J. The schools vs. education. *Saturday Review*, April 19, 1969, pp. 59-61; 80-82.

Krathwohl, D. R., Bloom, B. S., and Masia, B. B. *Taxonomy of educational objectives: Handbook 2, affective domain.* New York: David McKay Co., Inc., 1964.

Rogers, C. R. *Client-centered therapy.* New York: Houghton Mifflin Co., 1942.

Toffler, A. *Future shock.* New York: Bantam Books, Inc., 1971.

Valett, R. *Effective teaching.* Belmont, Calif.: Fearon Publishers, 1970.

Warner, S. A. *Teacher.* New York: Bantam Books, Inc., 1964.

CHAPTER 3

Gardner, John W., *The recovery of confidence.* New York: W. W. Norton & Co., Inc., 1970.

Holt, J. Why we need new schooling. *Look*, January 13, 1970.

Joint Committee on Educational Goals and Evaluation, California Legislature. *The way to relevance and accountability in education.* Sacramento, Calif.: May 1970.

Jung, C. G. The development of personality. In *Collected works* (Vol. 17). New York: Pantheon Books, Inc., 1954.

Newsweek, October 25, 1972, p. 44.

Valett, R. E. *A psychoeducational inventory of basic learning abilities.* Belmont, Calif.: Fearon Publishers, 1968.

Valett, R. E. *Programming learning disabilities.* Belmont, Calif.: Fearon Publishers, 1969.

Valett, R. E. *The remediation of learning disabilities.* Belmont, Calif.: Fearon Publishers, 1974.

White House Conference on Children, 1970, Re-

port to the President. Washington, D.C.: U.S. Government Printing Office, 1970.

Wilson, C. *The outsider.* New York: Houghton Mifflin Co., 1956.

CHAPTER 4

Bloom, B. S. (Ed.). *Taxonomy of educational objectives: Handbook 1, cognitive domain.* New York: Longmans, Green & Co., Inc., 1956.

Dewey, J. *Experience and education.* New York: Macmillan Publishing Co., Inc., 1950.

Gevarter, W. Humans: Their brain and their freedom. *Journal of Humanistic Psychology,* 1975, *15*(4), 79-90.

Harrow, A. *Taxonomy of the psychomotor domain: A guide for developing behavior objectives.* New York: David McKay Co., Inc., 1972.

Heath, D. Affective education. *School Review,* May, 1972, p. 117.

Henderson, S. *Introduction to philosophy of education.* Chicago: The University of Chicago Press, 1947.

Krathwohl, D. R., Bloom, B. S., and Masia, B. B. *Taxonomy of educational objectives: Handbook 2, affective domain.* New York: David McKay Co., Inc., 1964.

Mahoney, M., and Thoresen, C. (Eds.). *Self control: Power to the person.* Monterey, Calif.: Brooks/Cole Publishing Co., 1974.

Maslow, A. H. *Motivation and personality.* New York: Harper & Row, Publishers, 1970.

Russell, B. *Education and the good life.* New York: Liveright, 1970.

Rousseau, J. J. *Emile.* New York: Teacher's College Press, 1956. (Originally published, 1762.)

Silberman, C. E. *Crisis in the classroom.* New York: Random House, Inc. 1970.

Valett, R. *Self-actualization.* Niles, Ill.: Argus Communications, 1974.

CHAPTER 5

Aspy, D., and Hadlock, W. The effects of high and low functioning teachers upon students performance In R. Carkhuff and B. Berenseon, *Beyond counseling and therapy.* New York: Holt, Rinehart & Winston, Inc., 1967.

Azrin, N., and Lindsley, O. The reinforcement of cooperation between children. *The Journal of Abnormal and Social Psychology,* 1956, *52,* 100-102.

Bandura, A., and Walters, R. *Social learning and personality development.* New York: Holt, Rinehart & Winston, Inc., 1963.

Black, W. Self concept as related to achievement and age in learning disabled children. *Child Development,* 1974, *45,* 1137-1140.

Bloom, B. S. *Stability and change in human characteristics.* New York: John Wiley & Sons, Inc., 1965.

Bloomfield, H., Cain, M., Jaffe, J., and Kory, R. *TM—Discovering inner energy and overcoming stress.* New York: Dell Publishing Co., Inc., 1975.

Borton, T. Reach, touch, and teach. In S. Coopersmith and R. Feldman (Eds.), *The formative years—Principles of early childhood education.* San Francisco: Albion Publishing Co., 1974.

Braud, L., Lupin, M., and Braud, W. The use of electromyographic biofeedback in the control of hyperactivity. *Journal of Learning Disabilities,* 1975, *8*(7), 21-26.

Bronfenbrenner, U. Soviet methods of character education: Some implications for research. *American Psychologist,* 1962, *17,* 550-564.

Brookover, W. B. *Self-concepts of ability and school achievement* (U.S. Office of Education cooperative research project No. 1636). East Lansing: Michigan State University Press, 1965.

Brown, B. B. Recognition of aspects of consciousness through association with EEG alpha activity represented by a light signal. *Psychophysiology,* 1970, *6,* 442-452.

Bryan, J., and Walbeck, N. The impact of words and deeds concerning altruism upon children. *Child Development,* 1970, *41,* 747-757.

Buhler, C. Basic theoretical concepts of humanistic psychology. *American Psychologist,* 1971, *26,* p. 378-386.

Bullis, H., and O'Malley, E. *Human relations in the classroom* (courses 1 and 2). Wilmington: Delaware Society for Mental Hygiene, 1947.

Character Education Program Report. Valley Vista, Calif.: Valley Vista School District, 1971.

Cleaver, E. *Soul on ice.* New York: Dell Publishing Co., Inc., 1968.

Cole, C., Oetting, E., and Miskimins, R. Self-concept therapy for adolescent females. *Journal of Abnormal Psychology,* 1969, *74,* 642-645.

Coopersmith, S. *The antecedents of self-esteem.* San Francisco: W. H. Freeman & Co., Publishers, 1967.

Coopersmith, S. Studies in self-esteem. *Scientific American,* February 1968, *218,* 96-106.

Dewey, J. Some aspects of modern education. *School and Society,* 1931, *34,* 583-584.

Eysenck, H. J. *The inequality of man.* San Diego: Edits Publishers, 1975.

Fraiberg, S. The right to feel. In S. Coopersmith and R. Feldman (Eds.), *The formative years—Principles of early childhood education.* San Francisco: Albion Publishing Co., 1974.

Franklin, B. *Autobiography*. New York: Books, Inc., no date.

Freud, S. *Collected papers* (Vol. 4). New York: Basic Books, Inc., Publishers, 1959.

Gesell, A., and Illg, F. *The child from five to ten*. New York: Harper & Brothers, 1946.

Getzels, J., and Jackson, P. *Creativity and intelligence*. New York: John Wiley & Sons, Inc., 1962.

Gevarter, W. B. Humans. Their brain and their freedom. *Journal of Humanistic Psychology*, 1975, *16*(4), 89.

Glasser, W. How can we help young children face reality and become responsible human beings? Address presented at the E.S.E.A. Workshop for Primary Reading Specialists, Los Angeles, August 17, 1966.

Guilford, J. P. *The nature of human intelligence*. New York: McGraw-Hill Book Co., 1967.

Harlow, H. The nature of love. *American Psychologist*, 1958, *13*, 673-685.

Harlow, H. *Learning to love*. San Francisco: Albion Publishing Co., 1971.

Harman, W. The social implications of psychic research. In E. Mitchell (Ed.), *Psychic exploration: A challenge for science*. New York: G. P. Putnam's Sons, 1974.

Hartshorne, H., and May, M. *Studies in the nature of character* (3 vols.). New York: Macmillan Publishing Co., Inc., 1928-1930.

Havighurst, R. *Developmental tasks and education*. Chicago: The University of Chicago Press, 1948.

Havighurst, R., and Taba, H. *Adolescent character and personality*. New York: John Wiley & Sons, Inc., 1949.

Heaton, O., and Orme-Johnson, D. Influence of transcendental meditation on grade point average: Initial findings. In *Scientific research on transcendental meditation: Collected papers*. Los Angeles: MIU Press, 1974.

Jacobson, E. *Progressive relaxation*. Chicago: The University of Chicago Press, 1948.

Jones, R. M. *Fantasy and feeling in education*. New York: Harper & Row, Publishers, 1969.

Jung, C. The development of personality. In *Collected works* (Vol. 17). New York: Pantheon Books, Inc., 1954.

Jung, C. G. The structure and dynamics of the psyche. In *Collected works* (Vol. 8). New York: Pantheon Books, Inc., 1960.

Keasey, C. Social participation as a factor in the moral development of preadolescents. *Developmental Psychology*, 1971, *5*, 216-220.

Kohlberg, L. The development of moral charac-

ter and ideology. In M. Hoffman and L. Hoffman (Eds.), *Review of child development research*. New York: Russell Sage Foundation, 1964.

Krippner, S. The use of hypnosis and the improvement of academic achievement. *The Journal of Special Education*, 1970, *4*, 451-460.

LeShan, L. *The medium, the mystic, and the physicist*. New York: The Viking Press, Inc., 1974.

Linden, W. Practicing of meditation by school children and their levels of field dependence-independence, test anxiety, and reading achievement. *Journal of Counseling and Clinical Psychology*, 1973, *41*, 139-143.

Maddi, S. Existential sickness and health. *The University of Chicago Magazine*, July/October 1971, p. 5.

Maslow, A. H. *Toward a psychology of being*. New York: D. Van Nostrand Co., Inc., 1962.

Maslow, A. *The farther reaches of human nature*. New York: The Viking Press, Inc., 1971.

McConnell, R. A. *ESP curriculum guide*. New York: Simon & Schuster, Inc., 1971.

McKnight, H. *Silva mind control*. Laredo, Tex.: Institute of Psychoorientology, 1973.

Meditation high in Texas prison. *The Fresno Bee*. January 11, 1976, p. 88.

Mitchell, E. *Psychic exploration*. New York: G. P. Putnam's Sons, 1974.

Murphy, G. *Human potentialities*. New York: Basic Books, Inc., Publishers, 1958.

Myrick, R., and Kelly, F., Jr. Group counseling with primary school–age children. *Journal of School Psychology*, 1971, *9*(2), 137-143.

O'Connor, R. Relative efficacy of modeling, shaping, and the combined procedures for modification of social withdrawal. *Journal of Abnormal Psychology*, 1971, *79*, 327-334.

Ornstein, R. *The psychology of consciousness*. San Francisco: W. H. Freeman & Co. Publishers, 1972.

Parapsychology *Newsweek*, March 4, 1974, pp. 52-57.

Petit, C. How adults assess their own high school education. *San Francisco Chronicle*, January 19, 1976, p. 6.

Poland, R. *Human experience—A psychology of growth*. St. Louis: The C. V. Mosby Co., 1974.

Raths, J. A strategy for developing values. In S. Coopersmith and R. Feldman (Eds.), *The formative years—Principles of early childhood education*. San Francisco: Albion Publishing Co., 1974.

Rice, R. Educo-therapy: A new approach to delinquent behavior. *Journal of Learning Disabilities*, 1970, *3*, 16-23.

Rice, R. Premature infants respond to sensory stimulation. *APA Monitor*, November 1975. pp. 8-9.

Rogers, E., and Vasta, R. The modeling of sharing effects associated with vicarious reinforcement, symbolization, age, and generalization. *Journal of Experimental Child Psychology*, 1970, *10*, pp. 8-15.

Rosenthal, R. The Pygmalion effect lives. *Psychology Today*, September 1973, p. 60.

Rosenthal, R., and Jacobson, L. *Pygmalion in the classroom*. New York: Holt, Rinehart and Winston, Inc., 1968.

Ross, S. Effects of intentional training in social behavior on retarded children. *The American Journal of Mental Deficiency*, 1969, *73*, 912-919.

Samples, R. *The metaphoric mind*. Reading, Mass.: Addison-Wesley Publishing Co., 1974.

Samples, R., and Wohiford, R. *Openings: A primer for self-actualization*. Reading, Mass.: Addison-Wesley Publishing Co., 1974.

Schwartz, G. Biofeedback as therapy. *American Psychologist*, 1973, *28*, 672.

Seeman, W., Nidich, S., and Banta, T. The influence of transcendental meditation on a measure of self-actualization. *Journal of Counseling Psychology*, 1972, *19*(3), 184-187.

Simpson, D., and Nelson, A. Attention training through breathing control to modify hyperactivity. *Journal of Learning Disabilities*, 1974, *7*, 274-283.

Staub, E. The use of role playing and induction in children's learning of helping and sharing behavior. *Child Development*, 1971, *42*, 805-816.

Suomi, S., and Harlow, H. Social rehabilitation of isolate-reared monkeys. *Developmental Psychology*, 1972, *6*, 487-496.

Swenson, G. Grammar and growth: A French connection. *Education*, 1974, *95*(2), 115-127.

Szent-Gyoergyi, A. Drive in living matter to perfect itself. *Synthesis*. 1974, *1*(1), 12-24.

Taylor, J. *Superminds*. New York: The Viking Press, Inc., 1974.

Toffler, A. *Future shock*. New York: Bantam Books, Inc., 1971.

Uri Geller. *APA Monitor*, February 1974, p. 4.

Valett, R. *Self-actualization*, Niles, Ill.: Argus Communications, 1974.

White, A. Humanistic mathematics: An experiment. *Education*, 1974, *95*(2), 128-133.

Williams, H. Experiment in self-directed education. *School and Society*, 1930, *31*, 715-718.

CHAPTER 6

Bronfenbrenner, U. *Two worlds of childhood: U.S. and U.S.S.R.* New York: Russell Sage Foundation, 1970.

Carkhuff, R. The development of systematic human resource development models. *The Counseling Psychologist*, 1972, *3*, 4-30.

Driscoll, F. TM as a secondary school subject. *Phi Delta Kappan*, 1972, *14*(4), 236-237.

Erikson, E. *Identity: Youth and crisis*, New York: W. W. Norton & Co., Inc., 1968.

Havighurst, R. *Developmental tasks and education*. Chicago: The University of Chicago Press, 1948.

Kohlberg, L. The child as a moral philosopher. *Psychology Today*, September 1968, pp. 25-30.

Krathwohl, D. R., Bloom, B. S., and Masia, B. B. *Taxonomy of educational objectives: Handbook 2, affective domain*. New York: David McKay Co., Inc., 1964.

Piaget, J. *The moral judgment of the child*. New York: Harcourt, Brace & World, Inc., 1932.

Rousseau, J. *Emile* (W. Boyd, Trans.). New York: Teachers College Press, 1956. (Originally published, 1762.)

CHAPTER 7

Alschuler, A., Tabor, D., and McIntyre, J. *Teaching achievement motivation*. Middletown, Conn.: Education Ventures, Inc. 1970.

Bessell, H., and Palomares, U. *Human development program*. San Diego, Calif.: Human Development Training Institute, 1973.

Borton, T. Reach, touch, and teach. *Saturday Review*, January 18, 1969, pp. 58-61.

Brown, G. *Human teaching for human learning*. New York: The Viking Press, Inc., 1971.

Brown, G. *The live classroom: Innovations through confluent education and gestalt*. New York: The Viking Press, Inc., 1975.

Bruner, J. *Man: A course of study*. Cambridge, Mass.: Educational Development Center, Inc., 1967.

Bullis, H., and O'Malley, E. *Human relations in the classroom* (courses I and II). Wilmington, Del.: Delaware Society for Mental Hygiene, 1947.

Dickerson, W., Foster, C., Walker, N., and Yeager, F. A humanistic program for change in a large city school system. *Journal of Humanistic Psychology*, 1970, *10*(2), 111-120.

Foster, C., and Back, J. A neighborhood school board: Its infancy, its crisis, its growth. *Education*, 1974, *95*(2), 145-162.

Glasser, W. *Reality therapy*. New York: Harper & Row, Publishers, 1965.

Goldstein, H. *The social learning curriculum.* Columbus, Ohio: Charles E. Merrill Publishing Co., 1974.

Gollub, W. *Summary of research* (School District of Philadelphia Affective Education Program). Philadelphia: Board of Education, 1971.

Jones, R. M. *Fantasy and feeling in education.* New York: New York University Press, 1968.

Knaus, W. *Rational-emotive education: A manual for elementary school teachers.* New York: Institute for Rational Living, 1974.

Long, B. Behavioral science for elementary school pupils *The Elementary School Journal,* 1970, 70, 253-259.

Long, B. Increasing depth of self perception in children through a course in psychology: A feasibility study of a teacher training program, and a model for elementary school behavior science as an agent of primary prevention. In H. Dupont (Ed.), *Educating emotionally disturbed children: Readings* (2nd ed.). New York: Holt, Rinehart & Winston, Inc., 1975.

Mental health in the classroom (Report of the Committee on Mental Health in the Classroom of the American School Health Association). *The Journal of School Health,* 1963, 33(7a), 3-36.

Mosher, R., Sprinthall, N. Psychological education in secondary schools. *American Psychologist,* 1970, 25(10), p. 11.

Munger, R. *Behavioral science education project.* Ann Arbor, Mich.: Washtenaw County Community Mental Health Center, 1975.

Ojemann, R. The human relations program at the State University of Iowa. *Personnel and Guidance Journal,* 1959, 37, 199-207.

Randolph, N., and Howe, W. *Self enhancing education.* Stanford, Calif.: Stanford University Press, 1966.

Winstein, G., and Fantini, M. (Eds.). *Toward humanistic education: A curriculum of affect.* New York: Praeger Publishers, Inc., 1970.

CHAPTER 8

Berne, E. *Games people play.* New York: Grove Press, Inc., 1964.

Bloomfield, H., Cain, M., Jaffe, D., and Kory, R. *TM—Discovering inner energy and overcoming stress.* New York: Dell Publishing Co., Inc., 1975.

Fundamentals of Progress (Scientific research on Transcendental Meditation). Los Angeles, Calif.: National Center for Transcendental Meditation, 1974.

Harris, T. *I'm OK—You're OK: A practical guide to transactional analysis.* New York: Harper & Row, Publishers, 1969.

James, M., and Jongeward, D. *Winning with people: Group exercises in transactional analysis.* Reading, Mass.: Addison-Wesley Publishing Co., Inc., 1973.

Knowlson, T. In Baughman, M. D. (Ed.). *Educator's handbook of stories, quotes and humor.* New York: Prentice-Hall, Inc., 1963, p. 93.

LeShan, L. The case for meditation. *Saturday Review,* February 22, 1975, pp. 26-27.

Rubottom, A. E. Transcendental Meditation and its potential uses for schools. *Social Education,* December 1972, p. 854.

Simon, S., Howe, L., and Kirschenbaum, H. *Values clarification—A handbook of practical strategies for teachers and students.* New York: Hart Publishing Co., Inc., 1972.

CHAPTER 9

Guilford, J. P. *The nature of human intelligence.* New York: McGraw-Hill Book Co., 1967.

CHAPTER 10

Carlson, E. Games in the classroom. In N. Postman and C. Weingartner, *Teaching as a subversive activity.* New York: Dell Publishing Co., Inc., 1969.

Castillo, G. *Left-handed teaching—Lessons in affective education.* New York: Praeger Publishers, Inc., 1974.

Coleman, J. S. Learning through games. *NEA Journal,* 1967, 56, 69-70.

Drummond, R. Personal correspondence, May 1974.

Emerson, R. W. Circles. *Essays* (Vol. 10), 1847.

Keeler, G. Whether they like it or not, these students must marry. *The Fresno Bee,* May 6, 1975, p. D2.

King, M. *Biofeedback in the high school curriculum.* Paper presented at the Sixth Annual Meeting, Biofeedback Research Society, Monterey, Calif., February 1, 1975.

Lerner, A. Poetry as therapy. *APA Monitor.* July 1975, p. 4.

Mayhugh, V. Supervisor of student-built Homes. *The Clinton* (Iowa) *Herald,* April 28, 1975, p. 13.

McCormack, P. Biggest education gap comes in job skills. *The Fresno Bee,* January 18, 1976, p. A17.

Miceli, F. Education and reality. In N. Postman and C. Weingartner, *Teaching as a subversive activity.* New York: Dell Publishing Co., Inc., 1969.

Peso, A. *Experience in action: Toward a psy-*

chology of human movement. New York: New York University Press, 1972.

Valett, R. *Getting it all together—A guide for personality development and problem solving.* San Rafael, Calif.: Academic Therapy Publications, 1974.

Valett, R. *Self-realization training.* Privately published, 1976.

Zunin, L. *The first four minutes.* New York: Ballantine Books, Inc., 1972, pp. 237-260.

CHAPTER 11

Azrin, N., and Lindsley, O. The reinforcement of cooperation between children. *The Journal of Abnormal and Social Psychology,* 1956, *52,* 100-102.

Ballard, K., and Glynn, T. Behavioral self-management in story writing with elementary school children. *Journal of Applied Behavioral Analysis,* 1975, *8,* 387-398.

Bandura, A. *Principles of behavior modification.* New York: Holt, Rinehart & Winston, Inc., 1969.

Barrish, H., Saunders, M., and Wolf, M. Good behavior game: Effects of individual contingencies for group consequences on disruptive behavior in a regular classroom. *Journal of Applied Behavioral Analysis,* 1969, *2,* 119-124.

Bettelheim, B. *The uses of enchantment.* New York: Alfred A. Knopf, Inc., 1976.

Buckalter, G., Presbie, R., and Brown, P. *Behavior improvement program.* Chicago: Science Research Associates, Inc., 1975.

Childs, C. Structure + responsibility = progress. *Teaching Exceptional Children,* Spring 1974, *6,* 145-146.

Clark, H., Boyd, S., and MaCrae, J. A classroom program teaching disadvantaged youths to write biographic information. *Journal of Applied Behavioral Analysis,* 1975, *8,* 67-75.

Csapo, M. Peer models reverse the "one bad apple spoils the barrel" theory. *Teaching Exceptional Children,* Fall 1972, *4,* 20-24.

Franklin, B. *Autobiography.* New York: Books, Inc., no date.

Golden grades. *Newsweek,* 1966, *67*(14), p. 62.

Goodwin, D., and Coates, T. *Helping students help themselves: How you can put behavior analysis into action in your classroom.* Englewood Cliffs, N.J.: Prentice-Hall, Inc., 1976.

Green, A., Green, E., and Walters, E. *Psychophysiological training for creativity.* Paper presented at the meeting of the American Psychological Association, Washington, D.C., 1971.

Greenwood, C., Sloane, H., and Baskin, A. Training elementary aged peer behavior managers to

control small group programmed mathematics. *Journal of Applied Behavioral Analysis,* 1974, *7,* 103-114.

Haney, C., and Zimbardo, P. It's tough to tell a high school from a prison. *Psychology Today,* June 1975, p. 30.

Harris, V., and Sherman, J. Use and analysis of the good behavior game to reduce disruptive classroom behavior. *Journal of Applied Behavioral Analysis,* 1973, *6,* 405-417.

Hart, B., Reynolds, N., Baer, D., Brawley, E., and Harris, F. Effect of contingent and noncontingent social reinforcement on the cooperative play of a preschool child. *Journal of Applied Behavioral Analysis,* 1968, *1,* 73-76.

Hewett, F. The Tulare experimental class for educationally handicapped children. *California Education,* 1966, *3*(6), 6-8.

Hewett, F. *The emotionally disturbed child in the classroom.* Boston: Allyn & Bacon, Inc., 1968.

Jung, C. *Civilization in transition.* New York: Pantheon Books, Inc., 1964.

Kazdin, A. Self-monitoring and behavior change. In M. Mahoney and C. Thoresen (Eds.), *Self control: Power to the person.* Monterey, Calif.: Brooks/Cole Publishing Co., 1974.

Kohlberg, L. Development of moral character and moral ideology. In *Review of Child Development Research* (Vol. 1). New York: Russell Sage Foundation, 1964.

Kurtz, P., and Neisworth, J. Self control possibilities for exceptional children. *Exceptional Children,* 1976, *42,* 212-217.

Levine, F., and Fasnacht, G. Token rewards may lead to token learning. *American Psychologist,* 1974, *29,* 817-820.

Lindsley, O. Experimental analysis of social reinforcement: Terms and methods. *The American Journal of Orthopsychiatry,* 1963, *33,* 624-633.

London, P. *Behavior control.* New York: Harper & Row, Publishers, 1971.

Lovitt, T. Self management projects with children with behavioral disabilities. *Journal of Learning Disabilities,* 1973, *6,* 138-150.

Mahoney, M., and Thoresen, C. (Eds.). *Self control: Power to the person.* Monterey, Calif.: Brooks/Cole Publishing Co., 1974.

Meichenbaum, D., and Cameron, R. The clinical potential of modifying what clients say to themselves. In M. Mahoney and C. Thoreson (Eds.), *Self control: Power to the person.* Monterey, Calif.: Brooks/Cole Publishing Co., 1974.

Milligan, B. Effects of self-recording on rate of disruptive behavior. Unpublished masters thesis, San Jose State College, 1970.

Mulholland, T. It's time to try hardware in the classroom. *Psychology Today*, July 1973, pp. 103-104.

Patterson, G., and Gullion, M. *Living with children*. Champaign, Ill.: Research Press, 1968.

Rousseau, J. *Emile*. New York: Teachers College Press, 1956.

Sarason, I. Cited in H. Eysenck, *The inequality of man*. San Diego, Calif.: Edits Publishing Co., 1975.

Smith, J., and Smith, D. *Child management*. Ann Arbor, Mich.: Ann Arbor Publishers, 1966.

Solomon, R., and Wahler, P. Peer reinforcement control of classroom problem behavior. *Journal of Applied Behavioral Analysis*, 1973, 6, 49-56.

Stiavelli, R., and Shirley, D. The citizenship council: A technique for managing behavior disorders in the educationally handicapped class. *Journal of School Psychology*, 1968, 6, 147-156.

Surratt, P., Ulrich, R., and Hawkins, P. An elementary student as a behavioral engineer. *Journal of Applied Behavioral Analysis*, 1969, 2, 85-92.

Thoresen, C. (Ed.). *Behavior modification in education*. (72nd Yearbook of the National Society for the Study of Education, Part I). Chicago: University of Chicago Press, 1973.

Trotler, S. Biofeedback helps epileptics control seizures. *APA Monitor*, 1973, 4(14), p. 5.

Valett, R. A social reinforcement technique for the classroom management of behavior disorders. *Exceptional Children*, 1966, 33, 185-189.

Valett, R. *Modifying children's behavior*. Belmont, Calif.: Fearon Publishers, 1969.

Valett, R. *Effective teaching—A guide to diagnostic-prescriptive task analysis*. Belmont, Calif.: Fearon Publishers, 1970.

Valett, R. *The remediation of learning disabilities* (2nd ed.). Belmont, Calif.: Fearon Publishers, 1974.

Valett, R. *Self actualization*. Niles, Ill.: Argus Communications, 1974.

Wilson, T., and Davison, G. Behavior therapy: A road to self control. *Psychology Today*, October 1975, p. 59.

CHAPTER 12

Bronfenbrenner, U. *Two worlds of childhood: U.S. and U.S.S.R.* New York: Russell Sage Foundation, 1970.

Casteel, J., and Stahl, R. *Value clarification in the classroom: A primer*. Pacific Palisades, Calif.: Goodyear Publishing Co., Inc., 1975.

Durent, W. *The story of civilization: Part I*. New York: Simon & Schuster, Inc., 1935.

Galbraith, J. K. *The affluent society* (2nd ed.). Boston: Houghton Mifflin Co., 1969.

Hutchins, R. *The learning society*. New York: Praeger Publishers, Inc., 1965.

Jung, C. Civilization in transition. In *The collected works of C. G. Jung* (Vol. 10, 2nd ed.). Princeton, N.J.: Princeton University Press, 1970.

Krathwohl, D. R., Bloom, B. S., and Masia, B. B. *Taxonomy of educational objectives: Handbook 2, affective domain*. New York: David McKay Co., Inc., 1964.

Marcuse, H. *Five lectures*. Boston: Beacon Press, 1970.

Mercer, J. *The development of adaptive behavior*. Presentation to the Special Study Institute for School Psychologists, University of California, Santa Cruz, August 5, 1971.

Pirsig, R. *Zen and the art of motorcycle maintenance*. New York: William Morrow & Co., Inc., 1974.

Plato. *The symposium*. New York: Heritage Press, 1968.

Rogers, C. Can learning encompass both ideas and feelings? *Education*, 1974, 95(2), 113-114.

Second report on Self Determination—A Personal Political Network. Santa Clara, Calif.: 1975.

Silberman, C. *Crisis in the classroom*. New York: Random House, Inc., 1970.

Skelton, N. Brown . . . I'm not a mystery. *The Fresno Bee*, February 29, 1976, p. C1.

Skinner, B. F. Beyond freedom and dignity. *Psychology Today*, August 1971, p. 42.

Slater, P. Cultures in collision. *Psychology Today*, July 1970, p. 31.

Toffler, A. *Future shock*. New York: Bantam Books, Inc., 1971.

Tolstoy, L. *Resurrection*. New York: Heritage Press, 1963.

Valett, R. *The practice of school psychology*. New York: John Wiley & Sons, Inc., 1963.

Wells, H. G. *Outline of history* (Chapter 15). 1920.

Woodward, K., and Lord, M. Moral education. *Newsweek*, March 1, 1976, pp. 74-75.

Zahorik, J., and Brubaker, D. *Toward more humanistic education*. Dubuque, Iowa: William C. Brown Co., Publishers, 1972.

CHAPTER 13

Amidon, E., and Flanders, N. *The role of the teacher in the classroom*. Minneapolis: Paul S. Amidon & Associates, Inc., 1963.

Aspy, D. A study of three facilitative conditions and their relationship to the achievement of *third grade students.* Unpublished doctoral dissertation, University of Kentucky, 1965.

Aspy, D. The effect of teacher offered conditions of empathy, positive regard, and congruence upon student achievement. *Florida Journal of Educational Research,* 1969, *11*(1), 39-48.

Aspy, D. *Toward a technology for humanizing education.* Champaign, Ill.: Research Press, 1972.

Aspy, D., and Roebuck, F. From humane ideas to humane technology and back again many times. *Education,* 1974, *95*(2), 163-171.

Brown, G. *Human teaching for human learning: An introduction to confluent education.* New York: The Viking Press, Inc., 1971.

Charles, C. *Individualizing instruction.* St. Louis: The C. V. Mosby Co., 1976.

Divoky, D. Affective education: Are we going too far? *Learning,* October 1975, p. 22.

The Esalen catalog: January-March 1976. San Francisco: Esalen Institute, 1976.

Ginott, H. *Teacher and child.* New York: Macmillan Publishing Co., Inc., 1972.

Glasser, W. *Schools without failure.* New York: Harper & Row, Publishers, 1969.

Gordon, T. *Teacher effectiveness training.* New York: Peter H. Wyden/Publisher, 1974.

Humanistic Education (Bulletin of the School of Education). Boston, Mass.: Boston University, 1975.

Koestler, A. *The ghost in the machine.* New York: Macmillan Publishing Co., Inc., 1967.

Krathwohl, D. R., Bloom, B. S., and Masia, B. B.

Taxonomy of educational objectives: Handbook 2, affective domain. New York: David McKay Co., Inc., 1964.

Levin, M. *Teacher preparation for affective education* (Affective Education Development Program). Philadelphia: School District of Philadelphia, 1972.

Meichenbaum, D., and Cameron, R. The clinical potential of modifying what clients say to themselves. In M. Mahoney and C. Thoresen (Eds.), *Self-control: Power to the person.* Monterey, Calif.: Brooks/Cole Publishing Co., 1974.

Perspective. Santa Cruz: University of California Extension, 1976.

Phillips, M. Education for non-manipulation: A model teacher training program. *The Affect Tree,* 1975, *1*(2), 2-3.

Pope, A. *An essay on criticism,* 1:15.

Read, D., and Simon, S. (Eds.), *Humanistic education sourcebook.* Englewood Cliffs, N.J.: Prentice-Hall, Inc., 1975.

Rogers, C. *Freedom to learn.* Columbus, Ohio: Charles E. Merrill Publishing Co., 1969.

Rogers, C. After three years: My view and that of outside evaluators. *Education,* 1974, *95*(2), 183-189.

Rossiter, C., Jr. Maxims for humanizing education. *Journal of Humanistic Psychology,* 1976, *16,* 75-80.

What is AHP? San Francisco: Association for Humanistic Psychology, 1975.

What is the purpose of the est training? San Francisco: Erhard Seminars Training, 1974.

Index

A

Accepting help, 151
Achievement motivation, 116-117
Achievement orientation, 194
Acknowledgment, 14
Active listening, 207
Adaptive behavior, 68, 107, 109, 198
Adolescence, 74
Alternative behavior, 162
Alternative education, 198
Altruism, 196
Anger, 85
Aspirations, 10, 150, 194-195
Assignments, 175
Association for Humanistic Psychology, 212, 214
Attention and concentration, 4, 13-14, 172-173

B

Baseline behaviors, 179
Basic learning abilities, 28-34
    conceptual, 30
    gross motor, 28-29
    language, 30
    perceptual-motor, 29-30
    sensory-motor, 29
    social, 30
Becoming, 37-40, 44, 136
Behavior(s)
    adaptive, 68, 107, 109, 198
    alternative, 162
    baseline, 179
Behavior modification
    principles of, 174
    records, 63-64
    systems, 171-173
Behavioral science education, 122-123
Behavioral Science Tape Library, 216
Biofeedback, 64, 157
    and self-control, 179-180

Biological determinants, 38-39
Body awareness, 159-160
Brain functions, 64

C

Canfield-Crescent Heights School, 3
Cartoons, 154-155
Center for Studies of the Person, 215
Character, 45, 66
Character education, 199-200
Childhood, 74
Citizens Council, 173, 177
Civil rights, 189
Cleveland job development program, 150
Clinton home construction program, 151
Clothing, 14
Coalitions, 199
Cognitive development, 11
Cognitive mastery, 16
Communication, congruent, 208
Concentration and attention, 4, 13-14, 172-173
Confluent Education, 121-122, 210
Consequences, 68, 107-108
Contact comfort, 60
Contemporary education, 1
Contemporary music, 152
Continuing education
    American Educational Research Association program, 214
    Esalen Institute program, 214-215
    extension courses, 213
Continuous progress, 3
Cooperation, 173
Correct (C) marks, 175
Creative expression, 15, 59-60, 79, 80
Creativity training, 180
Critical emotional concerns, 84
Critical thinking, 16

Cultural experience, 16
Curriculum, 39, 45, 74
  models, 209-210

D

Death, 88
Destructiveness, 99
Developing Understanding of Self and Others
  (DUSO), 133-134
Developmental stages, 60, 66
  affective, 23-24
  cognitive, 22-23
  psychomotor, 20-22
Diet, 13
Dignity, 18
Dimensions of Personality, 130-131
Discipline, 172
Discussion groups, 62
Divergent production, 16
Dreams, 92
Dropouts, 173
DUSO, 133-134

E

Ecology, 44
Education
  alternative, 198
  behavioral science, 122-123
  character, 199-200
  contemporary, 1
  continuing, 213-215
  health, 116
  humanistic, 1, 2-3, 7
  psychological, 124-125
  rational-emotive, 119-120
  Teacher; *see* Teacher education
Education Network, 214
Educational goals
  confusion of, 190-191
  humanistic, 2, 6, 9, 12-13, 27, 36-37, 43-46
  priorities, 45, 190
  pupil self-goals, 46
  system, 46
  teacher, 46
  traditional, 1, 10, 11
Educational Policies Commission, 45
Educational systems
  design of, 195-196
  effective, 197
  failure of, 193-194
  reorganization of, 28
Educator as cultural designer, 195
Ego states, 132
Egocentrism, 196
Élan vital, 34
Elementary resource materials, 143-145
Emile, 44
Emotional concerns, 61, 84
Erhard Seminars Training, 215-216
Esalen Institute, 214
Evolution, 9, 12
Expressing feelings, 53

F

Facilitative learning, 206
Failure, 208
Faith, 97
Family relationships, 153, 166
Feelings, 53, 61-62, 84-85, 161
Field trips, 149
Focus on Self-Development, 131-132
Freedom of choice, 186
Friendship, 67, 168
Frustration, 89

G

Gallup poll, 192
Games, 163-164, 173
Group problem solving, 165

H

Happiness, 37-39
Health, 14, 44
Health education, 116
High school graduation requirements, 4
History, human, 201
Hope, 86
Housing, 14
Human Behavior Curriculum Project, 209
Human development, 40, 57-58, 190
Human Development Program, 123-124
Human history, 201
Human needs, 9, 13, 18, 19, 53, 59, 61, 76-
  77
Human potentialities, 34, 39, 44
Human Value Series, 129-130
Humanistic commitment, 201
Humanistic education
  curriculum, 2-3
  definition of, 1
  principles, 6-7
Hyperactive children, 64
Hypnosis, 62

I

Immaculate Heart College program, 207
Indochina War, 189
Infancy, 74
Intelligence, 141
Interaction Analysis, 208
Interest finders, 157
Inside/Out, 4, 134-135
Inspirations, 155-156
Instincts, 61, 84
Intuitions, 61, 63, 64, 70, 84, 91-92
Involvement, 15

J

Job development program, Cleveland, 150
Joy, 16, 90

K

Kindness, 101
Knowledge, 10, 59, 60, 77, 81
Kohlberg Moral Dilemmas Test, 125

L

Laughter, 155
Learning abilities; *see* Basic learning abilities
Learning systems, 190
Legislation, 189
Liberty, 106
Life stages, 74
Lifeline, 138
Los Angeles County Alliance program, 150
Louisville experiment, 122
Love, 14, 59, 76, 79, 196

M

Magic circle, 124
Malnutrition, 197
Man: A Course of Study, 120-121
Marriage, 87
Materialism, 40
Maturity, 54, 74, 107
Meditation, 4, 69, 112
Mental health projects, 115-116
Mister Rogers, 142-143
Modeling, 62
Moral development, 44, 66-67, 73
  stages of, 17, 192-193
Motivation, 39, 44, 172
  achievement, 116-117
Myth, 91

N

National Training Laboratories, 164
Needs, human, 9, 13, 18, 19, 53, 59, 61, 76-77
New Orleans Center for the Creative Arts, 150
New York Civil Liberties Union, 172

O

Objectives, 47-49
Organization
  social, 9, 39
  value, 192
Orientation
  achievement, 194
  value, 44, 137-138, 192, 200

P

Parapsychology, 62-63
Peak experiences, 63
Peanuts comic strip, 153-154
Peer acceptance, 17
Peer observation, 180
Peer tutors, 69, 173, 179
Personal integration, 27, 34, 36, 38
Philadelphia Affective Education Project, 125-126
Physical security, 13, 59, 76, 78
Planning, 160
Poetry, 153
Poker chips, 175-177
Political movements, 13
Population control, 189
Posttest, 51
Potentiality, 34, 39, 44, 57, 197
Poverty, 198

Power, 10, 103
Premises for constructing human development
  program, 40
Prescriptive educational programs, 50-51
Pretest, 50
Primary resource materials, 142-143
Problem solving, 4
  group, 165
Program design, 51
Program evaluation, 183
Progress, 44
Progressive relaxation, 64
Project Alpha, 4
Psychic energy, 6, 36
Psychological education, 124-125
Psychological wholeness, 191

R

Rational verbalization, 206
Rational-emotive education, 119-120
Reality therapy, 117
Records
  pupil observation, 180
  weekly citizenship evaluation, 182
  work and reward, 175
Reinforcement
  intrinsic, 173
  physical, 175
  primary, 173, 174
  social, 172
  strategies, 184-185
  systems, 196
Religion, 44
Research, 59
Resource materials
  elementary, 143-145
  primary, 142-143
  secondary, 145-147
Rewards
  Gold Star, 176
  Honor Award, 174-176
Right and wrong, 117
Riverton social economics program, 151
Role-playing and modeling, 173, 178
  steps in, 179

S

Sanger family living program, 151
School reorganization, 43
Secondary resource materials, 145-147
Self, composition of, 34-36
Self Enhancing Education, 117-118
Self Incorporated, 135
Self-actualization, 46, 191
Self-assertion
  cards, 161
  and esteem, 5
Self-awareness, 53, 63, 64, 93
Self-concept
  evaluation of, 49
  positive and negative, 159
Self-confidence, 18

Self-control, 45, 63, 93, 98, 171
Self-consciousness, 93, 94, 95
Self-description ratings, 157
Self-determination, 5, 11
Self-development, 129
Self-discipline, 3
Self-esteem, 61, 66
Self-expression, 4
Self-gratification, 194
Self-image, 165
Self-initiated learning, 65
Self-judgments, 158
Self-recording, 173, 177, 179-180
Self-renewal, 4
Self-resolution, 64
Self-transactions, 162-163
Self-transcendence, 68-70, 111-113
Self-understanding, 4
Self-worth, 17, 59, 77, 83
Sensory exploration, 15
Sensory stimulation, 15
Service, 104
Social acceptance, 166
Social awareness, 93, 96
Social change, 189
Social commitment, 110
Social competency, 17, 59, 77, 82
Social cooperation, 67
Social goals, 45, 195
Social judgment, 167
Social Learning Curriculum, 119
Social organization, 9, 39
Social responsibility, 17, 68, 107
Social revolution, 40, 189
Social spirit, 68
Social systems, 190
  redesign of, 198
Soul, 39
Sublimation, 191
Survival, 11-12
Symbolic thinking, 22

T

Taxonomies, 52-54
Teacher
  attributes of, 67, 70, 172
  education of; *see* Teacher education

Teacher—cont'd
  as facilitator, 206-207
  personal qualities of, 205-206
  self-evaluation by, 183-185
Teacher education
  effectiveness training in, 207
  evaluation of, 217
  interdisciplinary model for, 210
  in-service, 200, 206, 216-218
  institutions in, 212-213
  laboratory experiences for, 209
  specialist programs for, 211
Teaching strategies, 54
Technological development, 109
T-group method, 164
Tolerance, 102, 174
Toward Affective Development, 135
Transactional Analysis, 132-133
Transcendence, 5, 24, 47, 107, 111-113
Transcendent functions, 62
Transcendental Meditation, 137-138

U

Unemployment, 192, 198

V

Value clarification, 138
Value conflicts, 191
Value organization, 192
Value orientation, 44, 137-138, 200
  case studies, 192
Value vacuum, 191
Values, 53, 57
  cultural, 66
  manners, 100
  personal and social commitments, 100
Vital energies, 63

W

Washington Union High School program, 152
Watergate, 11
White House Conference on Children, 28, 30, 36-
  37, 44
Wholeness, psychological, 191
Wishing, 155
Work, 45, 105